Inside the
Mass Movement
A political memoir

Inside the
Mass Movement
A political memoir

Raul E. Segovia

ANVIL
Manila

Inside the Mass Movement
A political memoir

Copyright © 2008 by Raul E. Segovia

Published and exclusively distributed by
ANVIL PUBLISHING, INC.
8007-B Pioneer Street
Barangay Kapitolyo
1603 Pasig City, Philippines
Telephones: 637-3621, 637-5141,
747-1622 (Sales & Marketing),
637-3874 (Publishing)
Fax: 637-6084
www.anvilpublishing.com

Book design by Arnold R. Ramos

Printed in the Philippines
by: COR-ASIA, INC.

ISBN 978-971-27-2048-2

Table of Contents

Acronyms

ABB – Alex Boncayao Brigade, an underground armed unit well-known in the 1980s.

ACC – Asia Coordinating Council, a partner of Brothers for All Men (BAM) serving Asia.

ACT – Alliance of Concerned Teachers

AG – above ground refers usually to legal activities of the left or open groups

AS – Armed Struggle

ASF – Alternative Social Formation

Bagong Lipunan – literally "new society," political party of President Ferdinand Marcos

BAM – Brothers for All Men (*freres de sommes*), a French partner NGO

BAYAN – *Bagong Alyansang Makabayan* (New Patriotic Alliance)

BCC – Basic Christian Community

BUNSO – *Balikatan at Ugnayan Naglalayong Sumagip sa Sanggol*; "*bunso*" also refers to the youngest child in the family

CACP – Citizens' Alliance for Consumer Protection, a nationwide NGO in the consumer sector founded sometime 1978-79; "cacp" is another NGO. The acronym stands for "Citizens' Alliance for Consumer Power," a creation of the 1978 CACP.

CARP – Comprehensive Agrarian Reform Program that started in Cory Aquino's time but remains incomplete in succeeding governments

CNL – Christians for National Liberation

COG – cause oriented group; earlier name for NGOs devoted to the libertarian struggles that openly flourished under the dictatorship

CPLA – Cordillera Peoples Liberation Army; an armed underground NGO in the northern Philippines that used to be headed by ex-priest Conrado Balweg

CPP – Communist Party of the Philippines

EDSA Uno, Dos, Tres – other names for the First, Second, and Third People risings in 1986, 2001, and 2003 respectively that occurred principally along the super highway named Epifanio Delos Santos Avenue circling Metro Manila; similar uprising also occurred in major cities around the country

EEA – Emergency Employment Administration, an office created under President Diosdado Macapagal in the 1950s to address the problem of widespread joblessness

FIG – Filipino-Irish group, a support NGO in Ireland during the martial law period in the Philippines

FIST – Federation of Ilongo Students

FFP – Friends of the Filipino People, an anti-Marcos U.S.-based NGO during the martial law period

FLAG – Free Legal Assistance Group, an organization of lawyers and legal personalities founded by the late Jose W. Diokno (a.k.a "Ka Pepe")

IBFAN – International Baby Food Action Network, an ally of BUNSO in the baby food campaigns

IGP – income-generating project

IFI – Iglesia Filipina Indepediente, the official name of the Philippine Aglipayan Church

IMF – International Monetary Fund

IOCU – International Organization of Consumers' Unions, now known as Consumer International or CI

IP – indigenous people or original natives

IT – information technology

KDP – Katipunan ng Demokratikong Pilipino (society of democratic Filipinos)

KM – Kabataang Makabayan (patriotic youth)

KMPI – *Kapisanan ng Mamimili sa Pilipinas, Inc.*; an earlier consumer group long linked to Ms. Julie Amargo

KMU – Kilusang Mayo Uno (May One Movement)

LOI – Letter of Instruction

LFS – League of Filipino Students

MABINI – Movement of Attorneys for Brotherhood, Independence, Nationalism and Integrity, a lawyers' NGO formed during martial law

ML – martial law of the Marcos dictatorship

MAN – Movement for the Advancement of Nationalism

MASAKA – Malayang Samahang Magsasaka (free association of peasants)

MDP – Movement for a Democratic Philippines, a coalition of student organizations, circa 1970s

MNC – Multinational Corporation

MNLF – Moro National Liberation Front

MTT – Mao Tsetung Thought, the Maoist ideology guiding the Filipino left Underground especially during the martial law period

NDFP – National Democratic Front of the Philippines

NFPC – Nuclear-Free Philippines Coalition, a creation of Citizens' Alliance for Consumer Protection; NFPC was active in anti Nuclear programs

NPA – New People's Army

NUSP – National Union of Students of the Philippines

OIC – officer-in-charge

PDs – Presidential Decrees, Marcos' dictatorial laws

PCGG – Presidential Commission on Good Government, an anti-graft body

PETA – Philippine Education Theatre Arts, responsible for training several street theatre activists

PKP – Partido Komunista ng Pilipinas, the old communist party in the country

PNF – Philippine News and Features, a news service NGO of Crossroads, Inc.

PO – political officer; PO is also short for "People's Organization"

PPT – Permanent People's Tribunal

PSG – Philippine Support Group

R.A. – Republic Act or legislated law

SAL – Structural Adjustment Loans

SCAUP – Student Council Association of U.P.; also Student Cultural Association of U.P., this latter group was founded by Jose Ma. Sison

SDK – Samahang Demokratikong Kabataan (association of democratic youth) circa 1970s; resuscitated in 2005

SME – small and medium entrepreneur (or enterprise)

TFD – Task Force Detainees, an NGO keeping track of the conditions of political prisoners and their families

UCCP – United Church of Christ of the Philippines

UG – underground; refers to non-legal groups or activities

WCOTP – World Confederation of Organizations of the Teaching Profession now called Education International.

Acknowledgements

THERE ARE MANY who helped me finish this book. I wish to acknowledge some of them. Others must remain anonymous as they themselves have requested. It took me more than three years to write the book, not counting some entries taken from my journal long started, and still going on.

My wife did a yeowoman's work cutting down with merciless ax on badly drawn syntax, winding Proustian sentences that hid unknown subclauses and suppressed sense. My daughter Raissa who now lives abroad introduced me to the PC and its mystification and how to use it with less patience lost.

I thank my numerous friends whom I consulted through the new "illiteracy" called "texting" where and whenever I was, even during midnight or early dawn, asking them questions. I owe them and ask their forgiveness for disturbing their sleep. The new high tech makes one wonder (about others at least) how they could write and publish books every two months. My rate was snailed pace by a problem caused by a hyped blood pressure that caused a hospital sojourn. I use only two fingers to work on the keyboard. I wish to thank also my two healthy fingers.

Abe Padilla, U.P. anthropologist, gave me an insight on the indigenous anti-government struggles in the North and peasants' resistance in the lowlands. Partylist Representative Satur Ocampo is a reservoir of correct information about people who visualize surrounding the cities from the countryside, why and how.

xviii / Inside the Mass Movement

Now it's time to mention names because these are not the ones alluded to above. While the writing of this book owes a lot to them, all errors of interpretation and missed facts, distortion of memory and recall are mine.

Among academicians turned activists and activists turned academics to whom I am grateful include former U.P. President Francisco (Dodong) Nemenzo and wife Anna Marie, son Fidel who is now a Ph.D. in mathematics; Partylist Representative Clarita Ann (Etta) Rosales was a colleague during the heyday of Alliance of Concerned Teachers where my activist umbilical cord has been connected after an earlier commitment with the militant consumer group; former Dean Marita Reyes of the U.P. College of Medicine, later Chancellor and regent, was a source about U.P. people who went to the communities to fulfil a Hippocratic function; Dr. Romeo Quijano of the U.P. Manila pharmacology department is a partner in the consumer movement who had to face bravely a P20 million suit for his anti-pesticide position; Roland Simbulan, former deputy chancellor of U.P. Manila and partner "street parliamentarian"; Atty. Greg Fabros who aside from teaching in Centro Escolar was also teaching, unpaid, in the street marches; wife Cora is also a lawyer and pro-life defender; and Dr. Elmer Ordoñez who partially edited the book.

Nathaniel Santiago kept my curiosity fed on how a people's organization like BAYAN could replenish the ranks with new blood. Many years have overtaken the mass movement and the young then have grown in years; so has "Nath" although he dropped out of school, I always kid "Nath" that the Philippine Christian University in Taft Avenue where he came from should give him a doctorate in Political Economy, *honoris causa*. No one in his rank deserves more. Many more like Fathers Joe Dizon and Ben Moraleda, Jeek Santos, Oca Francisco, Mila Aguilar, Steve Quiambao, Joel Rocamora, Walden Bello, Francis dela Cruz, Sister (now Mother) Mary John Mananzan, O.S.B., Obet Verzola, Joel Garduce, Gani Serrano, Miriam Ferrer, Liza Pulgado, Becky Marquez, Rizza Hontiveros, May Rodriguez, the rest of the Proprint staff like Rose, Cris, friends from the corporate sector Lia and Denise, and finally my peripatetic editor-anthropologist Pons Bennagen. I owe also abundant gratitude to friends who were once active in the underground who have now retired.

The time calls for this double-edged, circumlocution. *O tempora, O mores*. We passed that and aim to survive further down looking for an institution to house the mass movement as a permanent legacy to post-millennium democracy this side of the globe.

Foreword

ONE WHO WRITES a "political memoir" about the mass movements at this time does so at his own peril. But Raul Segovia who played (and continues to play) a key role as a mass leader has done just that.

Inside the Mass Movement is a book that will certainly invite mixed reactions because of the nature of the material he deals with – of what is history and what is ongoing. There will be questions of fact and interpretation likely to be raised by those who were active participants themselves in the various people's struggles on a wide range of issues. Their appreciation of the personages, events and circumstances may collide with that of the author who of course has already said that this is his own view as witness and participant, in fact, as chosen leader, in a good number of mass struggles.

Those who were not participants but interested observers who lived through the past fifty years (now a dwindling group) of the nationalist movement may have their own concerns about historical accuracy – but the fact that the book is a memoir, and thus a subjective account, should already mitigate that concern. Yet, the writer of a political memoir has the responsibility of checking and rechecking his facts, perhaps not with the rigor of scholarship, but conscientiously enough for credibility's sake. There is ample evidence that Segovia had gone out of his way to get first hand information on a number of aspects of the mass movement, particularly when his own observation and experience seemed limited. Even in this quest for truth there are a number of constraints, particularly when dealing with leading personalities and the inner workings of the underground.

Ostensibly the subject of the book is the open mass movement and his active participation in and perceptions of it. Undercurrents are readily implied in the title with the word "inside." Has the book provided the insights that enable the reader to know what has inspired and animated the mass movements? Ultimately this may be what matters beyond the historical contexts provided in the periodization of the last 50 years. And what has emerged is the crucial role played by underground cadres who have integrated themselves from the beginning in the mass movements.

As a somewhat older contemporary of Raul Segovia (I was a starting instructor when he entered U.P. Diliman as student) I can follow his rendering of the key events of the nationalist movement after the war. Even while I was abroad in the whole period of martial law, I knew albeit vicariously what was happening in the homeland. And when he dwells on the anti-dictatorship struggle in North America – through a resource person – I hold back the impulse to be another informant as one who spent the whole period of his stay in Canada doing what can be done abroad to hasten the end of the dictatorship. This is after all his book and perhaps I should write my own. Because of the all-encompassing character of the book, there are bound to be what he himself calls "aporia" – creating gaps that should compel other memoirs to be written.

Raul Segovia does not mince words about breakthroughs and shortcomings of the mass movement; he tries to grapple with the so-called split in the Left, particularly in its effects on the NGOs and people's organizations he was involved with in the open mass movement. The ideological, political and organizational schisms of the Left have not affected him as much as it has a few others who already have come out with books that appear to have axes to grind. Raul has remained whole from the experience beginning with his active involvement and leadership in the mass movement during the martial law period, starting with the formation of the Citizens Alliance for Consumer Protection that spawned scores of other groups in struggles continuing to the present. Of course, one's active participation is now constrained.

The author has made a signal contribution to the understanding of the mass movement as seen through the lens of his particular temperament. As a professor he may be inclined to lecture but all the reader has to consider is that it is still within the purview of a memoir. For all the academic mannerisms, the book is a compelling work to read. He is also in his element when he narrates personal situations like his sojourn with solidarity groups/individuals and kindred souls abroad, or the time of his being caught in a crossfire near the Palace in the twilight of the dictatorship.. One wishes there are more of these accounts but Raul Segovia manages to keep our eye on the subject of the open mass movement, and he does so magnificently.

– **Elmer A. Ordonez.**
24 June 2008

Introduction

THIS IS A PERSONAL ACCOUNT of the mass movement, not its history for the last fifty years. Others who have lived through the same period will fault me for remembering the wrong things. To survive the years is privilege enough; to remember everything is abuse of memory.

When my memory falters, I resort to theories that explain not history but experience. As this experience involved others, I cannot vouch that we will have the same way of interpreting it. Semiotician Umberto Eco warns about "over-interpretation" in his book of this title. The value we gain considering other people's way of seeing things is tolerance and knowledge, no matter how suspect the latter is.

Lest the book be taken for an act seeking forgiveness, nothing of the sort is found here. Rather it is the recognition of the need to fill the gap in the country's story of the mass movement. I try to describe experiences with NGOs (and other similar groups with strange names) where I've been a co-founder, an official or participant in their activities.

"Non-government organizations" was an expression of uncommon use during this time but it did not mean that it had no referents in the objective world; there were. There was just no naming them "NGOs." These novel formations we now call NGOs and sometimes people's organizations or POs had a lot to do with the advent of the mass movement.

The name's provenance therefore had another importance especially when linked to documents after the Second World War in the launching of an organization of governments called the United Nations Organizations; U.N. for short. That was where "NGO" was first mentioned. Hence, the book uses "NGO" thereafter in its generic sense as "any political-economic-cultural mechanism" outside the framework of the state and state organizations. This usually implies a dynamic meaning, of being an alternative social formation. Our failure to come up effectively with what it could do in the long term keeps us repeating old problems. This was also the original sense of Aristotle's "civil society" where its pristine unit was the family.[1]

There are occasions when this concept of civil society is distinguishable from its current abuse closely related to some people's organized opportunism. I refer to groups that carry rent seeking (cf. Glossary) to ultimate practice. The book calls them "civil society groups" (CSG). Many of their members look at the workings of the government they used to serve from inside. When they work from the outside, they are critical, ceaselessly carping. Recently, many quit the Arroyo cabinet, having failed to defend President Gloria Macapagal Arroyo as her alter ego. They messed up their government jobs where they enjoyed unprecedented perks in their lives. At this writing they are back in the streets as critics and carpers. If the mass movement is murky to some outsiders, this new bunch muddies it some more.

The mass movement is a collective political response, sporadic but persistent (like a bad cold) to the many failings of the government, of its bureaucracies, or of some people behind them. There would be some description of these CSGs as we go along identifying them.

This personal account will focus on how I see groups and persons view the mass movement as political language, as vehicle, as response to the objective conditions shaped by government decisions. This will explain why a transformation in the country has to happen in a conscious, organized, determined political way, why the political option is a principal element in a transition society like ours.

What we call today empowerment is a process as part of the dynamism of the masses resisting injustice. This gives them opportunities to realize what they are seeking, defining among their ranks each other's role and even aligning their interest with the broader, sometimes international movement. The mass movement is a collective way of making and acting each one's own story, a part of rewriting history.

---

[1] See *Basic Works of Aristotle*, Modern Library Paperback, N.Y., 2001, especially the chapter on Politics ff p.1114.)

Book Outline and Theme

My experience showed me how the mass movement has become a bridge, maybe a new language to understand the wishes embedded in People Power. The cause-oriented groups (COGs,) NGOs, POs, civil society groups, etc. were attempts at creating alternative social formations that I came to call ASFs. These would take over the traditional services/functions expected of the role of state bureaucracies as many are failing. To me this explains partly why progressive NGOs seem anti-government. In NGOs I was actively involved in, many tend to spread and increase every time the government fails or when perception of failure by the masses toward these official agencies intensifies. It was in this spirit that many NGOs attempted to fill the gaps created by these government failures.

Sometimes you see it as a raucous public "calling to account" what the agencies of the government are doing or not doing well.[2] People usually expect from government what they are taught to see, and there is plenty they see that ought not to be there.

My account covers a 50-year plus period of struggle for a nationalist and democratic society. The mirror I hold up does not exclude how others see things. But other mass movements outside the national, democratic struggles deserve another book.

Theorizing the State

I am an avid note taker. Often in observing the mass movement I cannot help but theorize by way of explaining to myself or explaining the political phenomena to my students in U.P. Manila where I taught, the theory went this way for more than half a century now. We have had these institutions in their modern form, mostly under the rubric of what were then the nation-states. The current version supporting the sovereign power of the state is what we inherited from the west, the monarchy having been dislodged 200 years earlier.

---

[2] French Catholic philosopher Louis Althusser used to call them *"repressive state apparatuses"* like the courts, police, prison houses and *"ideological state apparatuses"* like the media, schools, families, etc. See **Essays On Ideology**, Verso, London, 1971.

We got the republican state. Consequently, there is something new in the republican state that governs by representation. The people remain sovereign. The part of the envisioned change was that the elected representatives speak and act and live for the principal interests of the people who elected them and that the sovereign power supposedly inheres in the people. Regretfully, it has not always been the case. What has happened instead?

The government is ruled by the representatives of the dominant few. The masses through the political movement attempt to reorganize the faulted system. Alternative mechanisms are put up. The transition from COGs to NGOs, POs then to "development NGOs" was to correct the inadequacy, a process of political adjustment. But something else occurred.

There are other kinds of NGOs. These are the rent seeking "civil society groups." (cf. Glossary.) They mirror the changing consciousness and a new discourse by some people under an economy that want to gain without actually producing. This used to be called "cronyism" where one's economic, social, political weight depends on the person's proximity to power and the unwarranted exercise of that power. In the mass movement, these groups could also oust a president even outside the constitutional rules for changing presidents. I've seen these things happen.

My interest in these political movements has not differed much from my interest in the courses in Development Studies I used to teach in the university. I noted that my students were not only concerned about the course or about getting good grades. They were equally interested in the mass movement and how it could be theorized in their academic interests.

Semiotics of the Mass Movement

Again, my experiences in the mass movement and readings about similar movements in other places allow me to come up with useful concepts. "Semiotics of the mass movement" is one: new language, new symbols, codes, public signals, and new significations of old, day-to-day signs. They constitute a slew of tools that compel us (both as activists and academicians) to study more carefully the varied signals used, *the new semiotics of the mass movement.*

It is not new, except in name. Marx more than a hundred years ago described it this way: "The tradition of all dead generations weighs like a nightmare on the brain of the living. . .and just when they seem engaged in revolutionizing themselves and things, in creating something that had never yet existed, precisely in that period of revolutionary crisis, they anxiously conjure up the spirits of the past to their service and borrow from them names, battle cries and costumes in order to present the new scene of world history in this honoured disguise and in this borrowed language."[3] The "borrowed language" is usually in the field of the economy. The most deceiving and commodifying today is something that falls under the rubric of "market forces." "Who controls the economy?" is a crucial question.

I recall that at the end of the 1950s there developed a rising political emotion directed against the presence of U.S. military, political and economic interests in the country. World War II gave rise to this political wave; then post-colonialism was born.

By 1960 nationalism was on the agenda. The "church people," an expression that separated the institutional church from mavericks like Father Hilario Lim, S.J. and other church activists, became to mean a large number that used public prayers and vigils as tools to arouse the somnolent generation. Catholicism tried to redeem itself in a country where more than 92% of the people are Catholics. The church did it by aligning its activist priests with the simple joys and liberation of the poor. Hence, Vatican II ecumenism.

This undertow, I remember, turned into a major political wave. The students became more visible and audible in the classrooms and the streets. Unknown to many, the Mao fever from the north blew in from the cold.

To become effective, semiotics departs from being a science to mix with popular practices of the masses. The more creative handlers in politics pull out symbols, e.g. flags, the color red, crosses, sickle and hammer, a kind of local language, a red star, images of motion, new relationships. These stirred a great number of people, attuned the symbols and the symbolic to common referents in reality where the masses live and feel the burden of life. These made our practices useful in mobilizing people.

---

[3] "The Eighteenth Brumaire of Louise Bonaparte" from *Marx-Engels Selected Works*, p.96 Progress Publishers, Moscow, 1968.

Search for Political Line

At the start of the 1970s, Mao Tsetung's Thought or MTT was institutionalized not in the school curriculum but in the street marches and study sessions, in UG houses and other secret places. In spite of the influence of the churches, several students, seminarians and young priests were looking for a "political line" away from the blessed icons and prayers of Vatican II. For example, the underground Christians for National Liberation or CNL, a part of the not-yet-formalized National Democratic Front brought these pious protesters closer to Mao's *Red Book*. Looking back to that period, our enthusiasm for reading, studying, analyzing underground literature like Mao's writings remained undiminished. The more oppressive the government of Marcos the more we searched for alternatives. At that time, the only alternative was what we were reading from the *Red Book*.

The ideological transition did not make the students atheists. It honed them to become militant national democrats or NDs. Many of us did more public prayers especially during police dispersals than we ever did inside churches. We sang the *National Anthem* with fervor where everybody stood still as often as the military broke up our ranks during rally dispersals. The tactic forestalled arrest and gave time for activists to scamper and hide.

The decade found Marcos more nimble in his exercise of political power. He tightened control over the media, schools, and decision-making. He became overly ambitious by extending his term of office beyond what the Constitution allowed him.

What was to be done? Marcos' answer: change the Constitution, hold an election. Allow the approval of changes by recognizing raising of hands in the *baranggays* and mark for arrest those who were critical. Better still call them "communists." American officials pathologically fearful of communists were tightlipped but gleeful.

The continuing political undertow pushed the tide of civil resistance forward. It would further produce a wave of repressions by the police and military. In being a part of many demos, I was hoping my face would not become too familiar with the police. I think this was also the secret wish of every activist lost in the fray. Otherwise, one walks with bent head and a little nimbler when a policeman is around.

By the late seventies, martial law grimaced in the rictus of threatening the population, gun-roared against the increasing number of its critics. The 7,000 critics or more earlier arrested increased in one sad unfolding dawn. The country's killing fields became secrets with the military closing the radio stations and arresting snoopy journalists.

For many of those in the middle forces, especially the students, it was difficult to resist the underground call for armed struggle or AS, a practice uncommon in the sensibilities of many Filipinos unless absolutely necessary. (Later on the expression "middle forces" had become common with reference not only to income but to political orientation, principally anti-Marcos.)

In the organized consumer sector where my organizing efforts were earlier focused, it was no longer feasible writing soft letters through the press pleading for reforms of government rutted with cronyism and corruption, police abuses and military repression. We shared with our audience many speeches, mostly agitational, that were delivered before organizing them. There was a strong belief among us in the sector of the consumers that the MNCs especially the oil companies squeezed dry both the national government of foreign exchange and the consumers of their meagre earnings. The state mustering its repressive resources against us became a looming symbol of a tyrant and an exploitative master.

The armed struggle among those wanted by the state became a compelling option. The number of students who joined the underground increased. Not all hope was lost. The open mass movement maintained a position of creatively exploring the uses of semiotics. The open mass movement tactically aligned itself with the underground.

Semiotics and Class Analysis

Rhetoric, cartoons, songs, free verses, street theatres, masked dancers donned in indigenous garbs stepping on the beats of primitive drums, swinging to the strummed native instruments became effective tools. These projected the cultural struggles in the open. All these have become materials for the emerging political semiotics.

The mass movement created new, often stirring symbols used to by-pass censorship while these aroused the different sectors of the society to their condition, suppressed dreams, and hijacked freedom. Such a process in consciousness-raising (another name for popular education) became programmatic answering, "what is to be done?" Usually this preceded or was accompanied by mass organizing.

In some chapters of the book, like the sixties and the seventies, a political calendar summarizes separately the sweeping events of these decades. They give me a sense of the elements that converged to the common end of a mass rising that was thoroughly political. Others called this mix by a neologism even surviving the dictator—"a conjuncture." It's a merging of events in *medias res*. For me, political economy simplifies this complexity by asking the question: "Who is the exploiter and who are the exploited?"

Among the NGOs the so-called conjunctural events produced a "split personality" syndrome between those hankering for foreign doles (funds) and those biting between their teeth to maintain their emancipatory agenda; between those unwittingly aligned among the "Re-affirmists" and the "Rejectionists"; between affirming Mao TseTung or rejecting it. Many imperilled NGOs believed this ideological division was not supposed to affect their organizing but it did. The collective symptoms remained up to the end of the millennium. The ideological split in the underground, between MTT aficionados and free-wheeling Marxists became apparent in the historic acrimony among those in the Left.

As a close observer, I tried to describe the stormy days of the NGOs with the National Democratic Front. This is balanced, I hope, with an account of my international experience, networking among kindred political spirits in other countries. Foreign support of the mass movement came not only in terms of funds but also political and ideological backing.

The closing days of the 1980s under President Cory Aquino are remembered by a long list of missed opportunities when she had all the executive powers freshly legitimated by EDSA Uno or People Power I that the world watched with awe. Was it because the people surrounding her, many former street marchers, had fallen back? They continued to use the language of lawyers instead of being aligned with the dire needs of the resisting masses. Were these incompatible that even today many are still struggling over such legalese they inherited from the days of Marcos?

Laws like new wines taste strange when put back into old bottles. My observation confirmed this so often. The repressive laws made by Marcos could have been swept away or thrown into the dustbin of history. That did not happen. Even at this writing (the year is 2006) laws passed during the years of the dictatorship like Batas Pambansa No. 880 are still used by the police to disband or arrest street marchers, even if the latter were asserting their constitutional rights to public assembly.

Legal advisers close to President Aquino apparently whispered to her not to abolish those repressive Presidential Decrees as she might also need them; not to abrogate those foreign debts as her government might also need to look credible to its next creditors, etc. These were only a few weaknesses of the transition government at the close of the 1980s. Under Cory Aquino not democracy but *democracy manqué* was restored.

The same lawyers and finance advisers were active marchers in the terminal days of the Marcos government. They were not total strangers to progressive ideas. I look back to history and found that in his days Lenin threw away his attorney's mantle in order to become a revolutionary. This was when he saw his lawyering an obstruction to liberating his people. That was the lesson the monarchies of Europe trembled against as they watched over their fortresses threatened by the angry masses for the next hundred years. It was in this manner, not learning from history, that many of President Aquino's lawyers and finance mavens failed their nationalist and democratic curricula. One does not have to be a card-carrying ND to know the principal needs of the oppressed masses.

Ameliorative NGOs Vs Emancipatory

My involvement with the NGOs makes me conclude in the book about the nature of their general activities. There are here studies of individual NGOs and other ASFs. Historically, the NGO communities seemed to bifurcate since

1983 into (1) those pursuing **AMELIORATIVE** activities and (2) those pursuing **EMANCIPATORY** agenda as principal features. The one does not preclude the other. The unfinished agenda called for these two to come out jointly. The beacon of the new economics (which we called rent seeking) became persistent and tempting.

The picture became clearer in 1986 when funding partners (domestic and foreign) started to ask the question on every project proposal submitted for support: where or what was this NGO's self-reliance component? A challenging question indeed viewed with egregious effect on several NGOs. Many took umbrage. They said that even the whole country was wallowing in debts beyond the next generation's capacity to pay. It was not fair to demand from NGOs, less equipped as they were, for answers to questions about economic self-reliance when their objective was political. My disagreements with many foreigners sent to the country to oversee their political investment in some NGOs or social investment in the others highlighted the different frameworks: why some wished to help others and others merely wished to help themselves.

Disempowering of NGOs

Thereafter, the conscious formation of NGOs, where I was involved, was no longer principally concerned with the deeper structures of oppression and repression, with thievery and tyranny that the authoritarian regime left behind. Neither was everybody fully aware of the exploitative nature of capital. Many of these NGOs have become responsive to the problem of how to get as much funds for income-generating activities, for coop formation, for micro-financing, for marketing programs, for a range of dole-out functions the NGOs were beginning to wrongly assume as their public role before the disempowered communities. New activists joined the new NGOs, and brought new disappointments.

Somewhere along, I wish to detail stories for some of these NGOs where I had direct involvement as official or participant-observer or as one of the founding members. There are about eight or nine of these spanning a number of social sectors that were NDF-influenced but non-party (CPP) members.

We will locate them in the decade when they were most active like CACP, a consumer rights and protection group in the seventies, NFPC, earlier an environment group that turned anti-American military bases in the eighties. PEAN in the nineties was a political grouping of more than 140 groups looking for a way to save our rapidly diminished natural resources, etc.

There is a discussion on the underground mass movement. This is distinguished from the mass movement usually led by open personalities many of whom at the time were national democrats. Many of them composed the icons of the open mass movement. These were (NDs or non-NDs) the likes of Tanada Sr., Jose W. Diokno, Chino Roces, Cardinal Sin, Corazon Aquino and others.

The NDF's role focused on making a bridge between the UG mass movement and the above ground (AG) national democratic open movement. The latter tried hard to appear as a legal mass movement against charges by the military of its being "fronts." The evidence usually spanned from the flimsy to the imaginary. This hardly endeared the military establishment to many of those participants in the mass movement.

The mass movement or, rather the two culminations in EDSA I and EDSA II entered history from different entrances. The mass movement in the early 1970s to the second half of the 1980s was led by iconic personalities. Some are mentioned above. The mass movement that culminated in 2001 which caused the ouster of a head of state, in spite of the fact that President Joseph Estrada garnered one of the highest votes in the history of the Philippine elections, had scarcely a national icon among the ranks of people behind it.

Instead, the one in 2001 had several articulate handlers or spokespersons many coming from disparate groups. They had good control of their political presence before the mass media, an effective platform for political theatre. Many used to occupy elevated posts in government, in society, in the church. This was one skill an activist had to learn when leading a mass movement.

The senate that tried an erring President Estrada before the nation had disbanded itself for failing to come out with a clear judgment. It was during this crucial period in full view of thousands of TV watchers and radio listeners that the second mass movement culminated into a dramatic fruition, again the ousting of a president. People Power II entered political history.

The mass movement that caused Marcos to flee to Hawaii preceded People Power II by almost twenty-one years. The second mass movement was short lived. Many leaders of People Power I used to occupy prominent public positions even before Martial Law in the national government, in business, in the church, in the underground CPP. The second one toppled with dispatch a popular president, a movie icon close to the heart of the masses. Then the masses turned against this idol.

Nominally, that second mass movement was non-iconic in composition of its mass leaders. None occupied high public office. It was a job well done by the urban middle class with skills on the IT and control of the semiotics of mass organizing, texting, cellphones, etc. The emergent sectoral leaders linked to this second historic mass movement were until recently novices in the lexicon of open political discourse.

Many of these sectoral leaders in the 2nd Rising (a.k.a. People Power II) were steeled in other mass movements but they led less nationally prominent public lives. Examples included sectors like the women with Liza Maza, Nelia Sancho, Sister Mary John Mananzan (my co-founder of CACP). Church personalities included Bishop Julio Labayen from La Paz, Iloilo.

I could not recall marches I joined in where Fathers Joe Dizon and Ben Moraleda were not there. Nathaniel Santiago and J.V. Bautista represented the students and were arguing with the police as often as there were violent dispersals. The farmers and fisher folk always had Rafael Mariano and Rudy Sambajon with them. Nuclear Free and Peace movement, an earlier version of the NFPC found Roland Simbulan and Cora Fabros in the midst. Trade unions under Crispin Beltran and Angel Mendoza continued to fuel militancy in the streets. Teachers had Etta Rosales and sometimes this writer leading. Artists and movie directors had Behn Cervantes and Bien Lumbera. Lawyers had Arno Sanidad and Alex Padilla in the group. The mass media was inspired by Joe Burgos and Satur Ocampo writing anti-Marcos tracts, etc.

Because these faces were seen in the Martial Law years and after, some remained in the dreaded military "hit list." Many of these activists received the public acclaim of being members of the "Parliament of the Streets," regulars of open advocacy work.

A chapter on the semiotics of the mass movement and a writing that the two historic culminations of mass movement above—in 1986 and in 2001—will show how both successful expressions of political People Power, ended in an inglorious Restoration period.

Some questions concerned me. Among these: who controls the semiotics of power? Were the organized masses in control of them? What other influences did the mass movement have on the country's continuing democratization? What is the role of the new information technology or IT? What is the significance to the mass movement with easy access to the personal computers or other tools like the cellphone?

Included here is chapter on the international dimension of nation-wide mass movements around the world. Often the routes to national liberation take circuitous paths through borrowed ideas, political images and social exemplars from abroad.

Lastly, why call it mass movement? When I consulted several books on the subject, I could not find in the indices of hundreds of titles, here and abroad, the phrase "mass movement." But for "social movements" there's plenty. One explanation for it is that the changes Filipinos are seeking in a transition society are plagued with under-development in both political and economic aspects. There's the economic upper class that does not need much developing and the lower class whose development has been obstructed, retarded; latterly lies the masses. This socio-economic cleavage makes for the mass movement to run its course. Without this contradiction, there's no mass movement.

Writing this book as a personal account is like viewing the country inside a moving bus. There are other passengers who may see the same things but take a different sense of them. Add to this experience: the bus has not stopped. Often the writer feels he is a part of the masses and the moving scene he writes about.

Chapter 1

At the Edge of a Fading Ideology
1950s

AT THE TIME of the country's independence from the U.S. in 1946, I was Grade III in the public school. Our school building in Negros hardly survived strafing and bombing. I saw it with huge pockmarks on its concrete walls, and its G.I. sheets were twisted with dangerous sharp edges warning us children to play away from the area.

At that time, the climate of uncertainty settled in many families' lives probably less for mine, my father being a town doctor. It was not so for other families with uncertain livelihood. I learned three years later about this period that it was followed by armed resistance against the hegemonic U.S. influences especially in Central Luzon. But this armed opposition faltered and failed sometime at the end of the decade. The contradictions within society did not resolve to strengthen Filipino identity, but with Rizal's books and lives of other heroes in the curriculum, nationalism was finally on the agenda of the organized masses. This was where I was introduced to what would be called the mass movement.

My first taste of it was in the student group formed by high school classmates (my early idea of the "masses") behind me following in a formation on our way back to the classrooms after a flag ceremony. The "masses" behind me also stopped when I stopped on the track. A school contribution was imposed on students to support athletes from other places playing in the school on some athletic meet. Many of us grumbled against it. The teacher screamed at me to move on and why was I stopping? The issue was born. Looking back I tasted power with the "masses" supporting me; I also tasted the first scolding from the principal's office, thereafter symbolizing authority.

A few things highlighted my memory of the period. Three presidential icons cast their shadows politically in the 1950s: Presidents Elpidio Quirino (1946-1953), Ramon Magsaysay (1953-57), and Carlos P. Garcia (1957-1961). I remember President Quirino being thrashed for corruption of office.

Rightly or wrongly, these presidents, transformed the country *from a colony to a neo-colony*. The main features of that post-colonial status have all their roots in the 1950s. They sprouted new phases of the country's development. The post World War II brought us a new status, i.e., "third world." I was unaware of this political shift then but came to know it when I entered U.P.

I came to think that the major problem of that period was in the educational re-orientation, a post-colonial status, including my generation's failed search for a political ideology and organizing methods for the majority of the people. We were concerned about how the government handled the orientation of the school system after World War II. This concern keeps challenging the mass movement and its NGOs. I should know this as I was one of the hundreds of NGO organizers. Some of us ended up organizing lantern parades every morning of the Christmas season. Others went to organizing political parades launching the candidacy of their favorite mayor.

From Colonialism to Neo-colonialism

My assessment of that period runs like this: the 1950s was a decade chained to the consequences of World War II, with thousands of Filipino families standing up against the ravages of war. After the war that was not of its own making, the country was apron-stringed to the post "liberation" assistance and aid conditions of the Americans, a sign that Filipinos would not be truly free.

I remember there was the collective clamor for the payment of war damages. Much later I came to know that the Japanese were being made to pay war damage claims of families whose houses were destroyed. The effort to make Japan pay and the promised U.S. assistance (war damage claims and American aid) got mixed up in the minds of claimant families.

Conditions for war damage payment were set by the Americans long before the granting of the so-called 1946 Independence. To name a few: an economy open to the unregulated entry of U.S. products while Philippine exports like sugar were tied to the quota system favored by American businessmen but falsely fearful this might compete with their sugar beets.

I belonged to the generation trained and educated for strong attachment to America, "land of the free, home of the brave." The U.S. was a model for governing right, for running the economy, for advancing education and for standing up again in order to walk after the havoc left by the War. While political freedom was packaged as part of our July 4, 1946 Independence, I look at this now as a tattered leaving of an eagle's claw after it had fleeced its prey.

Colonialism and More Deceptions

I started to think that our history drags the country like a heavy anchor that moored us to an unresolved past, cluttered as it was by more contradictions than we are able to resolve. A brief review will help refresh our memory. Earlier than this suspect 1946 Independence, a Republic was proclaimed in 1898. History was a way of erasing its significance. There was a string of deception, fake battle, a pre-arranged surrender and an imperial sale of the whole archipelago for $20 million by Spain to America. Together with this grand slam was the simultaneous exile to Guam of many Filipino heroes who refused to cooperate with the new imperial "owners" of the country.

Generations of Filipinos were slow to grasp the significance of this colonial history. It manifested in ways that later took roots in the mind, in mine and in others. First, it was not our Filipino story we were made to read and study. It is a story of U.S. imperialism. Even the monumental 52-volume *Philippine Islands* by Blair and Robertson could not give a balanced presentation of that past documenting what survived after almost four hundred years under Spain. Second, what turned out to be the political culture of post-1946 Independence introduced by the U.S. became a training ground for the revolutionary tradition of the *Katipuneros*, Andres Bonifacio, Apolinario Mabini, Gregorio del Pilar, Miguel Malvar, et al, freedom fighters all but invariably called "bandits, traitors, or *landrones*" long inscribed in books that we read. Historians like Alip, Capino and Zaide did not help much to straighten up things. The revising of history books came later.

The re-writing of the country's 400 hundred years of struggle against Spain from the colonialist's point-of-view and of the 50-year resistance against the Americans took place in the cusp of the new American language and American-trained classroom teachers. Adding to these two, even the four-year guerrilla movement against the Japanese was cavalierly underplayed if not dismissed. The latter is remembered today only in expensive coffee-table books. What had happened was a case of systematically re-shaping the Filipino consciousness.

Many were hardly conscious that imperialism in the 1950s was already a problem. Its hidden claws were dug deep in the nation's insurance business, finance, mining, logging, shipping, oil imports, banking, extractive industries and exports. The shadow of imperialism's global reach had grown and advanced far during the decade.

I am aware that the people's responses to colonialism and imperialism were scattered, few and far between. Sporadic upheavals, assorted risings, insurrections, peasant rebellion and civil disobedience of the masses that marked the country's history were without coordination, ill-armed, separated by islands. This made organized resistance difficult to sustain and carry against well-equipped and organized imperial intruders. Yet today's mass movement has its roots in this tradition. In one occasion I had a talk with Bobby Malay, activist wife of the partylist Representative Satur Ocampo. She wondered aloud: why is it that the starting points of resistance in the country almost seem to locate themselves in the same place(s).

I ventured to add that in the case of Negros, Pampanga and Tarlac among sugar cane workers, the class division between the numerous "sacadas," farm workers and landless tillers on one hand and the few landowners controlling this life resource of many on the other are too stark to ignore. This does not explain fully the bloody and deadly clashes why this contradiction had to result in several deaths and injuries. The major tools of violence are in the hands of the police and military under the control and influence of the state and owners of capital. Might this explain?

Mechanisms of Colonial Control

In U.P.-Manila where I taught Development Studies courses, I used to explain to my students to get acquainted with some features of imperialism. This was how it went:

Installed in the country were the full forces of the ideological and repressive apparatuses (refer to Althusser) of conquering armies, empires, states, various sovereignties, operators of imperial powers. We come to know these traditional and hegemonic tools of power in various forms as the military, police, *guardia civiles*, *kempetais*, the bureaucracies, courts, prison cells, the schools, church, media and other agencies of control by the dominating entities. The ruling institutions prepared to enforce the regulatory laws, rules and social conduct over the dominated masses. The latter lived in its traditionally organized but otherwise inchoate life in scattered communities. All these apparatuses were in place in different times. Their effects took the form of hegemonic culture foisting the contradictory values of those wielding power and those against whom power was wielded.

Then I tell my students an exception would come from some native leader whose legitimate authority is challenged. Illustrating this was the ultra-nationalism of Commonwealth President Manuel Quezon. We remember him as having said, "I prefer a government run like hell by Filipinos to one run like heaven by Americans." This formed a piqued political autocrat, a kind of leader who could signal a re-grouping of the unorganized to rally behind that kind of personal politics and personalized leadership. The influence of this iconic leadership even today is very much behind the rise of the mass movement. Persons not politics take command, persona not people. To continue my explanation:

"Although World War II had ravaged our country, the economy and infrastructures the Americans had put up since that time were part of the post-war reconstruction. The strengthening of the bureaucracies followed and continued through massive war damage funding and reparations after the war.

"In the course of the next fifty years since Commodore Dewey's fleet entered Manila Bay, the U.S. had introduced the civil service, expanded public schools, spread the use of the English language and sent Filipino *pensionados* abroad. Many of them returned to head the civil and military bureaucracies. Through these ideological apparatuses in public services, the U.S. ably promoted, protected and controlled its principal interests with unchecked admiration from the country's national leaders educated under American flag.

"It was an education that a few were vaguely aware of its destructiveness to national identity trying to exist. This identity was a thing we all badly needed to develop and cultivate in order to strengthen our 1946 Independence. It did not happen."

Then I warned my students many of whom had the ambition of becoming scholars abroad. More Filipino scholars, I told them, went abroad to pursue higher education, learn market economics in America's ivy-league schools and hone on the American political system and practices. I told them:

"As if it were our fate that history swept under the rug those with no clear idea of what was most important to the emergent nation-state. They've become like dusts consigned to oblivion. There was constant obstruction to the struggle in order to gain or develop one's national identity especially in the cultural arena."

I remember in Iloilo where I finished elementary, even the speaking of one's language in our school, a teaching lab for normal college teachers was deemed lowly, "uneducated" and punished with a fine. A "recidivist" would receive a call to the principal's office.

This educational colonialism became part of my life and the lives of others of my generation. The culture of dependency on the U.S. included the founding of a center of higher education for non-Catholics by the Baptist missionaries in the present Central Philippine University (CPU). To its credit, CPU had produced courageous student martyrs in the national democratic struggle during the martial law years.

Two Opposing Economics

I observed that not everything went smoothly in this transition. There were Filipinos who wanted their lives dictated by past ways and customs and the resources nearest to them. Look at the Amorsolo masterpieces of the idyllic countryside, lo and behold, that was what everyone would feel should not be lost every time one's eyes were raised to the horizon. It framed the country's natural richness, embraced by the sunset, cooled by hundreds of species of fruit trees in the hills covered by rain forests. There was agriculture as the base of an expanding rural life, shorelines and seas teeming with fish for everyone's food growing, fructifying endlessly around. With nature's richness, there was no reason for re-organizing the economy. We just keep our households in order and its members resourceful and use our resources wisely, which was how Aristotle defined the old economics of the early otherwise pristine Civil Society.

But contrast the above picture with this: Americans wanted to spread commerce, trade and to continue colonizing the country aggressively. They looked at these resources as convertible to cash. So much of these—lands, mines, fisheries, forests—remain untapped, undeveloped, unconverted to tradable goods, without market. Money-minded neo-colonialists noted that Filipinos were not only good sugar, copra and hemp producers but also ardent consumers educated by the school system to desire imported goods.

The countryside was a potential source of cheap labor. Given Arthur Lewis's theory of economic development during that period, the Nobel laureate believed that such labor were trainable, mobilizable to provide the cheap muscle for industrial economy that had hardly taken off. Lewis was the economist used by professors in Iloilo.

During the 1950s, the contradiction of the above economies started to surface. Two opposite ways of organizing the national economy asserted themselves and started to define government policies. First, much of production in the countryside was principally for subsistence. The growing number of households, with the population increasing would require three square meals. Organized beggary as we see it in cities today was non-existent. The idea of producing more for the market had not captured the mind of the Filipino peasant. He worked to live and not the other way around. He produced but not principally for making money.

Meanwhile, the Americans focused on producing for commerce, for the money-value of products in the marketplace. This was the second way, a dominant one. The idea of development was transforming the material resource into money form of wealth. The place for such exchange was the market.

There was so much spare labor and the U.S. saw the growing middleclass as consumers willing to pay for their needs and the cost of life style appurtenances that their consumerist culture had spawned. Slowly, the traditional household producing the things for direct use was giving way to production for exchange. The cash nexus became a necessity.

People's Resistance called "The Hukbalahap Movement"

During the 1950s and 1960s the Americans invoked *The Domino Theory* to rationalize their imperial presence in the developing countries in Asia like the Philippines by saying that if Vietnam fell to the communists, the rest of Southeast Asia would follow. The massive U.S. presence in Clark, Pampanga and in the Subic Bay in Zambales was their rampart against "the spread of the evil Communism."

The political situation in some parts of the country was being organized differently. Although the country was economically and politically shaky from the effects of war, there was an expanding minority that fuelled the resistance movement earlier linked to the movement against the Japanese known as *Hukbong Bayan Laban sa Hapon* or HUKS. The same group at that time prepared itself against the U.S. A rising political agenda called anti-imperialism was looking for a niche in the lives of many Filipinos. Specific targets were the Americans who had gained a permanent foothold in the two military bases in Luzon, the most extensive in the world at that time.[4]

The 1950s brought back government institutions patterned after those of the U.S. Not every one accepted it. While the Filipino insurrectionary impulse was suppressed it continued to look for an organizing initiative and form suitable for the masses.

Those living in the mountains exhibited their indigenous ways of resisting tyranny and post-colonial corporate greed. These political initiatives illustrated the mountain people's movement in the Northern provinces. In the south,

---

[4] See Roland Simbulan's *The Bases of Our Insecurity, A Study of U.S. Military Bases in the Philippines*, Balai Fellowship Inc, Q.C. 1983.

also the Muslims and various indigenous groups called *Lumads* remained unconquered, unexploited except in some cases by their own kind. They would wage their own struggles.

Rise and Fall of the PKP

An engaging topic at the time was the PKP. This was connected to the rising movement of peasants and workers. An armed minority in Central Luzon, Manila and some provinces in the Visayas were consolidating their forces equipped with weapons left over by the Second World War.

The early leaders of this mass movement were patriotic socialists and church people like Gregorio Aglipay and Isabelo de los Reyes. Isolated surges of armed rebellion against the government were later conducted under the leadership of the Partido Komunista ng Pilipinas (PKP) founded in 1930. This group traced its roots to the earlier socialist ideas and formations. *The Memoirs of the Communist* by Jesus Lava gives the reader a proper bearing of this part of the PKP's history. This armed movement rose slowly and fell more quickly by the end of the 1950s.

Why did it fail? According to one account (hardly objective) by one who later denounced the PKP's leadership for indulging in "adventurism," a term used at that time as a revolutionary opprobrium. Read for example *Philippine Society and Revolution* by Amado Guerrero (preface, 3rd edition, 1979). Amado Guerrero is the *nom de guerre* of Jose Maria Sison.

Sison observed that the PKP once tried to justify an armed takeover in a precipitate judgment by its politburo. This included ordering all units of the "People's Army" to make a "simultaneous attack on provincial capitals, cities and enemy camps." (p.42) It was supposed to be on March 29, August 26 and November 7, 1952. The attacks on the first two dates were executed. The rest is history according to the version by Sison in the above-cited book. His critique describing the failure of the old CPP opened a new page in the history of the revolutionary mass movement.

Thereafter, "left romanticism" staggered against an abandoned genuine people's revolutionary agenda of the earlier PKP called "the strategic seizure of state power." This blunder signalled the mournful knell for the old Communist Party.

The government responded by arresting their leaders in Manila. Sison wrote in the **PSR** (p.38) that the putschist orientation of the Lava leadership brought the most crushing defeat on the Party and the People's Army. This blunder, if I get Joe Sison right, followed an over-extension of resources, for example, "soldiers and communication lines."

This idea of "quick military victory" of a faction of the CPP was later to be repeated in the revolutionary movement that would cause its second historic open split in the early 1990s.

I was in high school at the acme of the Lava leadership and remember too well how our house in Iloilo City was burned down in a fire that started simultaneously in several blocks of the city. It was suspiciously arson but not to collect insurance. It was a kind of 'political arson," if there's one in the books. The name Guillermo Capadocia (or, was it Balgos?) sent tremors among the Ilongos. The subsequent killing and arrest of the other leaders was a blow to the revolutionary mass movement of the Fifties. The cause was an early version of left romanticism by the intellectually led PKP.

My family moved across the street, a neighbor's house, where the city's second big conflagration mysteriously (or miraculously) stopped. We were staying temporarily in the house of Jesus Nava II who was a member of the militant workers organization *Federacion Obrero de Pilipinas*, the biggest and strongest trade union in the island of Panay at that time.

U.S. Imperialism was not clearly recognizable then in the consciousness of many people. Like the symbolic eagle scanning over its prey, the U.S. sought a favored presence over the country's natural resources, control over its fledgling economy and in specific strategic areas of its two military bases. Were these viewed as threats to our national interest? Not yet during this time with some national leaders still deeply grateful to their World War II "liberators."

The Witch Hunt

After the Second World War, the U.S. was pre-occupied with the threat of communism in Europe. Fear caught the minds and hearts of every American who read and listened to popular media. One politician took the throat of the nation with this fear that spread like a prairie fire. This period of collective paranoia would be named after this one U.S. senator.

McCarthyism resounded in the halls of our government institutions, unwittingly expanded by the mass media in the Fifties. To stop "the spread of communism" became the rallying call of any high country official just visited by one U.S. Embassy functionary. Our national malaise thereafter mirrored this post-colonial dysfunction.

It was at this time that the role of American agents who worked with local Gunga Dins increased to place under surveillance the civil libertarians in the country and their un-welcomed nationalism. The local struggle against American economic engulfment was tagged "communist-inspired."

We came to know that the nationwide witch-hunt was traceable to the secret activities of the CIA, the USAID, and the U.S. Embassy in Manila. The authoritative source is Joseph B. Smith's book *Portrait of A Cold Warrior, Second Thoughts of a Top CIA Agent* [1976 reprint in paperback by Plaridel Books, Q.C.]. Smith was an ex-CIA and this was his confessional account. It showed how often American officials sent to the Third World pre-empted the use of embassy political, economic and even cultural resources over that of weak governments they were assigned to surveille. Colonel Edward Landsdale cosseted warmly to the inner circle of policy-making especially during the years of Ramon Magsaysay, then Secretary of National Defence and later President.

The virus of anti-communism among Americans had spread throughout the country. The immediate victims were professors in U.P., editorial writers, columnists, and the broad-spectrum agnostics who were later called before the Committee on Anti-Filipino Activities (CAFA), a copycat of the American version, to testify unnecessarily of their not being communists. This made the country's civil libertarians hugely uncomfortable. McCarthyism was often in town, shopping for more suspects in the academe. About this time, some students went to the hills; their professors cooled off by taking leaves-of-absence.

At the time, some national leaders did not succumb to this anti-communist hysteria. One highly respected member of the Senate Claro M. Recto, took a strong stand against this gratuitous campaign against civil liberties.

Senator Recto Faces the Dragon of Neo-Colonialism

A closer observation will show that the tempers of the 1950s enabled neo-colonialism to bloom. My generation was the last to sing with patriotic fervor the "*Star-Spangled Banner*" and "*Land of the Morning*" every Monday morning and Friday afternoon. We faced two flagpoles (our young minds did not ask, why two when we had only one county?) muttering an oath that sounded (excuse the syntax) something like "in thoughts in words and in deeds."

With that background my generation's ideological preparation for the succeeding decades was complete. The country was no longer a colony but a neo-colony. The most important infra-structure supporting this was the school system. This personal background had to reckon with one's intellectual, emotional and ideological development as activist in the mass movement.

Senator Claro M. Recto shaped my memory of politics of the 1950s. He was a man of rectitude, of clear thinking and persistently determined to discover the errors the Americans were officially making in the country. His political perspicacity was a searchlight that scanned the rest of the darkening decade.

I used to stay in the bench inside the Senate hall watching him. Many of his peers in Congress listened to him seriously although hesitant to commit to his opinions, which on the surface sounded anti-U.S. policy although not necessarily against the American people. But most of Recto's views were critical and disturbing to many Americans and embassy officials in Manila. I think he was more concerned pulling the legs of Filipinos who worshipped the great White Father symbol.

When the Senate and the House of Representatives were still housed in the same building, senators, congressional representatives, and their staff walked past each other in the lobby and hallway. Up on the second floor, on the left, one took the elevator with rattling diamond-shaped folding grills. This left was reserved for the public. On the right was another elevator reserved for the Senators. There was also another elevator at the back of the building. Senators, avoiding their constituencies asking for job recommendations, usually took the ride here entering the back of the session hall. (It was a time when one did not hesitate to link the badge of respect to them. They were far from one's thought of being "suspect crooks and criminals."

Legislators were a different breed of humans then. They were not always suspected behind some malfeasance or evil doings as the many columnists gleefully describe them currently. It would be years before the mass media allowed that suspicion to become part of our mind set. Not yet, not always until one of them pronounced the devastating public truth uttered shamefully, like a revelation by Beelzebub himself: "*What are we in power for?*" The man who uttered these words was to become Senate president.

Rizal's Two Books and the Rise of Nationalism

Why do I mention all these? It was here in the old Congress Building that I started to be running around, waiting, and looking for schedules of my favorite boss of a congressman for whom I used to ghostwrite speeches, my second payless job being only an apprentice while still in college. Senator Recto sponsored a controversial bill. I remember everyone wanted to say his piece on the "*Noli-Fili*" issue as it was called by the press then. The heated discussion that ensued was like a lighted candle that ignited Lenin's classic open prairie.

Thereafter activists, still a minority, felt a burning sentiment spreading wildly as resurgent love of country, the way Rizal managed to portray it. His novels were the only Philippine classics that emotionally stirred the vision of a revolution that the author ironically did not like to happen.

The 1950s linked in my mind the rise of nationalism fuelled by the debates on the compulsory reading of Rizal's **Noli Me Tangere**, **El Filibusterismo** and his other works. It shocked the Catholic official complacent spirituality. It was disturbed by Recto's draft bill. This was peppered, disparate as this was, by Recto's intermittent jabbing in his usually correct authoritative voice at the U.S.

Embassy and its arrogant officials. This combination could easily set one's nascent nationalism on fire as it did many of my generation's. These issues, the "Noli-Fili" and America's grudging decision to free the country from her domination survived the decade of the 1950s. These went farther a-field in the country's post Second World War history.

The Catholic Church's objections to the unexpurgated reading of the *Noli Me Tangere* and *El Filibusterismo* in schools almost divided the country not according to those who wanted to read and those who refused to read but those who cared to read and those who were compelled. This last point was the central issue in Congress. The educated middleclass survived it. The bill is now law.

As Students, We Take Ideas Seriously

I enrolled in U.P. Diliman coming from its Iloilo City branch then. The air was already glowing with sectarian heat. The late Father Delaney, S.J. seemed to define the intellectual climate among the students on the campus. Since I was new, I sensed that one is either an UPSCAn (U.P. Student Catholic Action member) or a non-UPSCAn. I avoided this grouping sensing I was not that insecure for new companions. I was a plebeian and I liked being alone.

A lot of student leaders then were either under Father Delaney's influence, or ignored, or intensely against. Meanwhile, a load of agnosticism was weighing on my back. Philosopher Ricardo Pascual was not my teacher but an epigone of his in U.P. Iloilo was. While formal logic reigned during our freshman years, it was a time when one took seriously new ideas of other philosophers.

I spent my time instead reading Sigmund Freud. To my happy surprise, the Main Library had a complete set of his work. I borrowed as many as 9 volumes in one day just waiting for the student assistant to change at the exit of the book section. Books about philosophy of ideas intrigued me. So were a few newly found friends. The laundry woman spent time segregating under my dorm bed some of these books mixed with my dirty clothes for washing. I found this as a symbolic act in itself, about what we're reading that might need laundering.

President Vidal Tan's administration seemed to have intensified sectarianism on campus. An accomplished teacher in literature who later joined the nunnery came to an unfinished rescue of my faltering and attenuated Catholicism. All these as I recall preceded the radicalization of the campus. Marx and Mao were still in the horizon but the gathering cloud of student restlessness hovered among the checkered shadows of the acacia trees that lined the university main roads. Those interested with left literature were beginning to miss their classes. Sonny San Juan was filling up pages of the *Philippine Collegian* with long quotes from Kierkegaard, Heidegger, Sartre, Nietzsche and a smorgasbord of other Continental philosophers. I was associate editor of its magazine supplement.

Mass Movement Absorbs History

Political movements are seldom created by a single issue much less by a single idea but often by several issues that coalesce, pick up more adherents along the way, intensify, expand and consolidate. Every NGO organizer worth his salt knows this. This fuelled a lot of "agit-props." My intellectual idealism (read: love of abstractions) which reading of Hegel cultivated did not stop these issues. I learned this much later after a reading infection from Mao's simplistic translated prose.

The issue of nationalism is political, cultural, and economic. It connects a series of disparate circumstances that could stir a groundswell. The more people are affected the greater chance is there of this accumulation heaving into political turbulence, against symbolic institutions that repress or are made tools for economic exploitation. My recent reading of **The Tiananmen Papers** (compiled by Zhang Liang with Afterword by Orville Schell, 2001) abundantly confirmed this observation.

The reality of people rising is not only contemporaneous with us after two People Power "revolutions" but also a part of history wrought in the anvil of past domination. Campus nationalism was young, growing but uncertain of its pace. My intellectual responses were attuned less to the task at hand (U.S. imperialism) and more on getting acquainted with theories. Information technology was still vague. We were like ants peering at the edge of Bill Gate's drawing board at the future of knowledge acquisition.[5]

It will be thirty years later that many of the young will conquer this built-in skill in handling this new tool. This could prove to be transforming both for education and for our society in general. The recent popularization of computers in schools confirms it. But integrating it into a coherent master narrative we commonly call ideology or the "isms" could be an ominous possibility depending on what or who at the end controls the info-infrastructure. The most dominant of this ideology in our lifetime and the newest in our consciousness was and still is Capitalism. Ideas, the tools for transmitting them, and the objective condition were the triune in transition society that deeply interested me and my friends.

And what about nationalism? Meanwhile, the heroes of *Noli Mi Tangere* and *El Filibusterismo* and the rest who lined up the pantheon of resistance against Spanish domination were resurrected from the books. Memory had long accustomed us to believing that Sakay, Papa Isio and Ricarte were bandits or traitors as these are described in our history books. It was time for their re-writing. Foreigners or foreign-educated scholars wrote them for our schools. It was time for their re-evaluation, for the re-writing of our own history. This is the basis of a growing conviction held by the activists of the First Quarter Storm (FQS) that the revolution they were launching is the continuation of what Mabini, Bonifacio and the Katipuneros had started but left unfinished.

What's the singular impact of the decade on me as activist? In all kinds of mis-education, the mind is always the first casualty. That is why many of my generation believed during this decade that Filipinos should run the school system responsible in training the young. The opposite of this is a mental captivity called neo-colonialism, from which condition many today still struggle to be free. What has the last fifty years brought out in this historical chain?

---

[5] Read Obet Versola's *Towards a Political Economy of Information* published 2004 by the Foundation for Nationalist Studies, Inc, Q.C. Also, *Information Feudalism: Who Owns the Knowledge Economy?* by Pete Drahos with John Braithwaite originally published in 2002 by Earthscan, London. Reprinted in summary version as "Political Organizing Behind TRIPS," by The Corner House as Briefing 32, September 2004, U.K.

Semiotics in the Making of the 'Man of the Masses'

In 1953, President Elpidio Quirino was about to end his term in the midst of ceaseless media carping. Even his own Secretary of National Defence, Ramon Magsaysay broke away from him to run in a manner novel in Philippine politics at that time. The "man of the masses" was a newly invented mantra for winning in a presidential election. That did not happen during the elections of Aguinaldo, nor of Quezon, of Osmeña and of Quirino. With that slogan, I stepped into a new period in Philippine politics defined by semiotics that made and identified the sources of power from the masses.

Thereafter, politicians would run for public office invoking the expression that each one is a "man of the masses." It is a left-handed recognition of the political value of democracy, where the "masses" reflected more numbers than any social class. If we echo Hernando Abaya in his book *Betrayal in the Philippines*, democracy was never more betrayed than during the post-war period. Behind the baby kissing, leaping the puddle antics, eating with bare hands and hugging the poor and oppressed, behind the skulduggery was a worse picture of a national leader, the original "man of the masses" manipulated by the CIA.

The critical and behind-the-scene role of the CIA shaping our political life has since become part of our un-written history. One should re-read as part of one's re-education, *The Invisible Government* by David Wise. The Vietnam War was evidence of this CIA interference almost systemic in the internal affairs of developing countries like the Philippines, then and now.

My first patriotic rally was an embarrassment. I joined the late Pete Daroy. We went or were supposed to go to the Department of Foreign Affairs in Padre Faura where large numbers of protesters were assembled earlier. It was an issue triggered by the bombing in the Gulf of Tonkin and the sinking of one ship by the Americans without U.S. congressional approval. The ship turned out not *SS Cambodge* as emblazoned in our placard. With dispatch, we surreptitiously threw our placard into the nearest garbage drum. It was a lesson for future activists to get their facts right before leaping into marches and demos.

The "New" Journalism

The orinola (bedpan) issue and the P20, 000 gold (plated?) beds that nested in the innards of the presidential palace were news earnestly churned by the Opposition with the assistance of newspaper columnists under the wings of the Lopez business house. It was an early instance of Business telling politicians to leave off political choices, especially of the country's presidents. The stories continued to regale the public as one of gospel importance and therefore deserved more media time and space. In Iloilo where I grew up, the Lopezes were political and moneyed icons.

The rest of the population diverted their attention from the real problem of *neo-colonialism*. Nobody asked, "What animal is that?" The public was ready for more diversions.[6] The country's journalism turned politics into great entertainment and brouhaha. Those who desired rapid circulation unfailingly follow this formula. The success in circulation was in inverse ratio to enlightened and enlightening journalism.

The U.S. embassy through its CIA assets took advantage of the orinola-cum-gold-plated bed scandal. It foisted Magsaysay as "the man of the masses" against somebody "luxuriating" on a 20-thousand peso bed in Malacañang. Mainstream media at that time had sunk and possibly reached its nadir. Business-minded mass communication students today study this method of increasing circulation. There are positive elements here. Often the power of media expose' is what makes for the secretive government bureaucrat or politician to tremble. He or she is aware of what the mass media is capable of un-doing her/him or the competing business. This made the "press/public relations officer" or PRO a new, full time, well-paid professional in the bureaucracy.

---

[6] The same way as today's public, the majority of whom are low-earning employees, who are being diverted from the solution to their problems of high prices by betting on numbers a.k.a. *jueteng*; they are being branded "criminals" for getting into this unproductive alternative to an unlucky life until the government legalizes it by re-naming it "lotto."

Abandoning an Ideology; the IGP Takes Over

Let us conclude the decade with the note on what usually could happen to an abandoned ideology, or more accurately, to the ideologues that used to be committed to it.

By 1961 newspaper accounts portrayed the PKP becoming an effete formation. Its top leaders were arrested and the rest continued to be relentlessly hunted. Its armed component, many of whom were idealistic peasants with deep grievances against Central Luzon landlords, dissipated into armed bands. Their ideological veneer started to fade and their leaders started to indulge in income-generating "livelihood." These latter included sporadic holdups, ambushing of businessmen, bank robbery, gun-for-hire, and other activities that belong to the ignoble stratum of every revolutionary losing grip of his noble purpose. HUK leader Sumulong of the old PKP was known to lead the group. "Idealist" Bernabe Buscayno a.k.a. Dante lost faith and subsequently wavered. The military heat was too much.

It will take another seven years before the historic meeting would occur, between "the armed peasant looking for an ideology and an ideologue searching for an armed revolutionary." This expression was attributed to socialist Dodong Nemenzo memorializing the historic meeting of Dante and Joe Sison.

Political Undertow of the 1950s

Remnants of the underground re-organized themselves, boosted by initiatives of student activists from U.P., P.U.P. and Lyceum. The early features of the mass movement defined its nature by these hidden political dynamics.

The surface was deceptively placid. While people are important elements, history has taught us that they are as many "pawns and jumping horses," as in the game of chess. Their decisions zigzag according to circumstance. As Karl Marx wrote, "People make history, but they don't make it just as they please… not under circumstances chosen by them…" but more like the many other things they encounter in life's rough edges. What they aim to do is as much dependent on why they are capably equipped to surmount what is obstructing them. But most important, when theory informs and guides their practices.

Among the organizers and participants of the mass movement these tools of power are used in changing people's relations with each other. They invoke these to transform society radically. The mass movement (underground or above ground) is *sui generis*, one such tool for empowering the people. This is especially so when the legal institutions and services are not within the reach of the masses. Or when the masses are marginalized from exercising them or pushed back and denied.

A few militants started to look beyond the local political horizon, that is, outside the country. What they saw was a revolution that had achieved its goal: *a reversal of relations between the few exploiters (read: foreigners) and the mass of exploited Chinese people.* Some wanted to observe first hand what was happening there, and a few secretly travelled to China to take lessons or, as many did, shook hands and took group pictures with Mao. It was the first political photo-op in the story of the country's mass movement.

On the other end, there were early Filipino communists and socialists who took the Russian road. These two divergent routes seemed to replicate the international split that occurred later between Maoists in China and the socialists from Soviet Russia. That's no longer our concern. **Trotskyism** took care of this. (Please see glossary.)

It is the relation between the old PKP whimpering toward the sunset of its life and Jose Maria Sison's phoenix-like CPP rising from the ashes of the previous struggles of workers and peasants that mirrored in the later years the local ideological differences.

There are a few political landmarks I wish to present in summary calendar for the decade of the 1950s:

First, there was the final downfall of the PKP when it started its "parliamentary struggle" at the price of giving up its principles that used to be backed up by armed resistance. Thanks to the C.I.A.-instigated spread of the viral suspicion that anybody who is against American policy must be a dangerous commie. Our American umbilical cord had hardly disconnected at this time. My initial days in U.P. took the final cutting and replaced the same with restless intellectualism.

Second, the resurgent nationalism of Claro M. Recto invited a cloud of red scare that intensified in the following decade. The legislation on the **"Noli Fili"** was a critical breakthrough to the growing number of nationalist fledglings, many of them belonging to the labor front; but many more came from the State University. Ghostwriting for somebody who knew Rizal at least improved my respect for the writings of the national hero.

Third, the rise of new political skulduggery popularized in the new politics creating "the Man of the Masses" who turned out to be the handiwork of the C.I.A. maximizing the skills in press agentry. Neo-colonialism was restored with the bureaucracy, especially the school system, taking care of how it should spread, i.e., through the young minds of my generation.

We end this chapter of the 1950s by recognizing the talent of Jose Ma. Sison as a campus organizer. Among the earliest student organizations that had their impact on student militancy was the Student Cultural Association of U.P. This was initiated sometime 1959 by the future founder of the Communist Party of the Philippines. SCAUP was the early campus-oriented NGO that aimed to organize students while developing their militant nationalist orientation.

We recall the end of the 1950s as "the edge of a fading ideology" following the old communist party losing grip of the socialist principles.

Chapter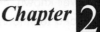

From Colonialism
to Neo-colonialism
1960s

Short-Lived Political Economy of "Filipino First"

Nationalism has its own economic-political terrain changing and affecting the lives of many people. Government policies instigate to change them. I viewed the "Filipino First" thrust of President Carlos P. Garcia as a reaction to President Ramon Magsaysay's almost sell-out to the U.S. The Garcia policy supported Filipino businesses threatened by increased American vested presence in the economy.

Filipino entrepreneurs were given priority in the use of foreign exchange. Garcia "filipinized" wholesale trade and labor employment. He required firms to submit lists of foreign personnel working in the hotel and restaurant industry. A Filipino-owned oil company was first formed under his administration.

Strictly speaking, the period 1957-1961 covered President Carlos P. Garcia's administration, a time linked to that memorable but short-lived political economy, critics of WTO today look back with teary nostalgia.

Two well-known economic theorists of the Third World development model guided technocrats of the period, even beyond. The envisioned "take off" to industrialization could not rely on mobilization of domestic capital. The prevailing theory by W. W. Rostow to whom experts of the period paid academic obeisance, observed that the early stage of economic development before "take off" was that the nation must muster savings before this could happen. Do we have savings to propel such a "take off"? This was the kind of economics I and fellow students in U.P. were regaled with.

Another way is to ask the question: under what conditions do we save as Filipinos? We save for weddings, for baptisms, for birthdays, for fiestas and desperately for our children's education but not in order for the country to industrialize. Filipinos are incorrigibly inclined to be happy people.

When I told the writer and bookstore owner Frankie Sionil Jose about my observation, he corrected me by saying that in many old, popular songs, Filipinos betray a sad, plodding and melancholy spirit. Start with "planting rice is never fun...." that reverberates in hundreds of Grade I classrooms in the provinces. This is reinforced by a massive cultural downgrading like "*Ang bakya mo Neneg ay luma at kupas....*" This mellowed my opinion about Filipinos being happy people.

Another western economic theory with productivist swing tried to wrest the country from this cultural base. W. Arthur Lewis, a Nobel laureate in the 1950s and a maven in the development theory of third world economies also observed that even when the "surplus labor" of the countryside were going to the cities, unless trained and educated to produce, this would only (prophetically enough) increase urban social problems.

Before the decade of the sixties ended President Garcia's "Filipino First" policy hung fire against the beacon of foreign loans with their "conditionalities." To jumpstart so-called economic development, a devastating "paradigm shift" happened on the way to Congress. The phrase was uncommon at that time but it would describe what had happened next when the new administration prepared for its implementation. In essence, the development could be made to start not by increasing domestic savings but by shifting to foreign borrowings. The foreign cash nexus took center stage from here on.

Foreign Borrowings and the Debt Trap

I wrote in my journal thus: "The country since then never got rid of that albatross (plus the burden of its unstoppable interests) around every Filipino's neck—the Foreign Debt. Thereafter, it would depend on the foreign law experts, on the foreign creditors who finally would choke to death the idea of the economy being steered towards self-reliance.

"This happened when the economic policies of President Garcia suffered a reversed gear under the administration of his successor President Diosdado Macapagal, the father of the Republic's most adept expert in neo-classical economics five administrations down the road. The "Poor Boy from Lubao"— the election mantra that brought him to the presidency—hastily declared "full decontrol" as the guiding light of the economy under him. It turned out that corruption in the country's economic history had been worse than the mythical seven-headed dragon.

The decision to 'full,control' favored immediately foreign companies and its currency speculators waiting on the wings. It resulted in the rapid depletion of foreign reserves. It cut short the development of domestic market, constricted opportunities for the locals, increased the unemployed and threw out into the cold Filipinos running fledging businesses for lack of dollars.

"In the early 1960s, U.S. accelerated pressures on the government to get capital from abroad. The willing creditors stood by, ready with their "conditionalities" like a taskmaster holding a whip. This brought the country into the historic indebted-ness known as Structural Adjustment Loans (SAL). It arrived with panache, mixed among the new vocabulary in the lexicon of saving the economy. The international finance institutions (IFIs) like the IMF, WB and ADB dominated the capital markets of the day. Thereafter, no economic development came out of the drawing board with the SAL stamped all over it."

The cowed, awed and often towed domestic technocrats trained in foreign schools were helping Macapagal "sell" the country to the foreign investors. With neo-classical economics on the drawing board, even today this thinking runs its course. The idea that Philippine development will have to rely principally on capital from abroad came from this skewed economic thinking.

It was novel at that time and inspired by the school of economics rooted on values of profit accumulation. If things could be produced with less, why not borrow so you could produce more, so runs the new economic rationale. Was it not the Wharton Business School that trained many of our technocrats? If only foreign money is within reach could we proceed with this productivist economics. Later in the day, the school of economics of U.P. made this also a hard fixture in its thinking. Was the direction of this policy irreversible? Where was it taking the country and the masses?

An articulate economist-businessman Hilario Henares was appointed to head the National Economic Council, the forerunner of today's NEDA, an important office where the country shapes its economic direction. This was to placate nationalist businessmen prematurely weaned from the "Filipino first" policy. They grumbled. I sometimes wish Filipino businessmen could do something aside from grumbling or threatening to grumble. The angry nationalists' interest could not be served by it much less the principal interest of the national economy in dire straits. It was a political gambit for President Diosdado Macapagal. He wished that a vociferous nationalist like Larry Henares could temper the impression created by his government increasingly cosmeticized to look pro-foreign and pro-U.S. if not a toady to IMF pre-conditions. But this equivocation did not pay. In the 1965 election, the U.S. smelling that Macapagal was following a "nationalist" line taught him a lesson by undermining his re-election. The U.S. embassy stealthily supported Marcos.

How did it happen that Marcos won? Was the "Poor Boy from Lubao" losing his wind with the masses that put him to the presidency? According to Joe Sison (more of him in the next decades) Marcos was "Macapagal's man Friday at that time cultivating the CIA and other US agencies linkages." He cited for source Joseph B. Smith's book *Portrait of a Cold Warrior, Second Thoughts of a Top CIA Agent.*[7] The student scholar Sison used this source later in an interview with the German journalist where he exposed this "Marcos liaison work with the Manila CIA Station". More of this can be found in the young revolutionary's book *The Philippine Revolution, the Leader's View* (p. 24). Larry Henares' nationalist line did not last very long. Like an orphaned theory,

---

[7] Introduction by Luis Mauricio, reprint Plaridel Books, Q.C., 1976

Larry and his economic nationalism mandolin were unceremoniously thrown out of the window. Larry went around in several symposia of the Left, explaining the economic ideology the country needed, and strongly unloading his spleen. Then finally, he quit the Macapagal cabinet like an honourable man.

The Sixties seemed to have prepared the ground for the country's major problems that still beset it up to the end of the 20th century. The sturdy roots of these issues were traced from this period. The Philippines entered the 21st century with all her major economic problems rising, growing more complex. For example: foreign exchange shortage, misuse of foreign exchange, the readiness to borrow, peso devaluation, unemployment, low exports. At the end of the decade, the economy wriggled out of the hands of Filipinos like an eel. Foreigners who held the dollars seemed to have greater control over it.

Meanwhile the implication of these unresolved issues already defined the political, economic and cultural tumults of the coming martial law years. The country was believed then to be sitting on top of a metaphorical volcano about to erupt. The abolition of tenancy, a major achievement of President Diosdado Macapagal failed to lift the farmers from their poverty and landlessness. The landlords resisted it and its enforcement slowed down and then halted.

The Rise of the Mass Movement

The semiotics for the rising mass movement in the country that arose from the economic crisis was fore-grounded by other events here and abroad. This presaged the critical political stage of the next decade. My activist years increasingly intensified.

What factors triggered the birth of the mass movement? There were many. Particularly the issues that militant students responded to included, that also created political turmoil in other countries in Asia, Africa, Latin America, the U.S. and Europe during this period. To illustrate: the Vietnam War was the most stirring of these issues especially the inflamed responses of student activists in Western Europe and the U.S.

The 1960s mass movement in the country was a response both to the loosening hold of the national political leaders on our economy. My own position at this time was that it was the absence of direction in our social and political life. Population was increasing rapidly. Urbanization was coming in with a highly commercialized imported lifestyle. Many could not catch up with the consumerist life style but instead created a visible mass of poor people. This further inflamed discontent. Government programs to alleviate economic suffering were far behind in servicing the needs of many people.

The mass movement grew out of this negative picture. The economy was in shambles. Students were easier to organize in the situation where solutions were needed but not found around. Marcos tried to provide a new vision calling it *ang bagong lipunan* (the new society). But he was instead increasingly hated. The mass movement organizers and ideological teachers came out with programmatic agenda directly addressing the needs of the broad, unhappy masses. Contacts with the UG were made.

What problems did the mass movement envision to overcome? There were three: the struggle for genuine sovereignty against the U.S., the threats to unity of the Filipinos against the local reactionaries, big buy-and-sell comprador class and last, the landlords who were driving their landless tenants to desperation. All these were classics in the repertoire of mass leaders and young street marchers.

The movement started on the sun-drenched streets of Manila. Its expressions were openly seen in the blank spaces of the city, in public walls, bridges, base of monuments, hangings on electric posts, writings that proclaimed angry opposition to foreign domination in the economy, in politics, in our cultural life. Many of us were expert in rapid wall "paintings" often with the police on our heels.

Many of these messages verged on the scurrilous that burned the blank spaces of public walls. It was an ambitious political enterprise lined up with inevitable ups and downs. It aimed for a "national industrialization, genuine land reform, and an efficient, honest bureaucracy." The vision lacked effective vehicle. Down the road, these issues were summarized in what the militants called "the three basic problems" to wit, "feudalism, bureaucrat capitalism and U.S. imperialism."

The social change was coming through a long, hard political process. It was the young Filipinos' version of the *Risorgimento* of the early 19th century Italy that produced a Cavour, a Mazzini, and a Garibaldi.

Social Movements in the Other Countries

It is important to take notice of what had been happening also in other parts of the world during these turbid ten years. More directly relevant to us as a neo-colony was how the Sixties linked to the irrational fear that gripped the American minds. It was their perceived threat of communism. The Korean War of the previous decade brought this to a boiling point. Anybody anti-American was a suspect commie. This was forty years ahead of the tiresome now Bush classic circa 2001: "If you're not with me, you must be a terrorist." The semantics sounded different but the pattern of thinking runs the same.

Anti-communism was the flavour of the decade as anti-terrorism was at the start of the 21st century. The rhetoric of anti-communism produced fear that fuelled more mass actions. This rhetoric replayed during the Republican National Convention in New York in 2004 where I found myself mingling with millions of activists in the avenues radiating from Times Square and Manhattan denouncing Bush and his corporate partners to gobble their civil liberties. This was how Americans played their counter-actions on the prevailing semiotics in the marches along democratic streets. In the decade after the New Millennium, terrorism replaced communism. The intensity of paranoia, its single-mindedness and blinkered outlook remained the same.

In the Sixties there were more of these collective political passions. There was the Feminist Movement, a call against the experience of women in society oppressed by patriarchy; the Civil Rights Movement when the blacks fought for equal rights in schools, in buses, in canteens, in public spaces, etc. Racist America was under siege during the period. Muslim black leader Malcolm X and his shifting battles against deep prejudices on his people almost deified him; same with Martin Luther King; the SDS (Students for Democratic Society) was rampaging against the immorality of the Vietnam War.[8]

---

[8] Paul Potter, SDS president at that time declared in a climax of a memorable speech: "What kind of system is it that justifies the United States seizing the destinies of the Vietnamese people and using them callously for its own purpose? We must name that System, describe it, analyze it and change it." It was high SDS rhetoric although Potter must have known what "it" is. One hundred years earlier Marx described it and analyzed it in his monumental three volumes, *Das Kapital*. See pp. 232-233 in *Democracy is in the Streets, from Port Horon to the Siege of Chicago* by James Miller, 4th printing, Harvard U. Press, 2000.

There were preceding political lessons. Filipino activists repeated the anti-imperialist and anti-colonial themes that were dominant as early as 1955. Patrice Lumumba in the Congo, Castro in Cuba, the Bay of Pigs aggression, the Indonesian struggle against U.S. intervention in West Irian. My friends in U.P., many of whom were knowledgeable of the above issues classroom wise were still unorganized. Theorizing the experience was different from seeking action; the organizing vehicle comes later.

Joema, Voltaire Garcia, et al

Among the student leaders who kept track of these developments was Jose Ma. Sison, an outwardly shy, lip-hanging undergrad from the state university. From his reading and experiences soon enough, he became a maven of armed struggle (AS) in his native backyard. Models were not lacking.

His first taste of jail was when he led a picket against U.S. President Lyndon B. Johnson at the Manila Hotel. The U.S. president was then in Manila mobilizing puppet states behind U.S. adventurism in Vietnam; adventurism here meant expanding capitalist interests wrapped in the tin foils of "defending freedom." The police detained the young Sison for six hours. The next day, according to his own account in a typical panache of the left romantic, he "came back with 5000 students and workers to demonstrate at the same place" i.e., Manila Hotel. (p. 24, Sison and Rainer.)

In another instance, U.P. student leader Voltaire Garcia launched the *October 24th Movement* with the large support of the KM. The student mass movement was born, a part of the worldwide social cauldron spilling its hot juices into the troubled streets of the cities. It was a prairie fire of political consciousness-raising among the young many of whom came from U.P., a favourite public university petty-bourgeois parents send their children to. Its liberal, agnostic climate became favourable to the training of militant students.

A lot of student activities were voluntary, self-imposed, not a part of the school. As Sison said, his work as activist involved ideological, political organizing. This pattern became the model of activities for militants wanting to be revolutionaries by organizing inside/outside campuses. They formed study circles, discussion groups, studied socialist theories and how Marxism could infuse the revolutionary spirit, methods and practices in the national democratic program of the growing mass movement. My acquaintance with Joe was superficial, except for what I gathered reading his books. It would be years later that I met him and wife Julie in Utrecht, already a revolutionary icon to generations of students.

In Joe's book, the students joined workers' movement, got involved in their direct political actions like pickets, strikes; explored other forms of concerted actions like marches, rallies; integrated themselves in several workers' struggles. Also, they organized seminars and put out mimeographed copies of political statements, distributed manifestos, studied and read more materials about national and international issues.

He wrote, "The covert discussion groups which increasingly developed into organized groups of the proletarian revolutionary party (read: CPP) became the hard core of the mass movement". The method, frequency and spread became enriched in due time. Sison was the first KM chairperson. He was in the forefront that shaped the ideological line of national democratic revolution. He assumed major responsibility in manning part of the country undertaking political demos. This included "training large members of cadres for the worker-led revolutionary party." (pp. 31-32).

During President Johnson's visit at the time of the Manila Summit, the youth responded to it by conducting teach-ins and some form of direct actions before the U.S. embassy. Schools, factories, section of communities joined to back up actions of aggressive trade unions in the urban and rural areas. Many of their members supported strikes and pursued defiant mass actions. (Sison pp 35-36).

An organization like KM was important not only for what it was doing during its heydays (1960-1970) but also for being an alternative social formation or ASF. It restored, revived, trained and enriched the militancy of the youthful cadres guided by revolutionary Marxist-Leninist theory and added to it Mao Tsetung Thought or MTT. This latter was compressed in the popular little red book that in China had been venerated by millions that the votaries of the Holy Bible could only envy.

The formal school system slowly infected by the witch-hunt virus slammed shut its libraries against selected speechless and writings of Fidel Castro, Lenin, Marx, Mao and North Vietnamese General Vo Nguyen Giap but filled its racks with handouts from the U,S.I.S. It was a battleground for the youths' mind that was heavily limited by the cost of good reads and the impecunious state of many students who were marching.

Several student leaders were not isolated from the activities that also enriched the workers' movement. CACP members were also attuned to it; sometimes we found ourselves in pickets joining with strikers. The account by Sison in this interview with Rainer Werning in a book cited earlier outlined his many activities and contacts with nationalist labor leaders like Ignacio Lacsina, Bert Olalia, Cipriano Cid. The last one was head of the country's biggest labor federation and became chairperson of the Socialist Party of the Philippines sometime 1965.

Jose Sison also got in touch with peasant leaders of *Malayang Samahang Magsasaka* (free association of peasants) in 1963. He lectured on the revolutionary theory, a refresher course, and "the national democratic line," His visits to the countryside allowed him to conduct social investigation (SI) and mass work preparing the bases for the underground mass movement when martial law was declared. Marcos was quick to the draw but Sison and the cadres were ahead. Looking back, one could only marvel at the students' foresight running ahead of the Marcos plan to rule the country under martial rule.

The Church, Nationalism and Mass Movement

Sometime in early 1958, a lone priest in his white soutane walked back and forth in front of the joint Houses of the country's law-making body, the building now appropriately occupied by the Philippine Museum. Two things looked strange at that time to any passerby. First, a priest saying the rosary while carrying a placard walking slowly in deep prayer. Second, the placard

---

[8] volumes, *Das Kapital*. See pp. 232-233 in *Democracy is in the Streets, from Port Horon to the Siege of Chicago* by James Miller, 4th printing, Harvard U. Press, 2000.

carried a text denouncing the ills of society. It was a novel publicity, a silent public prayer with words of denunciation written against a cardboard framed in wood for everyone to see and read. Coming from Zamboanga, Father Hilario Lim used to drop by our house every time he was in town. I accompanied him to the bus station on his way to central Luzon where he used to visit a fellow priest, another Jesuit expelled from the fold.

It would take another 20 years before this public piety and attention-drawing act started by Father Lim became widely accepted and practiced by many religious as adjunct to demos. This would be repeatedly used decades hence in public rallies. It was a tool for empowerment of the oppressed masses in this Christian country. Soon enough the urban poor, peasants, assorted professionals like doctors, lawyers, teachers, the rest of concerned citizens like mothers and even children who found fault in their government or some firms or officials would become accustomed to this method of expressing their grievances. The practice is now an institution outside the establishmentarian state. It has become the precursor of many mass movement tools.

As if carrying the message of the coming years, the ex-Jesuit Father Hilario S. Lim was a Filipino expelled from the Society of Jesus sometime 1958. He was a young maverick of the Catholic Church. He espoused nationalism in various forms (he called it "Filipinism") by demanding among others, that "American Jesuits must return to America as well as American soldiers and their evil officials…" he observed tendentiously that American Jesuits assigned in the country then hardly knew "ten percent of the writings of Rizal and Mabini". The year was preceded by the heated debate, by now a law, on the "*Noli-Fili*". (See previous chapter, The 1950s.)

All over again, Father Lim's voice was a replay of the three martyred priests' repressed voices in the history of Filipino nationalism. He was a product of that political milieu. We remember Father Lim today for his new method of publicly expressing grievances having just returned to the country from China drenched with left romanticism; didn't we ever miss a group picture with China's Helmsman! He gave me booklet, 3"x5" explaining his expulsion. It was in old, fading newsprint, hardly clean with a dedication to me. I still have to look for it inside my cluttered drawer, when needed. He took no small pride in showing my family a small picture showing him and some group of Filipinos with Chairman Mao.

Subsequent mass movements had institutionalized an open vigil, a public prayer that spilled out of the churches, a one-man demo started by this expelled Jesuit, an orchestrated rosary, and yes, for this Catholic nation there will be more prayers to the Intercessor, the Virgin Mary herself—all of these. It was nationalism awakened from the warmth of her holy garb.

It seems that the color of mass movement in this country has been determined less by nationalism than by the people's dominant religion. It will be 20 years down the road that the first People Power salvo was an immediate product of the clergy marching. Together with masses, they prayed and spilled into the streets with rosaries between nervous fingers and piety between quivering lips. It was a good cover for many middleclass activists against the accusation of being godless communist. So went the religious trace in the methods of the early 1960s mass movement. The practice has become increasingly common, often invoked like an angelus at the closing of a highly politicized day.

The composition and method of this mass movement would cover the whole country in the years to come. These were the Christian community lay workers and the disciplined young cadres energizing the marches and demos. This historic mix symbolically would become in the latter years a leaven to a broader struggle. This was the ground where the united front grew like an eager sapling.

Tondo served as an early illustrative base. Trinidad Herrera was the fearless leader of the Tondo area and used to be a lay organizer. In one symposium I attended, she narrated how she was brought to the military intelligence camp where she was undressed, interrogated, made to stand shoe-less on the wet floor where one live wire was connected. The other end, plastered to her body and for every question about her alleged link with the underground (which she denied) a hand dynamo was cranked making the flow of electricity all over her body agonizing. Every time she would tell this experience, her audience would gasp with terror and pity. I heard her talk in one symposium that ended with our skin feeling like electricity running along it. The picture of the military as "anti-people" usually gets a dressing down in this gathering.

Idealistic, realistic and not infrequently romantic challenges against political authority were launched on poor people's houses. Even squatter-residents in Manila's foreshore area long viewed as trapped in their ignorance, poverty and inertia formed an anti-ejection group calling itself Zone One Tondo Organization or ZOTO. The dynamic elements that supported the initiative of ZOTO were early small, localized version. The gathering energy that synthesized the formation of some NGOs related to CACP down the years picked up strength from here.

Other Option: The Underground

It was about this time (late, 1960s) that militant elements of the mass movement took the cavernous path of the struggle from above. Simultaneously, it became partly a mass movement from below. I missed a lot of friends in the campus; they were nowhere. I suspect the police also missed them.

The dynamics started to change from hereon. This transition reached another level of organizing the masses. The method changed but the perseverance remainèd unchanged.

The 1960s ended by gradually pushing the organized masses to the underground. The relation between those above ground and those below was not completely walled up. The pent-up frustration, anger and the youth's anarchistic, insurrectionary impulse directed against authority and its surrogate symbols took the day. The political energies of Joe Sison guided by the MTT found the field open for more studied organizing. His generation especially those who had decided to drop out of schools from which they believed they were learning all the wrong things about their country received Joe Sison like a hero. They were encouraged to peruse the *Red Book* with more than scholarly enthusiasm. A few young militants smelt gunpowder between its pages. My contacts with Joe were erratic, accidental. Sometimes I would catch a glimpse of him riding a public bus.

Consequently, many wanted to join the armed section of the underground. Not a few NPAs were dropouts from college. The hot blood of the young dropouts could no longer be contained in their revolutionary veins. Passionate and politically charged patriotism took the day. Many a young activist had made political decisions. The revolution started to look for a theory.

What happened to the old Partido Komunista ng Pilipinas (PKP) that was supposed to take a leading role according to the books? When many of its ranks were decimated and a few leaders hauled to jail, (thanks to CIA fingering into the local mess) the old communist party had turned effete (read: parliamentary.) Joe Sison once a member in it saw that the PKP had turned its back from the real struggle of the peasants they used to lead. Sison under a disguised name became founder sometime the second half of 1960s of the alternative political party inspired by MTT.

The young Sison mustered loads of moral anger and nationalist hurt against the old PKP leaders. He felt the old party of which he was a passionate part betrayed the masses. Most of the observations here are found in his interview account written with Sison by Weiner Rainer cited earlier. I met Rainer a German journalist married to a Filipina when he was gathering data for his book already late 1980s.

By the late 1960s, the mass movement gathered strength. There were contingent secretly armed groups not necessarily joining the street marchers but watching closely, or so I was imagining. Its moral influence to us could not be underestimated. It was usually a small group. Then thousands of soldiers blocked the road to the Palace. Often in marches and rallies, I would see the workers in rubber slippers, arms linked, lurching forward that reminded me of "The Charge of the Light Brigade" poem by Tennyson.

From Colonialism to Neo-colonialism

The guerrilla tactics of a few underground "soldiers of the people," remnants of Taruc's HUKs sometimes would conduct futile ambushes. If nothing else, it proved that they were still around. They could make government troops scamper and count casualties. It illustrates Che Guevarra's "foco theory," an idea not strange to activists who joined the underground in the late 1960s.

The New People's Army (NPA), a renovated condition of the armed group that used to occupy the hills of Arayat and other parts of forested Central Luzon continued to fuel the nationalist spirit of the mass movement. The presence in the minds of many activists of these sporadic guerrilla challenges meant the government was vulnerable. The thought echoed in the open marches and demos.

Did the "foco theory" succeed to strengthen the mass movement? Yes and no. although failing in many countries, Filipino activists looked up to the successes of the Cuban revolution and later the Nicaraguan struggle as models. Many South American countries pursued similar mass movements inspired by Che Guevarra but these did not ripen into a revolutionary turnaround. The new social mechanisms needed were not there; no alternative social formations (ASFs) were visible perhaps because the attempts were bound by the romanticisms of the young revolutionaries concerned with opposing and not with putting up a more stable structure to house and protect their fleeting gains. The early split between Maoists and pro-Soviet militants took off from this period.[9]

An apt summary of this chapter is also a good introduction to what comes at the advent of the next decade. The historian Eric Hobsbaum describes in his book *Interesting Times, a Twentieth-Century Life*, especially in its chapter 15 entitled "The Sixties." If nothing else, it suggests the international reach of what it was to be an activist during this period. Hobsbawm, an old horse of the English Left wrote about his times then: "...May 8, 9 and 10, the streets of Paris....were full of demonstrating students. By sheer chance the commemoration of Marx's (150th) anniversary coincided with the climax of the great Paris student rebellion. Within a day or two it was to become more than a student rebellion, namely a nationwide worker's strike and a major political crisis of the regime of General de Gaulle." (p.246)

That would have been their "EDSA" but the students and workers did not succeed in toppling the French government as intended or in driving out its President. In the Philippines nothing of the sort happened in the late 1960s. Most of what Hobsbawm was writing about had romanticized the Philippine Left. It included readings of the broad social risings in the U.S.

---

[8] See *The Imagination of the New Left, A Global Analysis of 1968* by George Katciaficas, pp35-37, South End Press, Boston, U.S.A., 1987.

Left Romanticism Takes the Youth

The First Quarter Storm (1970) was a political tumescence. Che Guevarra started to appear in T-shirts. The eldest son of Dodong Nemenzo was earlier named after the Cuban revolutionary coming down from the hills to boot out the corrupt Batista. Dante stickers were found in the book covers especially of the Left romantics from U.P. Diliman, Philippine College of Commerce and Lyceum of the Philippines.

The political climate produced a medley of symbols that fuelled the 1970 mass movement of the city streets mixed with dry dung left by calesas, etc. Newsmen leaving their desks patronized *Taboy's Sinko Litros* in Mabini Street. Everybody was a serious revolutionary in a childish way. The open mass movement crowded with middleclass characters rampaged half joyfully, half fearful and threatened. Left romanticism took the day and Jose Maria Sison now called "Joema" by revolutionary mavens was booted out of U.P. less for proselytizing MTT than for being· frequently absent from classes busy as he was spreading the gospel of the Left.

Subversion and Black Humor

When I took the bus from Diliman to Quiapo I usually got off at the corner of the Quezon Boulevard and Azcarraga street now Claro M. Recto where *P & P Bookstore* displayed in its narrow tight bookshelves a slew of leftist readings. The store was ensconced between nondescript old buildings that looked as if they would readily collapse even before the revolution. It sold cheaper reprints and left readings than other places known at that time. It was the usual source of writings that exuded the odor of subversion. The nationalist businessman Joaquin Po and his brother owned the store. A lot of books confiscated by the military during their mad raiding days came from this small store.

In the closing of the sixties there were more of these raids and confiscation that did not discriminate between Dante, the Pampango subversive from the author of *Divine Comedy*. The undisciplined Filipinos kept to their humors and ceaseless banter, a form of disguised cynicism, as means of surviving an emergent authoritarian state. For example, the seventies opened with a radio character ridiculing the Marcos slogan about "what the country needs is national discipline in order to progress." It runs like this in Pilipino, "*Sa ikauunlad nang bayan, disilinang kailangan.*" In less than 24 hours, the fellow was dungeoned for derogating the idea of "national discipline" with "bicycling." Ariel Ureta, to whom this incident was attributed, denied it ever occurred. But slogans about discipline filled the air as a preparatory to the authoritarianism Marcos had in mind. Filipinos heard it over the government-controlled radio every 30 minutes.

The jokes continued accompanied by repressed snickering. That was a signal the military was losing its sense of humor (if there was any). The UG people roared with laughter. The underground sector started thereafter to welcome satirists, humor experts, doggerel aficionados, and political versifiers into its ranks. This hodgepodge of memorable events in the sixties that contributed to the color of the mass movement can be synthesized thus:

Summary Calendar of the Sixties

1960, "The Mis-Education of the Filipino" written by Renato Constantino forced to look inside the classroom if not inside their soul how *colonial mentality* (a new name for an old pathology) was deeply implanted and became a systemic mental obstruction to the Filipino's liberation. Popular reading among the young, the essay was reprinted many times over during the next three decades. We had copies distributed at cost in many of our seminars.

1962, President Diosdado Macapagal under pressure by his U.S. patrons scrapped the graft-ridden exchange control; prices of basic commodities that shot up bedevilled Filipino consumers for a long time to come.

1963, looking back to this year, Marcos wrote in his book **Notes on the New Society** and claimed (p.19) that he saw in the year 1963 the formation of successive mass organizations like *Lapiang Manggagawa, Masaka*, KM and MAN.

1964, (Oct. 2) About 2000 students and workers attempted to gate crash Malacañang on the issue of U.S. Parity Rights and the Laurel-Langeley Agreement. The Presidential Guards dispersed them brutally.

1964, on Nov. 30 *Kabataan Makabayan* (KM, patriotic youth) was formed as a broad organization encompassing students, workers, peasants and professionals. It trained revolutionary workers; conducted several demos. The founding date coincided with the birthday of the revolutionary Andres Bonifacio.[10]

1966, Sison initiated the formation of MAN (Movement for the Advancement Nationalism) and became its secretary general upon its formal founding. It was "a broad united front organization that sought to bring together the organizations of the basic masses with those of the middle strata along the anti-imperialist and anti-feudal line." (Sison p.32)

1966, PETA, an important NGO group that trained activist modern theatre art techniques, much of which were participatory and inexpensive.

1967, (Feb. 6-7) The Movement for the Advancement of Nationalism was founded to "arouse, mobilize, organize" (*note the Maoist language sequence*). Although far from being communist it aimed to fundamentally alter, or at least substantially reduce" the undue foreign influence over our entire national life (*note the vacillation from* "altering" to "reducing").The elder Senator Tañada chaired this new group.

1967, or thereabout, Sison stopped teaching inside the classrooms because his secret peregrinations conflicted with his school schedules. His collection of speeches and studies published under the title. *Struggle for National Democracy* edited by Luis Teodoro, became in due time the youths' catechism for the mass movement.

1968, a pre-KMU group met in the cool hills of Baguio at Vallejo Hotel to broach the formation of a labor center; the bedfellows, now somewhat strangers to each other, were Gani Serrano, Angel Mendoza, the late Bert Olalia, Steve Quiambao, Ricardo Reyes. The composition of this group has no formation; this is different from the KMU formally launched on May 1, 1980.

---

[10] In a message on the 40th year of the *Kabataang Makabayan* by its founding chairman, Jose Maria Sison looked back with undiminished nostalgia how the KM fared during the last several years. "What had it done? It served as training schools for young revolutionaries; it joined the working class in fulfilling its revolutionary tasks, it worked for building the Workers' Party and the Socialist Party between 1964 and 1968; also for the Movement for the Advancement of Nationalism 1966-1968. MAN was the first broad national united front. It was supposed to be legal but the military and the U.S. Embassy in Manila loved to keep track of its members, thus thickening needlessly their dossiers on suspect communists."

1968, (March 18) Jabidah massacre (a.k.a. *Oplan Merkeda*). Several young muslims, in their thirties and below were recruited by the Marcos Government and brought to Corregidor where they were trained as mercenaries to invade Sabah claimed at that time by the Philippines as part of its territory. When the young soldiers refused, their trainers brought them to another area and killed all 28, except one who escaped to tell the horrendous tale. This incident gave way to conflicting versions. One observes that no military account in the ruffled history of the country had ever been accepted without questions.

This unresolved incident gave birth to the current Muslim struggles for self-rule. Two known Muslim movements that survived after three decades are the MNLF under Nur Misuari and MILF under Hashim Salamat.[11]

1968, (Dec. 26) Sison formed his own (new) CPP from the ashes of the moribund PKP. It was an ideological enchilada of Marx, Lenin and Mao. The Lavas of the PKP found this indigestible; CPP launched in Capas, Tarlac.

1969, *Pagkakaisa ng mga Magbubukid ng Pilipinas* (PMP, Unity of Philippine Peasants) members mostly based in Tarlac numbering 20,000 marched to Manila demanding land reform. This was a part of the 80,000 peasant mass base of the newly founded CPP. An open fierce campaign that killed PMP peasant leaders was launched by the military. In the same year, the New People's Army was officially established with 65 fighters with 35 guns. (See Weekley, p.27)

This continuing account of Sison about himself and his role demonstrated a marvel of perseverance, ideological politicking, unmitigated militance including sleepless nights and irregular eating habits. It's a wonder he did not catch tuberculosis. If he survived this national disease with a thoroughly democratic spread I attribute this to his care-giving wife, Julie.

---

[11] Source was a download from the internet, "Vol. III No.279, a Publication of the Mindanao News and Information Cooperative Center, 19 March 2005 calling attention to a similar massacre of recent date of Muslim prisoners in a military camp outside Manila. A good study source on the Muslim movements in the country includes *Revolt in Mindanao, The Rise of Islam in Philippine Politics* by T.J.S. George (Oxford U. Press). Also *Under the Crescent Moon: Rebellion in Mindanao* by Marites D. Vitug and Glenda M. Garcia (Ateneo Center for Social Policy & Public Affairs and I.P.D., Q.C. 2000.)

By the end of the Sixties, the mass movement picked up momentum fuelled by the national issues broadly affecting the country. These included the uncontrollable greed of the MNCs, the opportunism of government officials and the indolent, wasteful lives and the neglect of the peasants' welfare by the insensitive landowners. The student militants summarized these three basic problems as "imperialism, bureaucrat capitalism and feudalism." The slogan, a replica of Maoists' rallying call from China in the course of its revolution slowly seeped into the hot veins of student militants, dripped with the sweat of organized workers, and pulsated with the anger of left pedagogues and nationalist business leaders.

My mind at this time was far from the Revolution. It was still like, using the popular words of a weather forecaster, "a typhoon somewhere that had not yet entered the country's area of responsibility."

The times brought classmates in U.P., Iloilo and me looking for the virginal forested suburb and the brooks a couple of kilometres south of San Jose, Antique. This was about two hours rough ride zigzaging to the next province from Iloilo city. My activist days would start from another issue. Meanwhile, the romance of Walden Pond was the object of our search during those days outside the school. It was an alternative to drugs that bedevilled the next generation following martial law.

Chapter 3

Dictatorship and Beyond
1970s

    ORGANIZED STUDENTS fuelled more rallies and marches; leftist paperbacks and a crowded Manila heralded the coming political opera. This opened a full blown political theatre by the masses. In marches my group and no doubt other people belonging to other militant NGOs hauled, hewed, and harangued against the "Three Basic Problems" while the radical left turned secretly, silently, inconspicuously to armed struggle. The betes noires of the mass movement were and still are the non-productive, idle, big landlords, corrupt bureaucrats, and imperial U.S. This more or less characterized the mass movement of the Seventies.

About the first half of the seventies, my aunt, Dr. Pacita Abada offered me a course to teach at the Philippine Normal College (now PNU). The name of the course was "Socialism and Education." Imported McCarthyism and the rising domestic dictatorship forced me to change the name to "Cultural Anthropology." I taught it in the graduate school.

When decisions by government like an edict, executive order, or a presidential decree is issued, its real meaning is read more in the responses they will get from the people and less from print. They can be objectified as figures, numbers, units, proportions or percentages. I wondered if these numbers make for history much more a history about the mass movement.

As objective observer, I missed the excitement of marches. As a marching participant, I was likely to fail writing objectively. I had this dilemma all the years I was recording my observations about the mass movement. In mass movements there's hardly such a thing as objective history.

Student Risings in the Left

The time span from the end of the sixties to the seventies heaved with extraordinary turbulence. When I look back, EDSA Uno and EDSA Dos were already culminations of two major separate mass movements. What had happened in between left their marks on the ground upon which these two risings brought abundant lessons to myself and in general to the organized masses.

Already the country was shaken and shaking long before the historic People Power became real in every Filipino's life. As participant in many mass actions, I could not help but take notice how the moving scene looked to me as in the ringside of the country's history. My prescience tells me that living beyond the 1970s would allow me to say with a degree of finality, "I was there when it happened."

The decade of the seventies was a period of student rising. It was the springboard for the nation-wide mass movement led by young Filipinos from the school system. They eventually caught up and become sensitive to national issues. The base was mainly around Metro-Manila, the center of educational institutions, government offices, mass media, and business from which many decisions emanated that affected the whole country. This gained the metropolis an ungainly title of "Imperial Manila." The framework at the back of our minds as mass organizers was that among the oppressors was the hegemony of U.S. imperialism.

Below the placid social veneer was the intelligentsia in ferment. They were far from being communists but a few were steeped in Marxism, Mao Tsetung Thought, and Castroism; in Lenin, in Gramsci, in Trotsky and other left ideologues. I read these writers more as an academic interest than guides on how to conduct a revolution. I did not think I was immune from the viral impact that had affected my friends and contemporaries in the left. My NGO days, the secret meetings and study group sessions were filled with studying the revolutionary gospel partly hiding the way the early Christians went through their pristine Christianity inside caves.

I was not a member of the KM or any of the militant groups that were proscribed by military. I was with Alliance of Concerned Teachers (ACT), with the consumer group called CACP and other NGOs whose activities were principally limited to popularizing the issues I mentioned earlier.

With CACP, we were busy creating more progressive NGOs. There are about eight of these that I'll discuss in another chapter. Being on the agitprop wing of these groups, I spent a lot of times "speechifying" in many symposia. Like the eternal "lesson plan" of every elementary school teacher, no member of the audience leaves the hall without getting the lesson(s) on the Three Basic Problems. It was thus we spread the issues, clarifying them, making the people internalize what could be done, and how they will have to organize themselves to surmount if not solve these problems.

First, be aware, then organize. These two always preceded mobilization. It is not merely pushing, agitating the masses with the blindness of fanatics. That would be a mob. I think this was how people in power viewed the street marchers. The masses are people with ideas in their heads, with nimble feet and their brains burning with the passion for social justice. We were reformers and when things got worse a thin thread holds many of us from becoming revolutionaries. Did I follow this formula of being aware, then organizing and finally mobilizing with the masses? I did, and I usually went home with a sore throat and a slight fever after running through a drizzle.

Who's Afraid of Oil Price Increases?

I remember the oil price increases that occurred in the early seventies shook the country. The country's presidents have good reason to be scared of oil companies. From Marcos to the next four presidents, the crises brought by foreign control of this critical import taught the country a lesson it would not forget. Where prices of basic commodities are involved, organizing the thousands of unhappy consumers was like eating *pulvuron*. It fills your mouth but you don't have to talk.

The oil price increase was as explosive as the declared authoritarian rule. Both ignited a barrel of political issues against President Marcos, including the power of oil multinationals. Marcos failed to protect the Filipinos against the rampant price increases that characterized the crises of the 1970s. Oil price increases got thoroughly mixed up with the issue of academic freedom in that fateful day. More and more students declared their resistance against the foreign oil firms by putting up more road barricades.

One consumer group, CACP, where I was active as national chair at that time, conducted a series of symposia in Metro Manila's Catholic schools. One of these was in Assumption College in San Lorenzo Village where the country's future president Gloria Macapagal Arroyo was teaching economics then. GMA helped CACP organize a symposium in her school with Sister Mary John Mananzan, then the consumer NGO secretary general on the issue of oil price increases.[12]

Students were more frequently seen in street marches than in symposia. The groups marched, sang patriotic songs, spread their streamers across streets, and blocked the traffic. Not a few were inspired with the passion common to the "left romantics" of the decade. They brandished the hammer-and-sickle insignia and often drew it inside notebooks. Their ways exuded the sophomoric. Even in cultural programs, progressive songs (favourites: *Internationale, Bayan Ko*) accompanied by raising clenched fists marked street theatre of the young national democrats. These did not make us card-carrying communists although the intelligence community of the AFP and its paid infiltrators were busy taking pictures of the activists and presumably filing dossiers on us.

Jaypee Perez, a fellow activist, told me that in 1971 a U.P. SDK (*Samahang Demokratikong Kabataan*) member Freshman Pastor (Sonny) Mesina had joined a student barricade put up to condemn those behind oil price increases. He was shot and four days later died. He is remembered as a martyr by his surviving SDK comrades.

---

[12] GMA herself was the one who reminded this writer in 2003 that she was a "founding member of the CACP". Please see related CACP story.)

The youth's tragic end was the beginning of the gathering political storm now known as the "Diliman Commune." Down the road, SDK militants who are now in their 50s or early 60s recently commemorated Pastor's 35th death anniversary. I attended this rite on invitation of its founding chairman, Jaypee Perez.

A score of Ateneo students in Katipunan Rd set up a "sympathy barricade" during the Diliman Commune according to J. Perez, an SDK Ateneo High school member, now a doctor of medicine. A group of students on their way home in Bago Bantay, manned another barricade in lightning formation. The barricade fever spread to students in other schools connecting oil price increase with local or school issues.

Brief History of SDK; "Diliman Commune"

Its time to take a look at the brief account of the SDK and what lived down in student history as the "Diliman Commune". Aside from contributing a student martyr to its cause, the SDK's existence has to be explained when one is aware that there was already a *Kabataang Makabayan* (KM). The two have almost identical national democratic agenda. SDK's model was the Paris Commune of 1871, a two month old uprising then that sought to put up a proto-socialist government in Europe.

The students in Diliman put up barricades, seized control of the university radio and declared the U.P. campus free from police. But a phalanx of armed police came to break up the barricade. Some professors joined to reinforce the students' rank feeling that the police forcible coming in was a threat to academic freedom. Nobody clearly remembered if U.P. President Salvador Lopez came down from his office and negotiated with the students. The SDK-KM combine put up a short-lived *Alyansa ng Bayan Laban sa Pagtaas ng Presyo ng Langis/1971* (ABLPPL to be read fast as "*Abalapapala*", a play on the acronym which has the sense of "a delaying tactic." This was a precedent to the later CACP-KMU initiative CAOPI or Coalition against Oil Price Increase where I was a member.

One early member of the SDK was Sixto Carlos Jr., a maverick from the KM. His late father was the military court (JAGO) official who warned Jun "just be careful you're not caught by the military." This was the advice to a son from a father who like hundreds of parents at that time were helpless on their sons' and daughters' decision to join the rising in the streets. "Jun" Carlos told me about it when he and then wife Christine Ebro used to hide in our seaside house in Parañaque. SDK was then in its formative stage. "Jun" Carlos used to teach at the Philippine College of Commerce (now P.U.P.) in Lealtad. It was a street crowded with old pre-war houses made of dark aging wood about to collapse long before the rising turned into a flag-waving raucous revolution.

Sometime in 1968 the SDK had a strong inclination to pursue a "cultural revolution," while the KM or some of its members were already bent on "armed struggle." Early SDK core members included Luis Teodoro, Ninotchka Rosca, Perfecto Tera, Jr., Dick Ferrer, Vivencio Jose, Rolly Peña and not to forget an "original," the Muslim Nur Misuari. There were also those who came from U.P. in Los Baños like William Padolina and Ramon Sanchez.

Thirty years down the road of the revolution that did not happen, many of them became academic guardians, professors in arts and social sciences of the premier State University. (Nur still languishes in prison at this writing)

Although formed later in 1968, the SDKs held its first and only national congress in 1971. With the declaration of martial law in September 1972, many of its leading members went UG. There was a feeling among the original SDKs (formerly KMs in 1968) that the election among the KMs was "loaded." This was what started the SDKs view about Nilo Tayag's suspect election as KM chair.

Many SDK constituencies were in schools, mostly in urban areas. The group even organized a "back to school" program for the youths many of whom were dropping out of their classrooms. Unlike the KM that stayed long in the political arena, the SDK organized those who were both inside and outside the school system. This student NGO further followed what it called vaguely "multiplicity of organizing" even with the same sector. This open advocacy stopped all talks about merging with KM.

By 1975 the Martial Law repression went into high gear. SDK was dissolved as an organization and KM emerged as the out-of-school-youth and student organization. This time it effectively linked with the National Democratic Front (NDF). Several SDK members who were not absorbed by the underground movement inconspicuously dispersed and grew into practising professionals, parents, and grandparents serving civil society in their own separate ways, writing or hoping to write memoirs.

Leavens in Student Rising

Outside of the oil issue that triggered prices of commodities to go up in the 1970s, there were other active leavens to the student risings. These sent full blast the political romanticism of the left, mostly fuelled by progressive reading, revolutionary ideas one could read from cheap paperbacks, mimeograph sheets from the UG, students organizing in campuses all over the city and in provinces. Add to these were my contacts with the groups outside Metro Manila which were full of rich exchanges in information and experiences. Every sympathetic family was a political channel.

It was about this time that my travels to the provinces increased. These involved mostly organizing work or contracting other groups and inviting those linked with schools to affiliate with national organizations like ACT and with CACP for those bothered endlessly with prices spiralling.

The decade of the 70s opened with the spread of a new vocabulary for the left. The city was splattered with liberatory graffiti, the vibrating libretto of a forthcoming political opera. There were lessons gleaned from the *Red Book*, learned from integrating with the masses or observing Marcos officials and their noxious shenanigans.

The *Red Book* was very useful to the students. It was affordable, compact, and the translation was in simple prose. Its language and style was endearing to anyone in search of a solution to an oppressive government. To the militant, it spared him from reading Marx or Lenin in their English translation and emendation.

Role of Christian Churches

From what I gathered the largest student organization involved in the mass movement during the early seventies was the National Union of Students of the Philippines (NUSP) that numbered about 30,000. The NUSP was seen as "a moderate group." The other student camps in the movement were the militant KM, later SDK and students from the state university under the U.P. Student Council, and those from PCC now Polytechnic University of the Philippines. Jose Ma. Sison earlier formed the Student Cultural Association of U.P., (SCAUP) hijacking and converting the acronym of the U.P. Student Catholic action (UPSCA).

Student leaders, many of whom were Catholics, were looking for "a Christian political line," ecumenism having been found inadequate in order to rationalize the students' call for more direct actions. The NUSP led by Edgar Jopson of Ateneo (called "Edjop" by his peers) was preparing for a massive march to Congress on January 26, 1970. President Ferdinand Marcos was to speak in the opening session. I met Edjop much later when the police was already in hot pursuit of the 'moderate" student leader. He rapidly evolved into a national democrat militant.

The First Quarter Storm followed the historic melee on January 26, 1970 where students from outside Congress watched Marcos stepping out, and with a *papier mache* coffin that read "Death of Democracy" threw the bulky piece over the heads of the security. It landed smack into the security men surrounding the president.

Oca Francisco who told me this was a member of NUSP and one of those who later were called to Malacañang Palace with about 25 other student leaders for an audience with the President. The students would demand from President Marcos to keep his promise that he would not run for re-election. It was rumoured that the President's intention was to tell the students he was willing to give in to their demand. This report almost worried Joe Sison when he heard about it. He believed that Marcos was only pulling the legs of the students.

A few days later outside of the presidential palace, hundreds of KM, SDK and SCAUP militants not invited to an audience with the President were confronting the police with songs, slogans and stirring speeches against the government. Their violent dispersal by the police and military caused the death of four students. (By Sison's account six were killed.)

There were varying versions to this historic meeting with Marcos. What stood out was that "Edjop" demanded that the President Marcos put out his promise in writing. The media reported thereafter that for such effrontery, the President angrily dismissed the group and made a reference of the young Jopson as "that grocer's son." This presidential slur thereafter reverberated to the sensitive ranks of the middle forces in the streets.

The search for a "political line" Oca had alluded to earlier gave birth to the Christians for National Liberation (CNL). Vatican II was the source that infused the Catholic Church to locate her glory with the sufferings and joy of the poor; Mao Tsetung Thought (MTT) was the political *vade mecum* that guided the young to an emancipatory struggle. Both of these caused the country to take a deep breath with collective unease.

On the surface, liberation theology and Maoism were impossible ideological mix, a good trope for oil and water. Just the same, both mixed in bubbling, joyful, passionate creation that gave strength to a broad, vibrant solidarity presaging tumescence of the 1970s.

The means and methods of the mass movement broadened as the number of social sectors increased. As organizers we visited lots of houses, many were unreformed, uninterested friends' families. We exploited this friendship by using it to launch a discussion without being argumentative. I suspected we became "interesting" to them. Later the method improved so that we were able to reach out even to people unknown to us before. We were the ones learning more.

Members from different social classes interacted. Public speaking became a norm in explaining the dictatorship. No matter how little or undeveloped your communication skill, you become a member of a group that will develop it. There was maximum use of rhetoric, the mass media, street theatre; progressive cultural artists, nuns and priests in the frontline of street marches. When the situation got tight during the street actions, as police started to swarm the ranks at the call for forced dispersals, the hearty singing of the national anthem or the popular "*Bayan Ko*" would drown the melee into sudden and eerie silence. Everybody stood still out of respect for the anthem or the song in Pilipino until its fading, last beat. This usually sent a shiver in the marchers' nationalist and democratic veins. Screaming and scampering for cover quickly followed, the police on our heels.

Middle Forces, Tactical Alliance with NDF, Social Investigation

The organizing continued among NGOs where I was involved using new skills we acquired in the process. The trips to the provinces became more frequent. One week I was in Baguio, another week in Cotabato, then back to Legazpi City where I had been only two months earlier. With me were two or three staff members of the consumer group where I was head. What did I talk about? Most of the time common problems that afflicted the people in the places where I went. No other subject was more relevant to the masses than the difficulties that martial law had brought to their lives. And the solution? I kept on telling them they must organize.

After the open symposium, we sat down no longer in the public places but in some less visible setting in a private house. Usually there were some NDF representatives who would join us. That was time we came to know that the area was part of the politically NDF influenced territory. We acquainted ourselves with existing organizations, their problems, their close members, the issues that confronted them. We inquired about the people who controlled the resources of the place or the livelihood of the masses. What institutions were sympathetic to the people? Who were behind these? In what ways do people generally put across their grievances to the local authorities? How were these received? There were hundreds of questions (not interrogations) asked of each other. All of these fall under the rubric of social investigation, or what progressive NGOs fondly called "SI."

How could one afford all those trips? Several European human rights groups and funding agencies supported those peregrinations, the positive results of our applications for funding. Every NGO worth its salt has a battery of writers preparing these funding proposals. We wrote reports of the conditions in the countryside, of the people hurt by Marcos government, and its anti-people policies, of the obstacles the NGOs would encounter in their work with the masses, etc. The funding people believed us more than what they read about in the controlled media. A great part of the mass movement was bankrolled by the funding agencies, by human rights groups in Europe, by the assistance of the churches there.

A progressive NGO is not an office where every employee has fixed salary, stays in office from 8 a.m. to 5 p.m., retirement benefits, medicare, etc. Everything that a regular office is, the NGO is not. Every one works and thinks beyond the pay, is concerned, deeply concerned about reason why the organization was formed. Usually it is found in its mission-vision statements, strongly political in tenor and explicitness. I was connected in about eight NGOs as member and co-founder. Where the government fails where it should not, and the failure has affected the masses, the occasion gives rise to the birth of an NGO.

This is how I remember the 1970s political calendar of events:

1970-71 – (Jan. 26) 50,000 students and workers gathered before the Philippine Congress peacefully but police responded with physical force. Almost every week students, peasants, factory workers and militant women continued without let-up pounding the city streets. (Jan. 30) The opening salvo to the First Quarter Storm (FQS) exploded in Manila streets that brought death to 6 students during a police dispersal when the students assaulted the gates of the presidential palace. (Feb. 12) Students marched to Malacañang demanding justice for the violent death of their comrades. Demonstrations continued and did not peter out until martial law was declared. (Dec. 29) Lt. Victor Corpuz, an instructor at the PMA defected to the New People's Army after leading a raid of the country's top military school armory. (Aug. 21) Plaza Miranda liberal rally was bombed; Marcos quickly blamed the "communists". He suspended the privilege of the writ of *habeas corpus*. This was followed by more bombings tagged by the police as "July-August plan". In the same year Marcos called for a constitutional convention with representatives from every province. About this time guns for the underground landed and were unloaded from *M/V Karagatan* in Palanan, Isabela. News like this was not available to the public except to the military and some militants in inner circles.

1972 – Terrorism spread, with Marcos blaming the communist, but in many of these incidents, petty criminals out of extortion were caught, some of them military personnel; then more bombings.[13] The Constitutional Convention was wracked with a scandal following an expose of massive payola revealed by one Leyte delegate Eduardo Quintero. The idea was to extend the term of Marcos. The Philippine Constitution at that time did not allow Marcos to run again. (August 26) the Christians for National Liberation (CNL) was founded by a priest, Father Edicio dela Torre and added the church people as one more sector to the swiftly emerging National Democratic Front. Marcos' Defence Secretary Juan Ponce Enrile put up a mock car ambush of himself, blaming the communists. (Sept. 21) Marcos declared Martial Law; had his critics—about 7,000 of them—arrested.

1973 – (January) Marcos created the Citizens' Assembly (C.A.); (July 27-28) a general referendum was called by him which subsequently "elected" Marcos to continue as President beyond what the 1935 Constitution prohibited; the CA stopped the interim National Assembly from convening. On the same year, the UG gave birth to the NDF, "an underground mass political organization of the national democratic movement" with 14 mass organizations under it, including CPP and the New People's Army. The first draft of the Ten-Point Program was released; an "NDF Preparatory Commission" was tasked to develop the Party's work with the "middle forces"; much of the work was done by the religious like ex-priest Luis Jalandoni and once "moderate" student organizer Edgar Jopson. (April 24) National Democratic Front (NDF) launched. Marcos took effective control of the legislative power for the next seven years and ran the country by Presidential Decrees; (Dec. 30) Marcos' term as president supposed to end. It never did but instead went beyond another decade.

1974 – PKP entered into parliamentary accommodation with Marcos. TUCP organized as Labor Center "for the government."

1975 – The strike in October of about 500 workers at La Tondeña, a distillery, reinforced by church people, influenced other workers to strike in other places. Sister M.J. Mananzan and some CACP staff went to distribute sandwiches to the strikers. The dictatorship had become difficult to swallow by the people, except by the multinational corporations, big local business,

---

[13] See *Philippine Free Press* issue of September 22, 1972.

the Cabinet and the expanding number of cronies. The mass movement intensified.

Even the Supreme Court had become suspiciously soft and compliant. It allowed the dictator (so went the reasoning) to implement his own decrees since being Chief Executive he was responsible for these to become "enforceable laws." My father-in-law (a SC justice) convened the family to acquaint us with his dissenting opinion which he said Marcos would not take nicely.[14]

Radicalization of the Left

Many who used to be active in the open mass movement took to the hills. They used to populate the cause-oriented groups; not any more. The underground had become a more realistic option to them. I was missing a lot of friends who used to be seen with us in street marches. Many activists who used to believe reforms possible were disillusioned. They saw Marcos with lots of ugly surprises like a magician who pulled out more rabbits from a hat.

The life of Edgar Jopson, a young activist, had become exemplary for those who were once moderate in their ways of looking at the national situation but later decided to pursue radical ways (read: armed struggle) in transforming society. The young Jopson embodied left romanticism as an activist reformist transformed into a revolutionary. This romanticism is liable to underestimate the material forces of the state and the latter's readiness to neutralize (read: kill) perceived enemies.

Satur Ocampo and Edgar came to our house brought by another activist "Cora". If my memory serves me right, they were brought there sometime in the early 70's to broaden contacts among the middle forces. This was an introductory to all moderates about to enter the underground.

---

[14] Marcos allowed himself to be "elected" by indiscriminate raising of hands in the barangays (villages) through his own formed "Citizens' Assembly"; no such procedures were found nor allowed in the 1935 Constitution on how to elect a president. This lone dissenter was Justice Calixto O. Zaldivar, twice appointed to the Supreme Court, separately by President Diosdado Macapagal and President Marcos, himself.

Not any members of middle class families were prepared psychologically, much more ideologically, to support the armed revolution to which many youthful militants were openly committed. This did not mean they were not helping. Middle forces families remind me of John Milton: "*They also serve who only stand and wait.*" Middleclass houses at that time became haven to students seeking a refuge from the police or military. This happened usually after a violent dispersal. Our house in Parañaque was like a post-dispersal get-together assembly point for some activists.

What were the factors that contributed to this kind of personal convulsive transition in the mass movement? Of moderate activists turning radical? There were three factors. First, many of the student activists returned from China clutching the *Red Book*, so to speak, their travel tickets courtesy of the Association for the Philippine-China Understanding (APCU). Second, the payola scandal wracked the Constitutional Convention. This dashed all hopes of peaceful, honest change. Third and most important was the declaration of Martial Law. Given all three, 'the underground had become a more realistic option not only to the freewheeling and rampaging students but to other rebel individuals from the comfortable middleclass homes sympathetic to the mass movement.

Socio-Political Impact of the Oil Crisis

Briefly, the high prices of basic commodities triggered by rising prices of oil products roiled and riled both the poor and the middleclasses. Jeepney drivers, bus operators, thousands of commuters screamed helplessly against the oil firms. Relief was nowhere on sight. The first open resistance to the policy of the government religiously complying with the dictates of the IMF and the oil cartels opened the eyes of the militant consumer group, later known as the Citizens' Alliance for Consumer Protection (CACP). The latter held a public symposium in San Luis Street now Kalaw. For the first time CACP openly attacked the government "surrender" to the oil companies while the mainstream media were still shaking off the impact of many closures and arrests in their ranks. (See separate CACP story.)

Lest we forget, in the marketplace, the oil trans-nationals, also called the "Three Sisters" (Caltex, Shell and Esso-Mobil) were playing havoc on the economy. Immediately this triggered a historic increase of basic commodity prices that sent more than 90 percent of the population reeling with nobody resisting or shouting foul. It started in 1974 and went on and on. We started to live with the crisis.

Communists and Oligarchs

Marcos insisted on dividing the social classes opposed to him as (1) "oligarchs," referring to the rich who refused to endorse openly his Martial Law government but were perceived to be benefiting from it; and as (2) "communists" the rest who either were the underpaid but awakened organized workers in factories or millions of landless peasants from the countryside, agitated by student cadres visiting and catechizing them on the "Three Basic Problems."

I remember the effect of the student rebellion on January 30, 1970 was electric on the middle classes. The upper crusts of society not necessarily oligarchs (the real ones had long left for U.S. or Europe) were also packing their bags to leave. There was an exodus according to Pete Lacaba from the posh villages like Forbes Park, Dasmariñas, Magallanes, Bel Air, San Lorenzo making a ghost town the suburb of Makati. The well-heeled crust, wrote Pete, "had fears in their guts and guilt in their hearts holed up with hysteria in the big hotels" across EDSA certain that "their houses would be set afire by an avenging people." The avenging people did not materialize nor the houses set on fire. My family stayed put in the metropolis, most of the time pressing our collective ears on the radio.

Lacaba wrote lyrically about this highly romanticized rising. "The revolution was in everybody's mind, before everybody's eyes... (people) sat by the radio throughout that sleepless night, all in edge, thinking of the revolution... But the Revolution is not a Hollywood movie, its alarums and excursions completed at a fadeout. The long night of January 30 was so far the most violent in the (Manila) city's post war history, but it was not the Revolution."[15] Pete Lacaba, himself an activist, could not stop the Shakespearean wand of his pen. A

Marxist in his prose if not in his poetry, he wrote to date the best account of the opening salvo of the mass movement in his small book, *Days of Disquiet, Nights of Rage.*

Alternative to a Captive Press, the Other FQS

In the early part of martial law, Marcos was aware of how much his opponents were using this proclivity to critical reading plus the abundance of critical materials seeping through his censors. One of his early acts in declaring Martial Law on September 21, 1972 was to take full control of the mass media by issuing a PD taking over television stations, newspapers and radio from the hands of their corporate owners.

The coup on the mass media stunned the nation accustomed as it was to a freewheeling journalism. But this did not deter leaders of the mass movement of lawyers, teachers, student · activists, church people, doctors and other professionals from explaining their cause through other ways. These included the pulpit, the classrooms, lecture halls, study groups, and middle class vacation houses many of which are now forgotten but then had effectively served as the First Quarter Shelters, the other less known "FQS". They were especially good in hiding militants wanted by the police and military, even secret messages were sent in and out of prison cells that were holding arrested activists. The late Sister Marianni, founder of Task Force Detainees, used to hide message in written and tightly rolled papers in the hem of her habit or, believe it or not, behind her *postiso* (denture).

Other publications UG printing press and critical circles continued to run samizdat, mimeo sheets and tabloids. There were continuing exchanges between the UG groups and the legal organizations. Joe Burgos' *We Forum* was a classic in open anti-dictatorship publication. Many more were not necessarily illegal but closely watched by the martial law censors.

---

[15] P. xii, *Days of Disquiet, Nights of Rage*, 3rd printing by ANVIL, Manila, 2003.

Second Half of the 1970s

The other half of the '70s was "banner years" for the dictator but the country continued to be in a state of agitated uncertainty. More people were asking: "When would Marcos ever put an end to his martial rule?"

1976 – Satur Ocampo was collared by Marcos agents. Joe Sison was captured; so were Victor Corpuz and Buscayno a.k.a. Dante. The IMF-WB held a convention in Manila with 5 luxurious hotels refurbished using SSS/GSIS money and top-of-the line Mercedez Benzes were provided the delegates. Imelda enjoyed and jumped with "a towering feeling," an allusion to a once popular song. She took over Meralco and converted it into a foundation where popular belief confirmed she was the sole beneficiary. Senator Benigno (Ninoy) Aquino was convicted by a military tribunal and ordered shot. Ninoy dared Marcos to "shoot me tomorrow." This was good press in the underground. CPP instructed urban cadres to intensify labor organizing. Secret study groups flourished, unions became restive, followed by spontaneous strikes in other factories.

1977 – The "Ten-Point Program" of the NDF was re-issued with elaboration and explanations. Between 1977 and 1990 the Program seesawed from ten to fifteen and finally to twelve after a series of consultations with above ground legal personalities and groups. Horacio (Boy) Morales, at the night he was supposed to receive a national prestigious award, went UG and joined the NDF.

1979 – The League of Filipino Students was founded.

1978 – Marcos called for National Assembly (Interim *Batasan Pambansa*, IBP) elections. CACP congress was launched in Kalaw Street, Manila and denounced government surrender to the MNCs allowing prices of food and other basic commodities to go up unconscionably. Marcos hurried up another election for the interim Congress at the behest of the U.S. worried that the U.S. Military Bases could not be ratified unless the Senate was convened. Our Constitution says only the Senate can ratify treaties.

On the night of the "elections", a new form of concerted action by the middle Forces emerged popular: the *noise barrage*. This was an addition to the bagful of semiotic tools by middle class characters who were unwilling to show their faces in open street marches but dared to make noises with forks and spoons against their drinking glasses or drag empty kerosene cans behind their speeding cars.

Under Marcos' Iron Gip, COGs Mushroomed

One could not make a decent summary of a convulsive decade like the Seventies. Dynamic factors that affected the lives of many people have different origins. That's what the concept "conjunctural" started to explain, if not explain away when several things seemed to happen together but whose origins were traced to have come from different sources.

Otherwise, we try to summarize. We remember it now as a whirligig of a time that Marcos seized the country by the throat, abolished Congress, took hold of the Supreme Court, turned the Armed Forces of the Philippines into an expensive private army paid by people's taxes, cavorted with Catholic Church. And last but not least, *the decade made the mass movement a permanent institution of people's protest against bad governance in spite of, or because of the dictatorship.*

The late Seventies was marked by another development as a cumulative response to the dictatorship. The cause-oriented groups or COGs increased informally their members and consolidated themselves. More middle class personalities decided to join the mass movement. They were active, vociferous, creative, flair loving, flag-waving anti-Marcos. In the consumer group, we reached out to people who earlier never trudged the streets to shout their grievances. These were academic, lawyers, and small businessmen who had just closed shop, doctors and a slew of those belonging to the petit-bourgeoisie. The print media recognized them now as the "middle forces."

One looks back to credit the National Democratic Front for politically holding the medley of social forces together. A cementing work that no other institution in the country had done with plumed success. This will be another story in separate sections or chapters as told in the accounts of many NGOs and POs inspired by the NDF leadership.

The middle forces were challenged to put up alternatives to the gross errors of Marcos. The milieu was rife for alternative social formations to grow. People generally looked at government entities as failing. Again the articulation of these alternatives was strongly assisted by militants linked to the NDF, many of whom burnt candles into the night but many more, in Rizal's immortal line, "died without seeing the dawn."

Earlier, with the foresight of those who see the future standing on the shoulder of the past, Alejandro (Ding) Lichauco submitted before the 1971 constitutional convention a comprehensive, clear and perspicacious critique on imperialism and how this eroded the country's sovereignity. Let us get to its ringing conclusion:

"The massive and deepening poverty of our people, the rising unemployment, the inflation that has gone beyond control, the infantile state of our military and productive capabilities, the disoriented state of our educational system, the remorseless exploitation to which our economy is being subjected, and the social anarchy which these conditions have bred are all traceable, directly and ultimately, to our status as a neo-colony. It is a status which reflects the imperialist phenomenon in this country" [16]

The critique was the basis of what many COGs were studying when their discussion touched on imperialism in hundreds of semi-secret study groups. The shadow if not the substance of "nationalist industrialization" was already in its pages. "Ding" was a favourite resource speaker in many progressive NGO symposia.

But Marcos seeing his own mistake of completely abdicating economic policy-making to his U.S. trained technocrats like Paterno, Sicat, Virata, Melchor *et al* came out with his corrective *Eleven Major Industrial Projects* before the end of the seventies, November 1979. It was much too late, and ironically, too unbelievably clumsy and quick. It sounded like desperate propaganda. Even his economic technocrats shot down the economic dream. His own top economic adviser Cesar Virata admitted: "There was no financing, no appropriate investor and not viable."

---

[16] p. 76 in A. Lichauco's *Towards A New Economic and the Conquest of Mass Poverty*, printed by SSP, 1986.

As the dictatorship intensified through its repressive decrees and highly militarized *Bagong Lipunan* (New Society) the recruitment process especially among the young was sure and swift and the field for advanced organizing broadened.'

The relationship between the UG and the above ground (AG) mass movement was fluid. The UG mass movement was unreservedly supporting the Communist Party of the Philippines (CPP) while the above ground (AG) mass movement was attempting to openly broaden the legal opposition against authoritarianism. These two goals commonly converged into one immediate end i.e., the dismantling of martial law rule.

The Above Ground Option

Initially, the 1970s mass movement was an enterprise principally above ground (AG). As early as the latter part of the 1960s, student activism started to rise, publicly calling attention to its open, legal character. The history of the KM and the SDK and many others similarly organized can be located in this period. Young members invoked their constitutional rights as citizens like the right to free speech, to free assembly and to organize freely. They were the early student organizations that launched mass actions under the liberal climate of a few colleges and universities.

Public debate intensified in the early 1970s in verbal battles inside the Supreme Court questioning the constitutionality of the Marcos decrees and in the various freewheeling opinion and editorial pages of newspapers and other media. Systematic monitoring of these events were reflected later in the reports by human rights groups like the Task Force Detainees of the Philippines (TFDP) and Amnesty International, two conscientious groups that exposed how the new tyranny was being implemented.

Underground and Above Ground
Mass Movements Compared

The two distinguishing marks of these two movements, fluid as they were, could be drawn up in terms of *venue, ideology, methods and strategy* and *the class origins* of participants.

Venue

Generally, the open mass movement is stronger, more visible, better organized for mass mobilization purposes in the populated centers like Manila, Cebu City, Davao, and Baguio. They are centers of communication, of decision-making in business and politics, and education. These were accessible to organizers, militants and leaders of the mass movement. Meanwhile, I spent my time travelling to the provinces talking to the unorganized in the name of CACP.

Many of the things happening in urban areas also affected the lives of people in other parts of the country. The campuses were the foci of mass organizing in the early 1970s, peopled principally by idealistic students and academics. Disaffected professionals, and politicians became active critics.

I saw that most organizers and activists possessed superior rhetorical skills in both English and the local language. Give them a place to stand – a platform, an elevated ground, back of a track or jeepney rooftop with mike on hand, and they could stir and move a crowd. Many were leaders who organized in campuses and classrooms. Those who read, listened and kept abreast of events were politically sensitive. The Marcos-run government gave them enough fuel to ignite a curious, combative crowd and transform them into an aroused citizenry.

Campuses were common venues for news and analyses of the social and political situation providing an alternative to the controlled mass media whose owners were either scared or beholden to the dictator. Reading materials critical of the dictatorship but not necessarily illegal sheets circulated among anti-dictatorship circles.

On the other hand, the controlled media became the sole source of information coming from the government—much of which was military disinformation and official pronouncements of the regime. They made big headlines about the number of New People's Army (NPA) casualties, flattering economic reports, bright isolated news about economic prospects of the country after another multimillion dollar loan had been approved or debt-payment extended by the predatory IFI's.

Readership of the controlled media narrowed down to the business sector that wanted to keep abreast with official decrees, government press releases and legal notices. While the UG remained separated from the AG mass movement, the wall between the two was porous in terms of the free flow of information and analyses.

Ideological Sources

In the mass movement information chain, the so-called good news from the government were inevitably countered by scathing analyses, critical response and portrayal of the wretched condition of the economy and the continuing repression. These could be had through the writings and speeches of nationalist Senators Claro M. Recto, Lorenzo Tañada, and Jose Diokno, political analysts Renato Constantino, and a host of ascerbic columnists like I. P. Soliongco, Celso Cabrera, Luis Mauricio, and nationalist economists Alejandro Lichauco, Salvador Araneta, Hilarion Henares, and Walden Bello. Their socio-political economic critiques of the system constituted the ideological sources of influence in the open, mass movement. Our political officer gave repetitive lectures on the Three Basic Problems and the successes of armed struggle in the countryside.

If one were close to the UG, one gets an irregular copy of *Ang Bayan*, the CPP's official organ in light brown paper thrice folded tight. Its courier would reach down stealthily from the bottom of his basket a pressed copy. Sometimes this was given during street marches or in safe houses or study sessions. *Ang Bayan* was the "official text" of many political officers. This gave the other picture of the Revolution: news of successful ambushes, heroic escapes from Marcos torturers, arms taken from sleepy police outposts, casualties of government troops, etc. Their reading supported and boosted sagging spirits in the mass movement.

Some of these people in the 1970s (and up to the late 1990s) guided the liberal nationalist political thinking of many activists in the open mass movement. The U.G. militants continued to burn candles in safe houses reading classics like Marx's *Das Kapital* and *Poverty of Philosophy*; Engel's *The Origin of the Family*; *Private Property and the State*; Marx and Engel's, *The German Ideology* and Lenin's *Two Tactics of Social Democracy* and last but not least Mao's *On Contradiction*. During the 1970s all my copies of the above were borrowed. I was not in a hurry that they be returned ASAP. Not everything was a serious stuff. I had seen cadres and young UG personalities engrossed in *The Adventures of TinTin*, children's popular colored "komiks." My son who owned these "komiks" complained that some kasamas who borrowed his TinTin books never returned them, contrary to Mao's admonition about returning borrowed items.

In the 60's Jose Maria Sison, a younger contemporary, passed around his essays and revised speeches in the *Struggle of National Democracy*. Cheap editions of *Philippine Society and Revolution* by Amado Guerrero (said to be Joe Sison's nom de plume). Joe Sison became a bestseller outside of commercial book publishing.

If you were an activist during this period, you'd begin to feel the contradictions of Philippine society even before you have a clear understanding of this Marxist category of social analysis. One's ideological education starts with this experience, with left readings, radical friends and the guidance of your ever friendly political officer.

My participation in the open mass movement through the teacher sector from the earlier NGO in the consumer movement had increased my skill in delivering speeches before recruits in mass organizing. Etta Rosales,* first ACT national chairperson, I remember now, hardly started in her talks without exploiting the social contradictions. It was a sure fire starter. The method adds spice to the speech like condiment to a bland political menu.

Now Congresswoman, 2006.

Strategies and Tactics

In the cities, the main task of the mass movement was "to build small core organizations" and (CPP) support. I got this from reading the 1978 U.G. paper of Clarita Roja "Grasp the Principle of Revolutionary Mass Movement." It was used extensively as an underground discussion paper. Reporter Carol Arguelles from Mindanao later published it in **Talamdan**. The method is similar to the above ground mass movement except for the explicitness of the armed struggle tacitly (but not operationally) accepted by few above ground militants. This was what Roja (a *nom-de-guerre*) called "the broadening of the revolutionary mass movement" but also touching close to the open mass movement.

All mass movements have a similar function, in that they provide political support to a revolutionary (armed or unarmed) struggle of the masses. This is the achievement of EDSA II in 2001 that ousted President Estrada for different reasons but the same mass movement methods and radical impulses of an outraged class.

EDSA III on May 1, 2001 was not a nation-wide mass movement but a short-term mass rising of the jobless. It lacked sustained, broad organizing, continuing recruitment, and popular education (read: ideological training). This abruptly ended because of inadequate strategic preparation and disorganized free-for-all tactics of Estrada's shoe-less and rubber-slippered sympathizers from the heartland of the squatter areas. Its leader Ronald Lumbao was later wrongly arrested. He was formerly of the militant Filipino ideology group formed by Nilo Tayag of the ML period. Earlier Tayag had become a bishop of the breakaway group of Aglipayans. Tayag's epigone, the young Lumbao, was hardly supported openly by the pro-Estrada middle class coteries watching television from the comfort of their living rooms.

Later, down the road that the mass movement had traversed, the same inadequacy in EDSA I and EDSA II would show why these did not metamorphose into a real social revolution. Both ended in an ugly bureaucratic, business-as-usual **Restoration**. Such inadequacy haunts all other mass movements up to this writing.

The semiotics of the revolution, its collage of signs and symbols that gloriously occurred in EDSA I, II, III should not substitute for the reality of the national democratic changes the masses longed for. The latter involved more social mechanisms to replace traditional institutions. The machinery for this change was not there or rather is still being tested. Remember ASF?

Neither were the people conscious of the coming socio-economic juggernaut called the **Restoration** that would only put in place what they were strongly against before and during the risings. It was as if society did not move and that the old vehicle stalled. It was not replaced. The new driver merely followed the old rules along the same old routes and these served those already in power.

In all the three stages of the mass movement which include (1) arousing consciousness (2) organizing people (3) mobilizing them every step of the way, the honing of militants requires method and ideological tempering, sometimes called attitude-building.

In Stage 1, called consciousness-raising, we included information exchange, constant study and reading of not-so-conventional ideas about the status quo, propaganda, inspirational (religious) talk, writing, printing and distribution of handbills during mass gatherings, rallies and study sessions; streamers screaming with condemnation of the ills of government, lots of flag waving, etc. this collectively was called education work for all militants. Its major features include high visibility, dynamic imageries, stirring texts, auditory public presence. All senses were engaged or politicized. In the contemporary scene the Internet practically globalizes Consciousness-Raising.

Stage 2, that is organizing people, has never been supremely proficient as it is today when aided by a free, democratic, critical press rapid in its news transmission in the hands of the mass movement organizers. Information technology makes easy as fast for organizers of mass movements, separated by distance, to exchange information swiftly, to conduct simultaneous marches. These could congeal into big pressure groups with moving presence in public spaces.

Stage 3, is mobilizing people. The issues have become society-wide. When news from the other side of the globe used to take weeks, days or hours to reach us, now their simultaneity with us witnessing what's happening somewhere is a matter of course. Events and analysis of events occur before our eyes at the time they are happening. The absence of these during the 1970s and up to the late 1980s explains why it took the open mass movement more than two decades to oust Marcos in 1986.

Class

The underground mass movement focused on the class character of Philippine society, describing it as constituted by those who exploit and those who are exploited. That's another method of analyzing the contradictions in the country usually used by but not limited to the UG militants and their political officers. Organizing people on this line is not only easier but also makes the social picture and relations of people appear more volatile and contradictory. The fractious features trigger a desire to change things radically. One is awakened to one's oppressed situation.

Landless peasants and wage workers (there are 90% of these combined elements according to 'Clarita Roja's study are conscious or could easily be made conscious of their oppressors who are merely a 1% minority. With it the urge to mobilize has reached the level of instinct to survive. Recognizing this fact is not only the correct start of their political education (Stage 1) but also of organizing them (Stage 2) for a goal that follows mass mobilization which is (Stage 3) toward a revolutionary national democratic mass movement, armed or unarmed.

However, directing components of the current mass movement are in the hands of middle class people unable to transcend their class origin. The desire to control and dominate still persists. Many of the leading elements are still enmeshed in the comfort of as economic system dominated by profit-making and other dictates of the market.

When I was in U.P., I learned that people can never be indifferent; he can only be different. It is a credit to a few leading cadres in the mass movement that some of them rebelled against family ties. Many have deep roots in the many layers of the feudal past, in the military establishment, in landlordism or in plain greed that frequently bristles and breezes in capitalist practices. To name a few: Jose Maria Sison with landed parents; Luis Jalandoni from a landed and religious circles; Victor Corpus from a near bourgeois and teaching background in the country's prestigious military academy; Edicio dela Torre from the priesthood class, or Boy Morales from the academe bristling with technocratic values.

Added to the above list are pre-ML newsmen Satur Ocampo and the late Tony Zumel from the rambunctious media, Sixto Carlos from a military and rentier class; Maita Gomez earlier married to a shipping magnate. Their socio-economic background provided iconic pedestals the masses look up to and often view them as models. These people were strong cogs and consciences to the mass movement. Their presence in marches and demos served as iconic symbols of struggle.

While their enriched social and educational background were largesse to the mass movement, some of these participants and popular leaders remained a drag to the real goal of *a reversal of relationship between the class they came from and the class they wanted to serve and liberate.* It was not easy to start a revolution and neither was it any easier to survive detaching oneself from one's class roots.

Chapter **4**

Thorny Transition Out of the Dictatorship
Toward Early 1980s

THE CPP LAUNCHED what it called the "three magic weapons" of the Revolution. These were (1) the party (2) the army and (3) the united front. This was a long agonizing process but by the late seventies they were more or less shaping up. Some of us took this formula with a grain of salt.

If you were an activist undergoing a regular orientation by some friends from the UG, you would be told that the revolution is "a protracted war." The social classes leading principally are the peasants and wageworkers. I learned my mass movement ABC from the kasamas (comrades) in the same vein. The incredulous middleclass person (that I was) looked at this unlikely mix with wide eyes and mental reservation.

The expert on this is the Political Officer or PO who would pontificate in his nice way on the three stages which are the "strategic defensive, strategic stalemate and the strategic offensive." (Corpus also explained this is his book, pp.27-30) One often leaves the UG study session a little groggy with the language of revolution ringing with unfamiliarity for the novitiate emerging from the cocoon of the educated middle class.

Historic Strike in a Tondo Distillery

While the idea of party formation recognizes the CPP as leading element, it was peopled with middleclass characters in the center of decision-making. It claimed to be a party of the wage earners a.k.a. "proletariat" and of the wage-less, landless peasants. Meanwhile it continued to carry the whole cultural baggage of petty bourgeois thinking. Its members loved to argue to the wee hours, a mistaken notion for dialectical exercise.

I was told by one who used to be a member of the CPP Central Committee that UG cadres had started to organize in the foreshore areas of Manila long before martial law. This corrected the impression that Trining Herrera, the squatters' leader had done the initial work to resist eviction especially in Tondo. This created a corollary impression that it was also Church-aided. The case was that the UG organizing support in Tondo "might have slumbered but was never absent," my informant told me.

In trying to recall all of this, my memory is aided by sources that have the time to analyze, compare, and synthesize the general conclusions of the period. Australian writer Katleen Weekley maintained (p.113) that the Tondo resistance could be "a cross-cultural affair," meaning that cadres from the Church and from the UG were equally involved in organizing it. A forceful illustration of this joint effort was in the historic strike in the distillery sometime in 1975 during the repressive heat of the regime. The affair reportedly involved 5,000 workers.

The strike in La Tondeña together with workers' caucuses and pickets was launched with the above ground Catholic activists and CPP direction. Luis Jalandoni, an ex-priest, and Sister Mary John Mananzan, a co-founder of the Citizens' Alliance for Consumer Protection (CACP) had regular presence in the picket line.

What made the La Tondeña strike historic in the annals of the mass movement? It put together 5,000 warm bodies in open rebellion against their employers. It spurred other spontaneous strikes especially in Manila and environs. It may not have been a wake-up call to the dictatorship but it was to the collective courage of organized workers long subjugated by some unnamed threat to their lives and livelihood. It was the first of its kind since martial law repressions began three years earlier.

The Manila-Rizal regional committee of the communist party showed the importance of organizing workers like "the other basic sectors." This was an idea in opposition to the reigning ideological bias about "the workers as the leading elements in the revolution" and was strongly objected to by the hardliners in the party. The masses in the territory agitated and were rising. They believed this could already derail Marcos. It was a popular line among the group led by the late Popoy Lagman. Some of us in the CACP took this with reservation. This did not prevent a few nuns and priests with us from reinforcing the ranks of the distillery strikers.

In the mid-seventies, the cadres returned to the areas, especially Tondo where Manila's unwashed and dispossessed worked and lived. Cadres joined the work of the Basic Christian Community (BCC) to intensify the social justice issue and expand organizing work. Perceived moderate activists Edgar Jopson and priest Luis Jalandoni were more than tolerated I think because the dictatorship had an ambivalent relation with the Catholic Church, a phenomenon shown by the late Jaime Cardinal Sin's "critical collaboration."

Open Mass Movement Disagreement with the UG

The UG theoreticians were prone to explain and argue often sticking to the books. This only hastened the party's own undoing with future above ground democrats. Earlier the CPP was having some tactical disagreement with itself, at least with some members of its central committee. This was outside of its continuing open defiance against the government's military forces and of Marcos. As it turned out, there were for the CPP more fronts to fight than the dictatorship.

In 1978, Marcos started to loosen control. Meanwhile, the country's democrats and nationalists were building up steam over his "constitutional authoritarianism." He called for an election for the "National Assembly" a.k.a. the *Interim Batasan Pambansa* (IBP). Marcos never failed to use old legalese, this time "nativized" the law-making body to give you a feeling that you were living under no strange country. The legal profession was mesmerized by it.

During these years, thousands of college students seemed to be taking up law or at least pre-law courses. It was a college course of choice under the dictatorship. Many wanted to be smart like Ferdinand Marcos, hardly an honest model.

The political opposition, both in the open mass movement and those still stuck in the traditional political party, was inveigled to run in the coming elections. The UG did not believe Marcos was serious in giving the elected people a free choice when they become members of the national assembly. He still held veto power over the decision of this body. The UG (also influencing many of us in the open) maintained a healthy doubt that no meaningful change could happen out of this election. This was a terrible misreading of the Filipinos' love for elections. It was like cutting the umbilical cord of the masses from the source of their political power. This was where the CPP committed a historic blunder.

It was a surprise to me that others in the aboveground, some of those in custody of their military guardians, acted in strange contradictory ways. Ninoy Aquino leading his LABAN Party decided to run inside his prison cell; Alex Boncayao and Trining Herrera, the latter of ZOTO campaigned in the election; Nilo Tayag and Bernabe Buscayno also decided to run inside their jails for provincial seats. (More from Weekley, p.117) All these were not intended to win seats but to probe how far Marcos could stretch his authoritarianism and in the process show that it was being challenged.

Popoy Lagman of the UG Manila-Rizal Regional Committee wanted to exploit "this contradiction in the ruling elite" believing this would advance tactically the cause of the revolution aimed at seizure of state power. The CPP did not accept this kind of analysis and Popoy was later removed from his committee and replaced by Edgar Jopson. (Weekley, p. 117)

As mentioned, it was obvious that the CPP was in constant struggle not only with the cleverness of Marcos but also internally with some of its ranking members. In the mass movement, the differences in analyses and tactics were the root cause of this uneasy situation. Among the aboveground activists, especially those openly organizing the communities, the difference could easily occur because of the individualistic outlook of militants coming from the middle class families not having yet internalized the Maoist ways. The PO from the NDF adeptly handled this problem among many activists who were putting high value on their individualism.

By end of the 70s and beginning of the 80s, organizing in the open mass movement took a dramatic turn in its practices. The mass movement shifted organizing work from a locus known then as "territorial" or community or area like what Popoy Lagman's cadres were doing in Metro Manila in contrast to the concentration in union organizing.

Saul Alinsky

My own reading of the radical American activist Alinsky earlier in the decade of the 70s was that his popular approach to community organizing broke up old thinking and contributed to new methods. It was his idea to open the way and reach out to the masses. One should not focus, it says, on trade union organizing, starting inside the workplace or factories (as the CPP would have it). A better way was with the broad heterogeneous number of people even outside the unions. The Tondo foreshore struggle illustrated it well with the effort of BBC and church people.

This did not preclude multiplicity of issues where the masses could be made collectively to respond directly, immediately even outside the sector. When I was with ACT, this was a common criticism of my leadership; it was too focused on education issues. Further, the decision to tackle multiple issues would dog several legalists prominent in the national democratic above ground struggle. Marcos often anticipated their efforts. After all he made the laws like PDs, LOIs, directives, executive orders, etc. in the course of protecting his own political nest and the cronies' economic interests.

The leadership in the UG targeted the government. The Alinsky idea suggested to the community organizers to target specific persons or personalities for destruction, often mistaken for personalizing the problem. Criticism of armed struggle replaced the struggle for arms. As Gani Serrano described it, "the CPP was structural" while the others echoing the American radical were "actors-oriented." Alinsky's influence re-defined the nature of community organizing from trade union organizing to tackling multiplicity of issues among the masses outside trade unions. The mass movement lurched forward differently thereafter.

Unnoticed Countryside Organizing

What was not normally seen nor heard in the open mass movement centered in cities and big towns was the intensified organizing of the peasantry. The underground mass movement tirelessly reached out to the oppressed masses, the workers both in factories and farms; also the starving families living at the edge of big lands they didn't own. One NGO that addressed itself to these people started in Manila and later spread nation-wide was a consumer protection group that I co-founded.

What is the CACP?

The Citizen's Alliance for Consumer Protection (CACP) has been a part of a worldwide social movement since its founding days in the 70s. it is among the few consumer groups in the country that used to be members of the Consumer International (CI), formerly known as International Organization of Consumer Unions.[17] This body has consultative status with the United Nations. It was a source of secret pride among its early members that the group was as close to an international body like the U.N. as to its many community-based members.

CACP came to light under objective conditions both complex and critical for the nation. I will explain later why this initiative had to give birth to several other NGOs (at that time called cause-oriented groups). The launching arena covered various fields in trouble: political, economic, environmental, education, human rights, nursing mothers and children, nuclear plants, etc. In all these, the organized masses became central to CACP interest.

Originally known as the Tuesday Club, CACP was organized by housewives, drivers, academics, nuns, students, and a mix of human rights activists. At the time no public or private group came out openly to oppose the

---

[17] Among them included CFGP, KMPI, NFWC, etc.

anti-people decisions of the U.S.-backed dictatorship. This was in the late 70s when the nation was beginning to be paralyzed, unable to think and act with the horrendous effects of martial law in *medias res*.

The secretariat was (and still is) headed by Sister Mary John Mananzan of Sta. Scholastica's College who later became the school's dean and president, simultaneously Secretary General of CACP. The militant organization had a nucleus of activists called Study Action Group or SAG. Its special operational tasks included joining or helping organize other NGOs many of which reflected consumer-protection function and rights protection. This effort caused the formation of many other COGs where members of CACP board also performed decision-making functions. The expression "interlocking directorate" became popular in the language in NGO communities often because the same militant faces were seen in many other COGs.

Among the NGOs that CACP had a direct hand at helping to organize included the Nuclear-Free Philippines Coalition (NFPC), the National Coalition for the Promotion of Breast Feeding & Child Care (NCPB-CC) the local acronym spelled BUNSO, Philippine Environmental Action Network (PEAN), State Colleges and Universities Faculty Associations (SCUFA). The CACP was active in GABRIELA and the Alliance of Concerned Teachers (ACT). It was a founding member of the international group Pesticide Action Network (PAN). This was formed in Malaysia. Many of these NGOs eventually became independent from CACP with their separate charters, organizational structures, officers and areas of operation.

Some of these NGOs are treated separately in this memoir. Suffice it to say that their dynamic existence contributed much to have the advancement of the mass movement since the 1970s. In not a few of these areas, these NGOs made a difference.

A political vignette is worth re-telling at this point. Sometime in 2003, I was with Bobby Tañada's Fair Trade Alliance delegation that paid a visit to President Gloria Macapagal Arroyo. CACP is one of the FTA convenors, representing Filipino consumers in that workers-manufacturers-producers-exporters-farmers consortium. During the social amenities and shaking hands with President Arroyo, I had occasion to ask her if she was still interested in the consumer movement. Was I surprised when she looked up at me and threw me back the interesting question: "I am a co-founder of your CACP, remember?"

The only reaction I could give was no little embarrassment which, when out of the People's Palace, caused me to trace the provenance of this unusual claim.

Before we go further, let it be known that CACP has had lots of glittering personalities in the line-up of its 36-year history. To mention a few: Vice President Tito Guingona, our CACP pro bono legal counsel, Senate President Nene Pimentel, a member of the board; late Supreme Court justices J. B. L. Reyes and Calixto O. Zaldivar who advised CACP in several matters of great import during the Martial Law years; the late Human Rights Commissioner Mary Concepcion Bautista, and former COA head and anti-graft chairman Euphemio Domingo. Several other politicians out in the cold also joined the decision-making body of CACP.

Sometime in 1978, the year CACP was formed, it decided to broaden the anti-oil price increase campaign. The "Big Three" oil cartel brought the country to its knees with its unbridled price increases of oil and its by-products. This triggered increased prices of essential commodities practically every week with no end in sight and no one shouting, "Stop!" So the prices of things important in the Filipinos' lives continued to rise. The mass media controlled by Marcos were terrifyingly mum.

CACP undertook organizing work with Catholic schools in Manila. CACP General Secretary Sister Mary John Mananzan, O.S.B. went inside the Assumption College in San Lorenzo Village where GMA was once an instructor in economics. *The petite teacher now president of this republic helped us in the name of CACP organized that symposium denouncing the Big Three Oil cartel.*

Beyond Cheap Prices

From the start, CACP was more than aiming for cheap prices of goods or their improved quality. We were not aspiring to become Ralph Naders. We believed the country needed a different solution to its problems. For instance, the group did not waste time counting how many pads there were in a roll of toilet paper or how much fat and harmful preservatives there were in the *longaniza* or other such coloring-laced products in the shelves of supermarkets. It wanted to go to the roots of consumer problems like what or who were responsible for these goods of dubious values or how to detect them by informed consumers themselves; what policy decisions harm the consumers?

We had unanimous agreement within CACP that all these involved mass education, organizing and action strategies. These points steered the organization not only to expose questionable goods and services but also to oppose the institutions that promote, protect and cause harm to consumers; or worse, cheat them. It was not pure luck that all those who joined CACP were alert in analysis or nimble in their activist feet that we went beyond consumerism.

The Nation in Crisis

When martial law was declared, everyone was unhappy, threatened, silenced possibly with the exception of the Marcos families and cronies. All freedoms were suspended except the freedom to agree with the government. At this time, the country was ripe for organizing, re-orientation, and mass mobilization. The CACP was in the midst of these.

The first that gave impetus to this NGO was the price increases by the oil cartels, with the government monkey backing on the company through its onerous taxes on gasoline and other oil products. The processes had started in the early 70s. We saw Marcos to be the strongest man in the country but *vis-à-vis* the U.S., the IFIs and the oil TNCs, and before the eyes of the people who were unprepared to give up their nationalist and democratic values, Marcos had caved in to these foreign pressures. He used terror, sloganeering, legal cleverness and his foreign-educated technocrats to ride the crisis the country was going through. But it was ordinary people who felt more and more oppressed everyday.

Cold War and the Mass Movement

With all these nation-wide difficulties, Marcos blamed "the communists and the oligarchs." The dictatorship in ten years finally started to point an accusing finger on the influential Catholic Church because many of its members had expressed sympathies and started to join the growing mass movement. Nine out of ten people who fuelled the street marches were mass-going Catholics, swinging their rosaries. Not far was the report by military intelligence that many cause-oriented groups were "front organizations" meaning, "of the godless, atheistic Communist Party." The CACP, a militant group, fitted well into this wrong picture. So were the many anti-dictatorship COGs of the times.

In 1978, the population was 47 million; the rate of increase (2.2 %) was one of the highest. Rich natural resources that included fertile lands, forests and mines were no longer in their stable renewable and productive condition. Within the next decade, multinational companies, ambitious landlords and what the activists used to call the big compradors exploited these without heeding their future effects, the Marcos government nodding in secret approval.

Aside from economic and social exploitation, Filipino consumers were (and still are) victims of 'unjust arbitrary pricing', hazardous government 'development projects', many deceptive policies, corruption in the bureaucracies, misleading propaganda by TNCs and mis-education by the state of the broad masses of Filipino consumers."[18]

Those who bore the brunt of these problems were the workers, peasants in the countryside, students, housewives, low-income professionals, and small Filipino businessmen. To go beyond sectoral interest, CACP pursued a perspective that was nationalist, gender-fair, protective of the environment, and an advocate for human rights.

In relation with other countries and business institutions, the CACP upheld the national interest as principal focus. It calibrated its responses guided by participation of active members and consultation by the government with sectors that are directly affected by its official decisions. It called for fair trade that generates mutual benefits. On page 16 of its *Consumer Handbook* cited

---

[18] *Consumer Handbook*, p. 10, CACP, Manila, 1981.

earlier, the CACP declared why it was important for it to be a part of a militant mass movement:

(1) to help in changing people *from* being passive to becoming active in asserting their rights; *from* being unaware of these rights to having developed knowledge of them; *from* asserting these rights individually to asserting them collectively; and

(2) to effect a series of linkages of organized people pursuing self-protection: *against* dangerous additives, drugs, pollutants; *against* individuals and entities that profit from misrepresentation, deception, cheating, adulteration and other trade malpractices; and *against* a system dominated by corporations (foreign or domestic) that are relentlessly profit-oriented and heedless of the adverse consequences on the masses and the country.

In reality the CACP is remembered more by its organizing activities outside of traditional consumer issues. During its heyday, it formed other COGs and NGOs in sectors like energy, environment, urban poor, education, children rights, peasant women, and foreign military bases. It closely worked with contacts from the legal wings of the NDF whose cadres were traversing the legal and illegal lines, exploiting their ambiguities, and often piquing the patience of the police and armed bulldogs of the military. It was in this way that CACP mothered several NGOs thereafter.

Chapter 5

Turbulent Half of the 1980s, and Beyond

THE MIDDLE FORCES increased their organized protests; school reforms turned education into business. Political convulsions lurched ferociously but some middle class people weakened the emancipatory agenda of street protests by following a divergent path. This is socio-economism that took the day of many NGOs under the flag of "rent-seeking economics."

The Rebel Church:
Toward a new national democratic revolution

The old national democratic politics proved inadequate in the face of U.S. imperialism. The new politics had to undergo the necessary passage from infancy to (political) maturity.

The early attempts to define a new national democratic politics (anti-imperialist and anti-feudal) had to contend with a multitude of problems like suppression by the colonial state, revealing the need for a clear grasp of armed politics; the question of united front: how to link the politics of the masses with the politics of the nationalist elite, and Marxism still had to undergo its incarnation into nationalist and mass politics.

The struggle of Christians and church people to define their politics was at an even greater disadvantage, because it was divorced from the new secular politics. Hence, the efforts for Filipinization and democratization of the churches (both Protestant and Catholic) tended to be hostile to the new national democratic politics.

The relatively young national democratic movement (after the Commonwealth) soon faced two successive tests: Japanese colonialism and US neo-colonialism. It successfully waged armed politics and united front politics against Japanese colonialism. It failed to handle the same combination against US neo-colonialism and suffered strategic defeat in the 1950s.

It is in this context that we can understand the brief resurgence into leadership of the old national democratic politics in Recto's anti-imperialism and the struggle for Filipinization of the churches in the 1950s. The students' Second Propaganda Movement signalled the revival of the new national democratic politics, again anti-imperialist and anti-feudal, again advocating both armed politics and united front politics. It asserted the need for a new leadership to replace the inadequate leadership of the old nationalist elite.

It is in this context that we should understand the response to what CNL represents. Christian and church people seek to offer the resources of the Christian faith and church to the people's struggle. In the process, we seek to liberate both faith and church from their captivity in imperialist, feudal, and even fascist politics. We seek the transformation of the churches into more Filipino and democratic institutions. (Quoted from *Christians For National Liberation 2nd National Congress Documents*, 1981, pp 7-8)

I recall that Martial Law was lifted on paper by 1981. This was one of Marcos' wily tricks while his dictatorial decrees had become a part of the law of the land. Law professors and their students started to quote them with unabashed eagerness. This repressive jurisprudence was in place any autocratic Napoleon Bonaparte could only envy. All this time the dictator's claws were deep into the country's political being while his cronies were crawling all over, busy harvesting the economic largesse for collaborating. Deception by a slew of legal chicaneries was the operational theme of the Marcos rule. Meanwhile his military continued to kill, torture, and arrest suspected activists who waddled like commies. What were going on in the open sectors? It was about his time that my activities shifted from the consumer sector to the teachers.

School Reform Turns Education into Business

The 1980s found many of our student organizations existing separately, disunited and demoralized. This followed the arrest at the Task Force Detainees office of militant youth icons like J.V. Bautista and the late Lean Alejandro. Meanwhile, something else was turning about in the schools. The organization of college editors (CEGP) in every tertiary school level remained half-free, half controlled by authoritarian administrators; so were the student councils.

One bill in the Marcos-controlled Congress caused the students to re-organize, re-group and consolidate their ranks. Since the time many students opted to go underground during the 1970s, those groups that existed above ground had remained in disorganized condition. This reform legislation handed a historic movement to the students its authors had not anticipated. The Education Act of 1982 became law two years later.

The revolutionary climate triggered by the First Quarter Storm (FQS) directed itself to the bankruptcy of society. Those directly involved in the school-based convulsion focused attention on the Education Sector. When I think of it now, it was the wrong time for coming out with an education bill neither needed by students nor asked for by parents and teachers. But the bill was badly desired by many private school owners who envisioned education as principally a business enterprise, a fertile source of cheap, trained labor. It neither improved the curriculum nor the condition of teachers. That's how the militant Alliance of Concerned Teachers (ACT) saw the draft school reform bill.[19]

The education law was the government response to the Gustav Ranis International Labor Organization report. It encouraged an overhaul of the education curricula in order to focus on vocational and technical training. Its output was badly needed by the TNCs aiming to invest in the country's rising unemployed.

The organized students saw the bill in another light—as an attempt to take hold of the whole school system into a manageable bureaucracy serving as collateral to another World Bank loan. Such loan application was pending

---

[19] See *What's Behind the Education Act 1982?*

before the World Bank then. In due time, it was immediately approved. Instantly the country's debts increased by $100 million.

ACT launched its first congress with (of all people) Jaime Cardinal Sin officiating during the historic salvo of "*The Year of the Teacher, Year of Struggle*," ACT's campaign slogan. The aim was to recover the economic and democratic rights of the teaching and non-teaching employees in schools and intensify organizing in the education sector. The presence of the cardinal helped dispel the armed forces-instigated fiction that ACT was a communist front. Membership increased hugely when the militants received an unexpected blessing from the Cardinal.

Meanwhile, the economy was turning from bad to worse. At the Philippine Normal College the organized teachers there headed by Rene Romero, confronted the former head of the Central Bank Jaime Laya. He was just moved to the Department of Education, re-named the Ministry of Education Culture and Sports after having been caught by the international finance watchdog of window dressing the government finances by $600 million. This infuriated the teachers and Mr. Laya started his office completely losing the respect of thousands of militant teachers.[20]

On the other hand, the student organizations nationwide became united in strongly opposing the so-called "education reform bill." My fellow teachers in the mass movement spent the two-year hatching period of the draft bill before it came law to organize, agitate and educate our ranks.

The open mass movement gained a fiery dynamism and consolidation the Marcos government did not realize until 1983. Following this, the students organized nationwide as a response to the bill that the school militants saw as ominous. One participant in the sector was young Fidel Nemenzo who in one of the scuffles with the police was shot at the back. Fortunately he survived and later finished his study in Sophia University, Tokyo where he earned his doctorate.

Etta Rosales, then ACT chairperson, who came from a private school knew like the palm of her hands how many of those schools were run principally for profit. Campus leaders lost their innocence about private schools as many

---

[20] This economic technocrat excused himself as reported by the press by saying he did not personally profit from this shenanigan.

of these became the subject of many symposia attended by activists. The Marcos government looked at the restless students first, as ornery people, then as troublesome, and finally as "communist-led." A few were dangerously "upgraded" to the military hit list.

The political turbulence continued in other areas of Philippine society. The Alex Boncayao Brigade during this period gained moral ascendancy in the public mind for killing some of the notoriously corrupt and abusive men in uniform. The ABB guided masses to believe that the political climate was ripe for a "swift takeover" and should be accompanied by rapid re-organization of the underground. This meant that the campaign for arms and battalion-size formation should intensify and those in the mass movement should start locating themselves in the struggle. My understanding or reading of it was that this was contrary to Joe Sison's "protracted armed struggle" and "circling the cities from the countryside" taken from MTT Thought.

It was about this time that Popoy Lagman, allegedly linked to the ABB, came to the house one early morning. A woman activist named "Cora" and also a family friend brought them. Popoy was accompanied by another person, tall healthy-looking, of secretive mien; perhaps, Popoy's later replacement? Were they mapping the middle class consciousness-raising terrain?

Popoy and companions were brought inside the library. He walked around my table, surveyed the shelves behind me and said, "Manong, *may mayamang karanasan tayo* (we've our own rich historical experience)," impliedly pointing to the irrelevance of the books in my shelves.

I took this as a criticism of my bookishness, so I told him: "Popoy, this is my *hanap buhay* (livelihood). I am a teacher." It was a 20 years later down the rough revolutionary road that I saw on TV when he was gunned down by unknown assailant{s} in the University of the Philippines campus.

The turbulent 80s was a decade that saw the mushrooming of people's organizations. No longer happy with each COG or NGO operating or being organized separately in the open, sectoral manner, the social formation found another innovation that would allow for consolidation of mass movement forces. One could observe them in the organizational banners of COGs, NGOs and POs during long marches. Those behind the mass movement had become selective, politically sensitive and sharply discriminating. The need to unite against an overwhelming power in the hands of one man was at the top of every activist's mind.

Unexpected Mix in the 1980s

The alternative formations gave rise to unexpected socio-political mix in the early 1980s. In organizing work, we in the open mass movement were sensitive to shades of the politics a person holds. Here's some:

If you strongly disliked Marcos but not the U.S. you're only anti-fascist. You may join a group that reflected this sentiment. You liked to watch and cheer and possibly join (since every one was a joining one group or another those days) a rally but not when this turned to Roxas Blvd. screaming epithets at the U.S. Embassy. Cory Aquino used to lead this group during marches before People Power I in the early 1980s.

If you dislike the dictator but found it difficult to hate the landlords because you're a landowner yourself, there's a group for your kind. Look for it because it fought or carried another issue that tried to protect your rights against foreigners who were extended the right to buy huge tracts of idle land.

If you could not stomach Marcos but wanted to pursue some business undertaking (e.g. import/export) and earned a thousand pesos a day or oodles of dollars compelling your workers to work harder (but not paying them more because this would erode your profits) you're not only a bourgeoisie but "a national *burgis*" and possessed an element of being a nationalist carrying on the economy which you saw as being perilously handed to the TNCs or the Americans. You admired the group rallying behind the "Filipino First" policy that President Carlos P. Garcia was unable to save 20 years ago.

If you could not hate a corrupt, oppressive government because you're a part of its bureaucracy but envy its military minions, generals and colonels who owned palatial homes in the posh villages in the suburbs and who kowtow to JUSMAG ("advisers"), your nationalism was piqued. You're not only desperate for alternative ways of surviving the regime and still continue through the commission or bureau where you sought livelihood. Consequently this rationale for making a little greasy cash that came from under your official desk got into your system earlier than retirement or before Marcos falls (whichever comes first). You would not like to listen or join the marches who scream, "*Ibagsak ang Burukratang Kapitalismo!*" Even your frankly false Filipinism would not survive it.

All these people hated Marcos but could not fully accept the "Three Basic Problems" that fired the mass movement. They posed a dilemma to organizers and those that were NDF-linked. This was the unexpected mix in the struggle of the 1980s.

COGs, NGOs, POs Increased in Numbers, Paving Way to Coalitions

How had the NDF viewed the rising organizational issues? Popular education, broad organizing and mobilization were going on. The common target was the country's three basic problems in its classic formulation: "Feudalism, Bureaucrat Capitalism, U.S. imperialism." In the mass movement, many of us involved in organizing were conscious how the PO would address correctly the issue of relationship with other NGOs.

An intense political heat in a cloud of uncertain future could burst like thunder from the sky. An example is the murder of the popular Senator Benigno Aquino in 1983. Aquino was an explosive icon who visited people with different beliefs to rally out of intense anger, frustration and fear. Another good example was the declaration by activists of the country as "Nuclear Weapons Free." The political implication of these two disparate events was immense in the future of the nation and the movement.

The campaign against U.S. Military bases pulled together broad COGs alliances and a medley of anti-Marcos groups. Some alliances did not start explicitly as anti-bases campaigns. But one such coalition, the Anti-U.S. Bases Coalition (ABC) in 1983 was launched as anti U.S. bases. Former Senator Jose (Ka Pepe) Diokno, initiated and led the campaign. Ka Pepe was an incisive handler of prose, concise, and to the point.

He visited my in-laws in Magallanes Village, a few blocks from his own place then. He had a draft of what he was writing about, "The First Years of Martial Law" showing it to my father-in-law who was a Supreme Court justice; and seeking his support. It was jointly signed.

Coalition building became the norm as early as 1980. The Nuclear-Free Philippines, (NFPC) founded in 1981, was one such COG earlier formed by the Citizen's Alliance for Consumer Protection. The NFPC became instrumental in the campaign against the nuclear plant in Bataan. Although the new 1987 Constitution did not have a blanket prohibition on nuclear power or nuclear energy, the campaign against the Bataan Nuclear Power Plant was based on the provision that was long demanded during mass actions to be included in a new Constitution.

Sec. 7, Article II, of the 1987 Constitution says: "*The Philippines, consistent with the national interest, pursues, and adopts the policy of freedom from nuclear weapons.*" Roland Simbulan was its chair and Cora Fabros its secretary general who were actively leading the NFPC; both reminded me of this critical provision.

The mass movement gained historic strength during this period; the Kilusang Mayo Uno (1980) and the Alliance of Concerned Teachers (1982) were not simple workers' unions and teacher alliances but dynamic centers for mass education, organizing and mobilization.

Women NGOs

GABRIELA, named after the revolutionary Gabriela Silang was a formidable formation of female fighters against the fascistic regime. Several militant women's groups rallied against the dictator. Formed in 1984, Gabriela's early composition were the *Kilusan nang mga Manggagawang Kababaihan* (KMK), the KMU women workers movement, *SAMAKANA*, housewives and urban poor with Petit Perido as first president; Center for Women's Resource (CWR); Parents' Alternative, Inc. (PAI).Women Media Circle and also Women Artists Circle; *Kalaya-an*, an anti-U.S. bases research group studying the conditions women prostitutes around the American military bases. Actively involved in the research were the late Raquel Tiglao, Oye de Dios, Aida Santos Maranan and many others.

In time more women from the middle class rallied behind the widowed Cory Aquino in their sunbright, blinding cotton yellows, with wide brimmed hats tied in feminist ribbons, during the presidential campaign early in 1986. Among them were Dr. Mita Pardo de Tavera (who was with the CACP board),

Fely Aquino as GABRIELA's general secretary, Senator Tecla Andres Ziga, Nicky Coseteng, Mary Concepcion Bautista, and others. All were die-hard anti-Marcos dictatorship just like Cory but not all were anti-U.S. imperialist.

When Cory Aquino became president (1986) the groups split between the anti-Marcos but not anti-U.S. imperialist coteries and the anti-fascist Marcos and fiercely nationalist women members. Included in the first group were Fe Arriola, chief convenor of GABRIELA, and Imelda Nicolas. These two women left the organization to join Cory Aquino's cabinet; both were anti-Marcos but not anti-U.S. Source of this data was Nelia Sancho, herself an active, militant member like Liddy Nacpil also a GABRIELA and widow of murdered Lean Alejandro, a militant U.P. leader in the student sector. GABRIELA later served as an acronym for *General Assembly Binding Women for Reforms, Integrity, Leadership and Action.*

The spirited participation of these women in mass mobilizations gave color to the movement that indicated the direction of history had not always been in the hands of men. Many of those who used to rock the cradle were also rocking the Marcos government if not wrecking the peace of mind of the dictatorship.

Many of these women were later absorbed into Cory Aquino's cabinet or rewarded with government positions.

During this part of early 80s, other formations and alliances developed, including the militant Nationalist Alliance for Freedom, Justice and Democracy (1983), Justice-for-Aquino, Justice-for-All or JAJA (1983); Coalition for the Realization of Democracy (1984); Bagong Alyansang Makabayan (1985).

There were others, small and short-lived although in Manila they often occupied the headlines because their leaders were adept in holding on to the new semiotic messages inherent in creating media mileage. These leaders were usually academics, political has-beens or businessmen who fell into the laps of the Left behind several mass movements. Many of us in the progressive NGOs partied with them in their plush houses and felt like socializing Marxists.

Not understanding the real nature of the masses, these leaders ended up disappointed not knowing why the crowd was not always following what they were told to do. Not a few withdrew in typical middleclass reaction of denial, and a few tragically took their own lives. Marcos often had a better understanding of these bourgeoisie-bred activists. He scared them with the smell of gunpowder and roar of tanks. My brother-in-law used to call these people "radical chic." They had transient following from the middleclass and higher middleclass. Among these were the BANDILA, KAAKBAY, *Manindigan!* (Take a Stand!). Their members alluded earlier were articulate, educated, individualistic anti-Marcos votaries.

Their contribution to the mass movement should not be belittled. Aside from adding their voices to the "Marcos resign" calls, they were leaders and personalities in their own circle of friends and among their office employees. In a period of intense organizing, no one person or group or class or sector is insignificant that could not be made to join and contribute to the downfall of the dictatorship.

Ninoy's Death and the Big Leap Forward

The open mass movement gained a momentum and rapid consolidation that the Marcos government did not realize until that fateful day of August 21, 1983. Senator Benigno Aquino was assassinated when he decided to come home and became a martyr.

In some parts of the country, especially in Mindanao, there were more killings by the CAFGUs, a militia organized by the AFP recruited from among the jobless in the communities. Their stories of depredation splashed the front pages of newspapers. A massacre was reported in the town of Escalante, Negros Occidental. Vigilantes were running around in southern Philippines in a festival of gruesome killing. In one place, gross cannibalism on an Italian priest's brain was reported.

The velocity of the political processes increased in the year 1983. Even Ninoy Aquino foresaw his death in many interviews he made with the international press before his plane departure. If an important member of the Philippine Senate, a former award-winning journalist and part of the scion of the landed class in Central Luzon could be cut down with such impunity, no one else (in the elite or those aspiring to be a part of it) was safe.

The fateful day was stomach turning among the middle class activists and sympathisers. Award-winning movie director Lino Brocka had a yellow scarf, waving it to us teachers, encouraging us to be at the airport or form a line along Roxas Boulevard to welcome Ninoy Aquino. Being less sentimental that I was, I could not understand how events could turn around having a piece of yellow kerchief tied on a tree. The suppressed fears of the years gave way to a retching anxiety that Marcos was capable of doing worse. That fateful signal escaped us for a while.

The Filipinos' celebratory response and love for remembering their dead opened the fields for a historic march. The field of symbolic images was never broad as it was during the historic funeral of the late senator.[21] All, signs, symbols, syntax and forms of signification were on hand to point singularly to the "brain" behind the murder. The bandwagon meaning was not in the monumental 15-kilometer cortege but spread beyond the immensity of this collective mourning. It singed deep in the heart of every middle-class Filipino.

I recall other deaths of mass movement martyrs. These were Mountain Province native leader, Dulag Macli-ing's, Doctors Johnny Escandor's and Bobby de la Paz's, labor leader Lando Olalia's, young priest Father Rudy Romano's and many more. The deaths of some urban organizers and hundreds of peasants, now freshened up in the troubled consciences of many. They re-ignited the memory of a somnolent population that started dangerously to believe the dictatorship was tolerably normal and acceptable. This absurd sentiment was not uncommon especially among the middleclass. They were lulled by martial law propagandists because many were unexposed to actual repressions.

The Turning Point

The assassination of Senator Aquino was like a high-octane tank truck ramming an electric post. It set the country on fire. A segment of the UG believed the revolution was at hand. Those in the aboveground precipitately thought the end of the dictatorship was around the corner.

The message outlived the medium. Such martyrdom that deeply disturbed the moneyed middle forces sent tremors to the rest of the country. Their contribution to the mass movement thereafter was more than the bags of sandwiches and cash they gave to the thousands of young "parliamentarians"

[21] Ninoy Aquino's funeral was recently compared to the funeral of another popular character, a movie hero's death in Fernando Poe Jr. FPJ's death followed his presidential defeat in the 2004 elections.

in the streets. Funding agencies here and abroad were bankrolling the mass movement in many disguises. Such reaction changed the pace of the struggles. It was a turning point.

The rhythm of the mass movement followed a pattern: two steps forward, one step backward. There was rout in victory, advance in defeat. Joema's "protracted war" seemed to come true but in reverse. It was the city that was starting to surround the countryside. Then the country's population increased in leaps and bound and mass migration led to cities bursting in the seams. People lived in crowded hovels and even populated street marches. It was said that the NPAs were active in 62 of 73 provinces.

Meanwhile, a rubber stamp Congress was institutionalized in the Batasan. It was dominated by the shameless armada of Marcos yes-men. The bankruptcy of KBL started to surface and to smell starkly. There was no way seeing the government doing right. You name a problem out of this spreading miasma and an NGO grew out of it. The parlous days of the early 80s continued to paint the sky with ominous clouds. With that kind of political weather, NGO and POs continued to sprout like mushrooms.

How Does One Unite a Heterogenous Mix like These?

A direction-less gathering like KOMPIL (*Kongreso Ng Mamamayang Pilipino*) was a short-ended political candle that burnt its wick too soon. The August Twenty-One Movement (1983), an urban petty bourgeoisie group, principally Makati-based was formed by Butz Aquino as an immediate response to his brother's assassination. This group later split with more members joining BAYAN. (See Sison/Werning, p. 116.)

These new broad formations were wracked with organizational problems. When BAYAN was formed, some pro-U.S. but anti-Marcos elements attempted to grab some organs of leadership out of proportion to their memberships (Sison/Werning, p.116). But the attempt failed and they formed a separate group called BANDILA. A surviving leader like Guingona who later became the country's appointed Vice President in 2001. KAAKBAY, a group mostly of U.P. academics and radicals, was chaired by "Ka Pepe" Diokno. This also took a typically middle class independent existence.

Presidential decrees, letters of instruction and various military directives remained; so were the symbolic hateful barbed wires across Mendiola Bridge, checkpoints, the hateful CAFGUS. Abusive militias continued to run wild in the provinces. Marcos continued to threaten and terrorize the people with secret infiltrators, police operatives, intelligence units, curfews. And he was supposed to have lifted Martial Law in 1981.

During the second half of the 80s, more especially after 1986, problems of consolidation rose among the different anti-dictatorship formations. There was a perceived weakening to the political agenda in the mass movement. Meanwhile, the pattern of struggle characterized by the conscious pursuit of the *ameliorative agenda shifting away from the emancipatory agenda* by the many COGs, NGOs and POs was slowly and visibly established. This would be repeated in the above ground organizing in the years to come. It was not the case with those in the underground. The Communist Party, leading the underground mass movement, insisted that thereafter all struggles would be done in the name of the Revolution (read: seizure of state-power) and not of reformism (read: patching up what's wrong with the government or with people running it).

Prioritizing the armed revolution was rock-hard party decision. The cadres were unaware of romantic elements of this strategy. The theoreticians of the mass movement (UG and AG) were not fully conscious that the state is a sovereign machine that could turn and crank for more power by itself or in cooperation with other states. Its arms, trained soldiers and other appurtenances of its sovereign might would remain unmatched by the revolutionary underground.

The middle-class elements read this phenomenon usually in its psychological dimension. No objective dialectics was involved under Marcos' iron hands. The leaven of consciousness started to rise but the various open organizations were still groping before an uncertain future. They grouped together although with incoherence, and ultimately re-defined agenda for the next stage of the struggle. What was this new formulation?

The Peace that Refused to Happen

From 1986 to 2004, fitful attempts, one after the other, of peace negotiations failed. What had happened since President Cory Aquino opened negotiation with the NDF starting 1986 was actually a series of disheartening uncertainties. The fault was less of Corys' than of her recalcitrant military that she was unable to effectively control as its Commander-in-Chief.

While Cory was supposed to lead the national government after her triumphant People Power I, her AFP seemed to act independently from a line of command that should start from her. Her Secretary of National Defence was plotting against her. This made negotiation with the rebels more difficult. A part of the AFP launched a coup that emanated from the lobby of the Manila Hotel. There were continuous arrests of members of the UG. These arrests were taken as violation of an understanding that nothing of the sort should be resorted to while peace negotiations were going on. This was a costly lesson the NDF learned later in dealing with the government.

Often little political "victories" happened not in the negotiating tables but in press releases, where the public was entertained with half truths and military disinformation. The game was equally played with skill by the CPP spokesperson Ka Roger hiding in the fastnesses of the Sierra Madre. He remains a marvellous maven in mass media riposte. Eighteen years were spent on the "on-again off-again" peace talks with the UG forces but nothing substantial turned out. Thereafter, another stage in the series of failed negotiations was under-taken by non-combatants: neither CPP/NPA nor GRP/AFP. There were mostly church people, NGOs and 23 COGs calling themselves Coalition for Peace.

During this period, especially in the mercurial months that followed the People Power I of February 1986, the political clouds had become fast moving and volatile. The socio-political weather was rapidly changing. It seemed that the dictatorship was receding. The mood was taken over by mass euphoria principally middleclass-created. How did NGOs respond? New groups were born and new coalitions launched.

Having the past seemingly out of sight did not mean the infrastructures of state repression were dismantled. They were not. This had been the predicament of many militant social formations, including the so-called Peace

NGOs. They wanted to build a broad swath of networks that would last longer and secure the safety of the population. The military was not cooperating with that thinking unfortunately.

Why should NGOs and other coalitions of NGOs take this initiative and not the government? Simply put, the new government of President Cory Aquino had not exactly extricated itself from the *base* of the previous dictatorship, i.e., its dependence on and continuous toadying before the United States.

The widow of the murdered senator might be a stirring symbol for driving Marcos and his cronies out; of military subalterns on the run but the country had to move forward on some new badly needed strategy, that it should take off from another plain. There was none.

The people around Cory Aquino were former stalwarts of the mass movement. But sometimes naïve nationalism and patriotic piety could blur their vision. They were not clever enough to discover how to address and act with decisiveness on a series of political power grabs from within the military, starting with Cory's own Secretary of National Defence. The seed of more putschist power grabs was cultivated in this garden of hesitations, uncertain with its "Freedom Constitution" while the 1974 Marcos Constitution was not completely stamped out.

The Years Beyond 1986

The EDSA Uno rising was historic for two reasons. First, it installed the concept of "people power" as a legitimizing political process never dreamed of by UG advocates of armed struggle. Many in the Left called it "new risings" of the masses. Subsequently, the expression "people power" was made popular by the international media. It echoed in the corridors of the twentieth century, being first of its kind at least in the last 500 years.

Its historical significance also lies in how it influenced the succeeding "revolutions"—endless demos, marches, rallies—against the beleaguered states in some parts of the world. One finds it symbolically in the fall of the Berlin Wall (1989) with the accompanying toppling of rulers and dictators in Eastern European states, and ultimately, the break-up of the 75-year old empire of the Union of Soviet Socialist Republics. The people's revolution that exploded in

Tiananmen Square, Beijing also came about this time (1989) although brutally suppressed. I was in China two months before this happened where I travelled in the so-called "Prohibited Territories." These were regions mostly in the northwest that were either military areas or vast lands with gruelling poverty.

But beyond the shores of its birth place in the streets of Manila, People Power found havens in the downfall of other dictators and authoritarians in Georgia, in Kyrgyzstan, in Venezuela, in Columbia, in Ecuador, etc. It is now a natural thing for the masses awakened, organized, and powerful to pull down their abusive, corrupt leaders without the benefit of national elections. The People Power in EDSA preceded all these and international press projected the local unarmed, massive risings like a new-found political discourse. It was a lesson equally learned by other peoples under repressive regimes. Several elements in the eighties had their different origins. The conditions that brought them forward may be different. Their confluence in that decade compels us to recognize the role each played.

Beyond the repressive PDs and assorted administrative fiats there were the military mind-set of law enforcers, barbed wires (old hated symbol) blocking the passage to the Presidential Palace, and check points put up in the provinces. All these were deeply cultured in the attitudes of those who could not easily shed the cruel, anxiety-laden years of suppression of freedoms.

How did the NGOs and other emergent political but non-party formations respond? As mentioned earlier new voluntary formations were born, new coalitions launched, and old sectoral organization re-grouped. The historic split in the underground surfaced in a process of public purging of "enemies within." This issue had not limited itself to the CPP. This had affected not only the UG but also many legal organizations and persons that had long been influenced by the NDF. Bad memories that were part of the dark past were like jetsam bubbles before one's eyes. Books like Robert Garcia's *Suffer Thy Comrades* remind us of these unfortunate events of the past.

Even then, the organized consumer groups were still watching the behaviour of the oil multinationals. Militant teacher groups honed their skills away from the traditional 3-Rs and the classroom alphabets for the kids towards the pedagogy of human rights. They now focused on authoritarian administrators and profit-hungry private school owners. Thanks to the badly conceived Education Act of 1982. Alternative news agencies started to gain readership, National broadsheets including those formerly ran by the Marcos cronies, also proliferated. (See chapter on PNF.)

Farmers started to forcibly occupy land abandoned by big landlords as a result of the slow implementation of the land program. The fisher folks organized under the militant PAMALAKAYA continued to fight for fishing rights in the inland and coastal waters exploited by large foreign vessels.

Even nursing mothers were slowly discouraged from breast-feeding their babies as milk MNCs started to hype many of the dangerous milk substitutes their cancer-causing leaden canned milk. (See chapter on BUNSO.) Other emancipatory struggles continued long after martial law had been lifted carried out by many people's organizations under the leadership of BAYAN.

The eighties opened with the mass movement gaining large ground. This was especially true when more militant organizations, non-party but highly politicized formations, emerged as mass poverty and repression deepened in the countryside. It was no longer effective to just call for ousting an authoritarian leader. The hidden face of the problem remained. Nationalist economists Alejandro "Ding" Lichauco and Hilarion "Larry" Henares and political analyst Renato "Tato" Constantino in various writings and speeches during this period continuously critiqued neo-colonialism and U.S. imperialism.

NGO Organizing Shifted to Rent Seeking

The COGs began to call themselves NGOs to highlight the difference. They distanced themselves from the graft-ridden government system. When Cory Aquino won the elections in 1986 after the massive risings in EDSA, funds, grants, and other financial assistance, poured into the government and much of these were shared with NGOs. A great shift in the lives of NGOs took place. It defined a new mode of profit making without being productive. This is rent seeking. The latter formations started to call themselves "development NGOs" supporting a variety of socio-economistic enterprises. These unwittingly occluded over the crimes of Big Business, e.g. unpaid debts, behest loans guaranteed by government. They started to believe there was no more need for marching in the streets and demanding for a new, just social system to carry out a pro-people's agenda.

Many COGs sold out to the new and biggest consortia of NGO network originally gathered by a Canadian funding agency. These groups bundled themselves to capture foreign funds. Aside form Canada, Australia, the U.S., Japan and some European countries contributed. Much of these funds were intended to support the foreign policy of their respective country-donors or church sector and secondarily to help the poor and the "wretched of the earth" (my apology to Frantz Fanon).

The new consortium was called Caucus of Development NGOs (Code-NGO) which became notorious when two decades down the road its financial mavens became involved in a multi-billion bond scandal. Two keywords that characterized the scam: bonds and commission. (There is abundant literature on this, and should be read in relation to the kind of economics called rent seeking that started to be dominant in the second part of the 1980s and up 2002.) The Code NGO operation demonstrated this highest form of rent seeking. (See Glossary.)

I remember in the late 1980s where NGOs submitted proposals for financial support. The first question raised by the funding agency was "Where is the self-reliant component of your proposal?" The question caused many of us to bite our lips. NGO and POs were not aware they were aligned with the exploitative economic programs of these IFIs the likes of IMF and the World Bank. The NGOs with us were far from racing with them much less saving the economy by their programs. We just had a different agenda, and that was principally searching for justice for thousands who were victims of the dictatorship.

What can an NGO do? The warning of Ding Lichauco in the 1960s came back like a ghostly voice. The fish we must catch for lunch is less important than taking hold of the fishing rod. Translation: the control of resources like land, skills, tools, seeds and other productive inputs are more pressing than all these dole-outs called "foreign assistance." Cory Aquino's triumphalist assumption to power fearfully presaged a restoration. The emancipatory agenda of the COGs was muted as Cory and the technocrats around her started to signal to foreign investors to take over the moribund economy against the provision of her own 1987 Constitution. Never had such opportunity for genuine liberation from neo-colonialism both in economics and politics been squandered.

People's Strike

Against this miscalculation the mass movement consolidated, envisioning another society. "*Welgang Bayan*" or people's strikes were launched. But another semiotic shift happened with the Cory-Doy team (the party of Mrs. Aquino and Vice President Doy Laurel). In joining mass actions they suddenly got lost as they made a turn around. This happened as soon as the screaming, angry marchers from Kalaw Street turned left towards the U.S. Embassy relentlessly denouncing American imperialism. Many in the Left viewed their act as a revelation of the duo's true color.

Suddenly Corazon Aquino changed her mind and stopped calling for boycott of San Miguel products as she did in the heat of the election campaign. San Miguel, one of the biggest locally created multinational corporations, was back on track. Overnight, neo-colonialism was restored unscathed, its feathers neat and unruffled. It was "business as usual."

The Conditions in the Underground

In the underground, the CPP was counting the increasing number of is forces with worrisome frequency decimated by arrest or killing by the military. Suspicion rose that the UG arrests were triggered by planted government assets, a.k.a. deep penetration agents. The belief was prevalent in Mindanao and Southern Tagalog provinces where many were caught or arrested by the military and were tortured, "salvaged" or killed outright.

The CPP reacted severely if not irrationally. It attempted to clean its ranks of suspect infiltrators by launching *Kampanyang AHOS*. There were varying names for this "cleansing process" (read: torture, especially psychological torture, in some instances forced confession and execution). It was called "anti-zombies" campaign in Mindanao, Operation Missing Link (OPML) in the southern Tagalog, and Olympia in the National Capital Region or "Kadena de Amor" in Quezon-Bicol region. The first of this was supposed to have been launched in July 1985.

The anti-infiltration campaign to cleanse the underground went wild and was stopped only in 1986 and 1988 in some areas. Restitutions were supposed to have been made to the victims and/or families of the afflicted. The number of those executed ran wild, commensurate only to the un-verifiability of the rumor. The military bloated the figures. It was good propaganda against the underground.

The kind of information we got among us activists in the above ground mass movement was at best wrapped in the category of rumor that spread in whispered, low voices. Often our political officer refused to elaborate. It was both hard to believe or disbelieve. The DPA issue troubled the UG as it had not in the long past. This was not supposed to affect the open mass movement *but it did.*

Some activists got lost, hid, absented themselves from NGO work, unaccounted, or rumoured to have been kidnapped by the UG on orders by the CPP. Boni Ilagan, chair of the First Quarter Storm Movement, had an explanation of it posted recently in the Internet extensively quoting the CPP side of the exaggerated magnitude of the deadly enterprise that plagued the underground.[22] Earlier, Cory Aquino selected her own people to draft a new Constitution. This did not receive a whole-hearted, wide and warm welcome from the above ground mass movement. The open mass movement was split into "Critical Yes" and "No" to her draft Constitution. Obviously, there was a confused message coming from or coming through the NDF guiding the mass movement.

Political Officer or PO

One person was playing an important script in the open mass movement— the political officer. In the UG lexicon, he/she was neither an officer nor was it a full-time occupation. But the PO was well known in the mass movement. He/she worked beyond 24 hours, usually with an NGO. His/her work was rewarded not by money but by a deep conviction that things were going right according to the books of the revolution guided by theory and correct practice. The correctness of his/her guidance was based on how the country's "three basic problems" were being made operational in one's activities as a militant in the open mass movement.

---

[22] Posted in Bulatlat.com. Compare this data with the experience of Robert Garcia in the book cited above.

A PO was friendly and highly knowledgeable but a deeply suspicious character depending on what social class you came from. There were only two classes: the disadvantaged and those taking advantage, the exploiter and the exploited. The PO possessed such political sapience he could not afford to be dogmatic although he/she might sound in his/her correct ways like a member of the Society of Jesus. The PO was embedded in NGOs or people's organizations or some other center of organizing the masses that has had an emancipatory goal, a strategic objective laced with democratic values. A PO could be mistaken as a full-fledged CPP member but often he/she was not. Being with the NDF made him/her a target for the military.

When the anti-DPA campaign was launched, the NDF tightened its hold on the open mass movement. Some POs got lost, or withdrew or were re-assigned elsewhere. This deepened our suspicion in the above ground that something chilling or uncommon in the mass movement was going on. The party paranoia was infectious. A distancing from the UG among above ground militants became inevitable.

Political Synthesis of the 1980s

What follows is my synthesis of the breath-taking decade of the 80s. Several NGOs and people's organizations shamelessly abandoned their emancipatory agenda in exchange for funds that ensconced their ameliorative short pursuits into the bosoms of their funding partners. Their annual reports with the enumerated achievements began to read like profit-and-loss statements. This happened when several foreign-funded cooperatives abandoned their liberatory agenda.

Ninoy Aquino's murder widened the space for democratization. Unfortunately this only prepared the country for the coming restoration of elite control both of the economy and the political system. It was "elite democracy" and still is to this day.

The political paranoia that seized the CPP in the late 80s left a permanent dent on the open mass movement. This presaged the public split between the UG and the AG mass movement in the next decade. Why did the split happen and what were the consequences? There were also benefits. Many concluded that the 80s was a period of restoration. I did not see any conscious attempt to put in more than the alternative political values like honesty, criticalness, alert accountability against public officials.

Restoration

The revolution attains its end according to the *Communist Manifesto*, when the exploiters shall have become the exploited. The tools of power taken away from their hands. There is a reversal of relations. This is only a half-real reversal because no one is sure how the tool in the other's hand would be used. That change of hand does not erase the picture of injustice, which was the original cause of the revolution. The capture of the machinery and tool(s) of power up to this point is the immediate political goal of any revolution. This will make us see clearly that the cause(s) of the revolution is distinguishable from its goal.

Who wields the tool is a more real and engaging problematic. The answer is not immediate because the new wielder of power can change or will change or, in a worse case scenario, refuse to change. A Machiavelli like Ferdinand Marcos could only worsen that kind of change no matter how much brush strokes he mixes on his political palette of re-naming the country "*bagong lipunan*." Hitler also did it and neither of them succeeded. Marcos painted a more benign picture in his speeches of what could come out from his *Eighteenth Brumaire*-like coup of the government and the whole civil society when he declared martial law in 1972. He ironically justified his autocratic rule in the following decade rationalizing his brand of "democracy" that would eliminate the "oligarchs" and drive away the "communists." Neither happened.[23]

Former President Diosdado Macapagal had a perceptive critique of that period in his book **Democracy in the Philippines** (Manila, 1978). He wrote that "... dictators resort to quaint devices of "democracy" in the manner of Fulgencio Batista of Cuba, Sukarno of Indonesia and Ayub Khan of Pakistan" invariably calling it "disciplined democracy", "guided democracy", or "basic democracy." Macapagal noted that "in the end, (these three) were deposed

---

[23] The capture of power without having changed hands is peculiar but it happened. Marcos did one 1972. It was in the *18th Brumaire of Louis Bonaparte* that this Napoleon of France foreshadowed Ferdinand Marcos. Marcos was an ardent student of history. For more of this political capture of power—a coup d' etat—when one is inside power, read *Marx-Engels Selected Works*, p. 961.

with the tragedy that after their ouster the people had to start all over again and to suffer the aftermath of the dictatorship..." (p.21). Marcos was not short of wrong models.

The restoration after the two EDSA risings should teach a lesson. It haunts us and maybe would continue until we shall have answered not how to attain a revolution but having attained this, how to re-conceptualize and particularize the real question: *after the revolution, what?* The question remained unanswered. Worse, it was never raised by people I worked with in the movement.

The Pathology Called Left Romanticism

I wish to repeat an observation that those varied elements in the decade of the 80s had their confluence here although they many have different origins. One such feature was left romanticism. It is a minor pathology that often accompanies a revolutionary zeal. It happens when one is motivated to act eagerly by the images, sounds, colors or by multiple messages of change and take them as new signs, a stirring of one's hopes. These signs take the equivalent of the real things in our minds, that is, of a meaning as signified by these symbols. Jean Baudrillard calls them simulacra, second level meaning.

When we keep interchanging this literal with the figurative because we wish to move beyond literalness of reality, when this happened, the normal person's vision turns him into a visionary. This is left romanticism, a political pathology.

Hence, the "revolution" is now spelled with a capital letter R; nobody does that with mere rising. I often use the phrase "left romanticism" in a pejorative way. The expression signals its own limit. It is neither left nor romantic. It is a reactionary waving a revolutionary flag; excusable and natural to young people learning a new vocabulary for an experience they did not have a name before. Note what political scientist Hannah Arendt said apropos of this reversal:

"It is well known that the most radical revolutionary will become a conservative on the day after the revolution."[24] This reversal reminds me of many "civil society" people who were screaming against President Estrada to

---

[24] P.64 *Crises of the Republic*, Pelican Book, 1973..

resign at the height of EDSA Dos, succeeded by then Vice President Gloria Macapagal Arroyo. When another group in another time screamed against President Gloria Arroyo because they perceived her to have won by "massive electoral fraud and cheating" these people were called "de-stabilizers."

Many neologisms picked up from the streets manufactured by marching activists partake of novelty that is not actually new. They are old names given a new twist and sound by the new often jumbled spelling. To illustrate: "*Kumpare*" is truncated to 'pare' syllabically reversed, shortened to 'Erap', the deposed president's moniker. When stamped on a wristband, the band piece becomes a ring or insignia in non-formal relations, evoking a feeling that one is with the common man. President Estrada popularized this use of the wristband.

He is also known for this exhortation in his inaugural address: "*Walang kaibigan, Walang kamaganak, Walang kumpare*" (neither friends, nor relatives nor...) as warning against nepotism in his administration. Since then his fall from grace did not diminish the value of the presidential wristband nor discoloured the street expression "*pare ko*." The popular romance with the word "Erap" triumphed over the historic fall.

When Jose Maria Sison was imprisoned in 1977, left romanticism especially among the youth was high. It was a measure of popular appeal of the mass movement with the deification of some personalities linked to it. Stickers of Commander Dante's image in covers of school notebooks of coeds and in study groups convening under the shaded trees and not in the classrooms, with Mao's little *Red Book* and later Joe Sison's *PSR* (Philippines Society and Revolution). For the left youth, deification of iconic figures illuminated the path ahead.

Restoration I

The description above defines the milieu before the close of the 80s. Slowly without being noticed restoration took place. The semiotics of the revolution should not be taken lightly. It fuelled the spirit as much as informed the mind what to leave behind (old ways, old thinking and old habits) or what were the new directions taken?

Romantic transformation in areas other than politics or ideology happens when language starts to control our thinking. In restoration whether of system, government or relation, the old structures are put back in their old places. For example, when government is "re-organized," bureaucracy "streamlined," cabinet "revamped" an old system is actually being refurbished, restored. The public mesmerized by concepts behind "re-organized", "streamlined", "revamped" etc. come to believe in the hastily legitimated restoration. Everybody stops questioning why an old suspect system, usual breeding places of old problems in this Republic, was back in place.

No questioning was focused on the powerful entities that legitimated all these putative changes. We in this mass movement confronted a goal we did not consciously wish to happen: restoration. In the two People Power risings, restoration re-appeared at their separate ends, after 1986 and after 2001. Was this restoration the goal of the mass movement with its militant, triumphalist agenda?

I believe the principal cause of this restoration was the failure of the national democrats and street radicals to problematize the issues of political economy. There was no coherent agenda after the mass rising of February 1986. There was an implicit trust the government of Corazon Aquino would act right on behalf of the organized masses that placed her there. The lawyers around her, although many were "street parliamentarians," pursued legalism to the hilt. Some insisted on continuing the dictator's PDs, LOIs and other martial law decrees. This made genuine change very difficult.

I remember how restoration happened after Cory Aquino took over. The old institutions, never having faded away after EDSA I, were the same that readily supported the martial law regime: same Congress, Big Business, and the U.S. Embassy-toadying Executive branch including the military. These were responsible for the restoration the day after the mass movement culminated with EDSA *Uno*.

Restoration II

In EDSA Dos, the so-called "civil society" groups found themselves in the bureaucracies, corporate boards, commissions and cabinet. They were one in calling to stop ("*Tama na!*") and shouted "enough of rallies" and demos. Some members of "civil society" groups were angling for more government positions and sinecures. The rest were waiting on the wings for posts here or abroad. But those who continued the unfinished business of cleaning up the government by more mass actions were already called "de-stabilizers."

How often had I felt a strong sense of *déjà vu*. Several public contracts signed before had become resurgent deals rancid with suspicion. This was true in the Ramos government, truer in the Estrada government. The Arroyo government inherited what had started in the earlier administration, and re-invented new ones of its own. Often these were molehills transformed into mountains not only as the public perceived them, but as the scandal-inclined media focused on the events. It appeared that restoration is not only a powerful but often a global wave among colonized and colonizers, between the oppressed and their oppressors. Restoration equally produces a political undertow that became apparent to the organized masses.

Below the surface, a wave sought to bring back a climate for justice or fairness for everyone especially the poor and marginalized. This is the sense of political philosopher Hannah Arandt's definition of revolution. It is the sense of the earth rotating around the sun. When things return to their proper places or when the nature of things is just and fair has been recognized and put back, thus do we think of a revolution.

The values I saw through all these are rich in lessons that kept repeating as they slipped away like a bad dream. I thought that institutions built by people are strengthened by positive laws not government decrees of an ambitious auotocrat or dictator. Yet many Marcos decrees are still enforced. They remain to nationalize institutions that have become corrupt and corruptible like the bureau of customs and the BIR, the police, and the military that continue to dominate the lives of Filipinos in the countryside or in poor urban areas. Include the courts that order homes of the poor to be bulldozed. People respond angrily. Their anger fuels more mass actions.

Mass actions are practical political tools that can change the ways of the bureaucracies. Government policies are difficult to change. Not even by elections but when the organized masses trained to be critical, and are free and the rules guiding them fair, they can define their interest and advance them.

Restoration I and II Compared; Middle Forces Split

Offhand, the two restorations involved large numbers of people unwittingly pushing. The national democratic mass movement developed with the masses taking initiatives through many direct political actions. Many NGOs projected an emancipatory strategy. By a strange twist of fate, things turned out differently. The forces of restoration have reserved energies to survive by other means. Many NGOs surrendered their emancipatory agenda to foreign grants. Their previous interest had turned into desire for funds and embedded themselves in so-called foreign assistance programs.

Others participated in the restoration process. Many of these people wish to stop any more mass actions, which they even called "destabilizing." They no longer admired the power of the organized masses like booting out two presidents.

As I see it, there's a contradiction within the ranks of the middle forces. There are those who view the EDSAs as triumphant but unfinished. Others view the two risings as the end of an autocratic regime of a dictator and the end of an irresponsible government with corrupt cronies in the inner circle of the movie-actor-turned president.

Former NGO activists who call themselves "Civil Society" became bureaucrats, managers of government corporations and economic mavens in President Arroyo's cabinet and councils. Another group of earlier "Civil Society" who pinched-hit on the side, were ardent watchers of the political scene and non-activists changed political faces and loyalties, and kowtowed to the Cory Aquino government when Marcos was toppled. This group is remembered with a sobriquet "balimbing," an allusion to the sour fruit that grows uncultivated nation-wide. They worked against the "enemy" before but now the same political "enemy" is their friend.

We have a lot of these "balimbings" in the bureaucracy and national life. In their innocuous way, the suspect goodwill of "balimbings" glosses over the temporariness of restoration government. Their leniency is mistaken for good PR. They look at the incumbents as no different from the people they had worked with. Old habits are hard to nip; they have deeper roots. Restoration has one strong feature. It tends to re-organize structures and social systems to fit its immediate needs, replacing them with accustomed ones. It is the matrix of a conservative philosophy. How does one replace, correct, or introduce innovations against a reigning conservatism? How does one communicate the message against it in the public domain?

The PNF Story

My personal involvement in the alternative news agency did not start from its founding days. Philippine News and Features is one NGO very active in the communication arena. Its contribution in the mass movement during the 80s was in providing alternative news sources to mainstream media struggling against official handouts, many of which were undisguised disinformation and self serving public statements.

After EDSA Uno repressive presidential decrees were still in force. The police had military infrastructures, e.g., checkpoints, raids, warrant-less arrest were all in place everywhere. Generally people critical of the government had never believed ML had been lifted or the dictatorship ended. The activists were incredulous. *De jure, yes; de facto, no.* No president in the country's history was cleverer in legal maneuvering than Marcos.

In the long period (1983-1999) that this NGO news agency operated, writing the news, editorials for the op-ed page and feature stories addressed principally for use by print media with national circulation, the PNF survived gloriously. The national papers were not exactly free as many of the editors were still groping for their accustomed "come-what-may" reporting shortly before ML. Others of course were level-headed. While one ear was listening to the exercise of press freedom as found in the Marcos' Constitution the other was attuned to the military camp radar scanning for "subversives." PNF stories

---

[25] Former PNF editor Sophie Bodegon, does not agree with this observation.

were less concerned about this putative and threatening wall that otherwise some media desks cautioned their own reporters from crossing.

On hindsight, it was this very appeal to the commercial media users that became the seed of PNF's own dissolution.

But to understand these practices of PNF's activist journalism, the context of the 1980s has to be kept in mind. Here, we would like to focus on some important points especially how PNF played its role in the mass movement. I was chairman of the board of PNF's mother corporation at this time.

The run-of-the-mill reporters wrote by looking at the events only as news when these were shaped by official pronouncements. That would be safe, factual reporting. What the writer chose to ignore was another matter. That part of course did not see print. When a breaking news came, like an interview with the commander of the New People's Army in the Southern Tagalog region (after years of a hiatus of reliable information from the underground during the 90s) only the PNF carried the story as "exclusive" news. No other source could be had and no newspaper could play this up as front page material except media subscribers of PNF.

The late Tony Zumel, a top ranking NDF official was reported to have waited for a PNF account before trusting stories about the mass movement in the country. Such large degree of reliance extended to PNF news stories was also observed among funding agencies in Europe keeping close eyes on the people's organizations (POs) in the Philippines energizing the open mass movement. Many of these were receiving support from these funders.

When the first peace negotiation between the NDF and the Philippine government broke out in 1987 exclusive interviews done by PNF writers with then NDF spokesperson Satur Ocampo. [Satur later became one of the top editorial writers of PNF whose political analyses, rich in insight of the mass movement, were frequently reprinted in the pages of mainstream newspapers that subscribed to PNF.]

The corrosive influence of Big Business and Government on impecunious reporters had popularized pejorative phrases like "AC-DC",* "envelopmental (with hidden cash) reporting." These blatant violations of journalistic ethics

---

* acronym for "attack-collect, defend-collect".

have roots in the heyday of the dictatorship. It was a time when writing skills had become a commodity for sale for public relations purposes. Underpaid writers for print media were particularly susceptible. Newspapers are run principally as business enterprises no matter how their editors claim they are independent from business pressures, especially their advertisers.

The travels of PNF editors abroad strengthened close relations with human rights organizations, church circles and other solidarity groups with Philippine-based partners. One time editor Sophie Bodegon told me that during her trips abroad sometime in the late 1980s funding agencies and Filipino networks abroad relied on much of their knowledge about people's struggle against Marcosian authoritarianism from PNF accounts. The PNF abroad became a regular source of contact for journalists wanting to be linked to NGOs and POs active in the mass movement.

The PNF stories often appeared in broadsheets like *Malaya*, *Philippine Inquirer*, *Manila Standard*, *Globe* (the forerunner of *Today*) *Manila Times* and *Manila Bulletin*. Soon thereafter the political commentaries of Satur Ocampo and Luis Teodoro became regular reprints in many of these national newspapers and drew the notice of the government sensitive to critiques of continuing crassness, repression, corruption and extravagance like that of Imelda Marcos's.

PNF had become a workshop for NGO activists desiring to work in print media. Later the training of the NGO writers, information officers, PRO's for this special purpose was taken over by PRESS, a "policy review and editorial services" NGO organized by columnist Conrad de Quiros. Earlier Conrad was in the PNF for a brief period.

Media users of PNF stories told me that PNF stories were printed without further rewriting and landed in the front pages. Many young reporters working in commercial newspapers interacted with PNF writers who sourced their materials direct from the crucible of highly politicized street actions and human rights violations by the state and its subalterns, especially the military.

From the 80s and to the early 90s environmental crises, illegal logging, pollution, health issues in red-light districts surrounding U.S. military bases, forced evacuation, labor strikes, exclusive interviews with the spokes-persons of the underground—all these were recurring materials in PNF journalism. PNF showed to mainstream media, still recovering from the effects of martial law the way to newsworthy stories even if their accounts did not come from the usual government sources or the military or big Business upon which reporters relied so much. PNF kept close to newsmakers by directly interviewing them; more often it kept tab of victims of government neglect or its corrupt practices especially victims of human rights abuses by the military.

Reports about workers' strikes and rally dispersals were no-no stories to big business whose advertisers would threaten to withhold ads in the pages of the broadsheets using PNF stories. I gathered these from friendly newspapers using PNF stories. An expose' on pesticides that hurt a chemical multinational corporation invited a P20 million libel suit against PNF and a warning shot to the desk of mainstream media sensitive to corporate advertisers especially MNCs. This suit was dismissed in favour of PNF after several months but this did not increase mainstream media subscriptions to. PNF.

The editorial desks of the national newspapers started to be sensitive to PNF stories about labor. strikes or anti-U.S. military bases stories in a nation strongly believing in the putative U.S. benevolence. PNF editors and writers were placed on the watch list of the Intelligence Unit of the AFP, according to friends closed to AFP sources. For example, PNF exclusive interviews in the 90s with Ka Roger, UG spokesperson, indicated direct contact with that elusive guerrilla commander. The critical opinions of its writers directed at wrongdoings of government officials appearing in the national dailies invited unwanted attention by AFP agents.

The fact that many writers of PNF emerged from the crucible of political issues tempered in "the parliament of the streets" enabled them to come out with stories and opinions implicitly supporting the mass movement. The members of the Board of Crossroads, the mother corporation of PNF were all street parliamentarians, respectable middle class, at one time or another, all anti-Marcos activists and professionals. In a sense these were the same people who were also responsible for forming other NGOs. They were not only opinion makers; many were national personalities in their own right whose words could make news. Not a few were activists, church people, and mass leaders.

PNF editorial policies hewed to pro-democracy, pro-people development themes.[26] When mainstream media got wind in later years of the methods of PNF, e.g. contact with underground, hiring activist writers or sending out reporters to follow leads that went all the way down to anti-government sources, the practice became easily replicable. The climate for this kind of reporting had relaxed. This journalism was perseveringly truthful and right for the masses and the national interest. *We Forum*, and later *Malaya* when it was still under the Burgos family, the early *Inquirer*, *Globe* and even the U.P. *Philippine Collegian* all these belong to this same tradition. The people who took their journalistic responsibility seriously are still manning the desks in many of these mass media up to this day.

In time contradictions in PNF began to surface—of being pro-people siding with the mass movement and being sensitive to the threatened interests of big business (as all commercial media still are).

The more big business ravaged the environment, the less visible stories of PNF were to the broadsheets whose very breath depends on the oxygen that business creates. The more PNF became objective and critical but still hew to the canons of good journalism, the less needed by some media were these stories, the usefulness of which (in their view) was tied to how they protect, promote and advance the interest of advertisers and financiers behind the business. These were a few pitfalls of good newspapering. You can count on the fingers of one hand those that survived in the practice of exemplary journalism. The dream of every honest newspaperman tired with being pleasant to the paper's owner is to put out even a small, independent, community-supported press. That day had passed.

This is how in its very success PNF as alternative source of news and feature stories had planted the seeds of its own slow dissolution. But the end is not final as long as courageous, truthful journalists exist. The market has become a negative terrain in supporting the values those stories or even the Crossroad policy (I was its board chair) behind their persistence. It was journalism beyond just being good writing. It was journalism behaving correctly in a terrain politically charged where it was expected to contribute to the

---

[26] Read the article "The Lord of the press" by Sheila Coronel in *The Philippine Media in the 1990s: From Loren to Miramar*, PCCIJ, Q. C. 1999..

advance of nationalism and democracy. Even PNF former editors disagreed with a large part of my assessment above when PNF went gently into the sunset.

Pictorial Section

A

A girl rallyist hits her head against the police shield as the rough arm of the law is used as repressive tool.

B

High-powered hose directed not to put out fire but to disperse the firebrands in rallies (pictures left and below).

C

A

More water power.

B

The youths confronting
repression and symbolic
greed and corruption.

C

The days of marches will return as often as the state fails the masses.

A

Celebrating the glory
of mass struggles.

B

Plaza Miranda is
hallowed less by the
imposing Catholic church
than by the number of
activists dedicated to the
pursuit of social justice.
It is one of Manila's
crowded crossroads.

An orderly march
that usually ends in
confrontation with
police-instigated
violence taking over.

C

A peaceful march to Mendiola Bridge that will end in a bloody aftermath.

The peace before the storm.

Mourning for a fallen comrade re enacted in street theater.

A

(a) Liwasang
Bonifacio's another
political crossroad
in Manila's rallyists
from north and south
of Luzon usually
converge, staying
until dark (b).

B

The melee following a
forced dispersal.

C

Mass education inside classroom (c) or outside (a) precedes effective organizing.

Open stage as political theater can mobilize millions (b).

Inhouse political education is usually located in borrowed auditorium of nearby university.

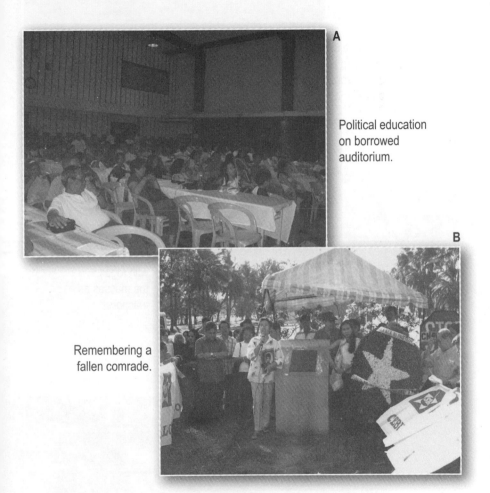

A

Political education
on borrowed
auditorium.

B

Remembering a
fallen comrade.

Beautiful
people taking a
breather from
mass action.

Mass education
with togas,
the masses as
teachers.

A bullhorn not pencil
is more useful in
popular education.

Street political
education is
exemplary.

Dramas on stage and on
the streets are tools for
mass mobilizing.

The dynamics of mass movements are found in the streets, in marches and in the imagination

I wish to thank Arkibo ng Bayan for lending me many of the pictures used in this section.

Chapter **6**

Stormy Days of the NGOs with the UG and Aboveground

From Colonialism to Neo-colonialism

I was an active member in some militant NGOs and often the contradictions among activists would precipitate debates during study sessions. Each one defended his/her strong bias. Those with closer experience with UG people stuck to their political agenda. Those with no contact were intensely "economistic." This meant that securing a livelihood was good enough. There were two major stages involved in this historic and social process in NGO bifurcation.

The first stage was pursuing what is principally a political agenda, usually NDF-guided. The second stage is pursuing primarily an economic program. We call this socio-economism. These two complement each other, but one has to be principal. These dynamic processes occurred, surging mostly in the decade of 70s and the 80s. There was no split the way I looked at it then. One principal element was political, and the economic amelioration of the masses was an integral call. The same active processes accompanied the non-party political organizations that joined the bigger stream of the mass movement. This community of NGOs had been constituted between the 70s and mid-80s.

The second stage, i.e., of pursuing consciously economic ends showed how the mass movement was veering away from the political agenda of the social revolution. Some political officers guiding its direction lamented this bent. What followed was that the socio-political revolution faltered. This occurred in mid-80, specifically after the People Power of 1986 and all the way to the 90s. By then the division of the two paths had become pronounced like one river taking two separate courses. As organizer and mass leader, I found this divergence heart-rending.

Urgent Task of the NDF

The influence of the NDF over the many NGOs and POs generally during the 80s was strongly felt by every militant activist. I thought of it so often when I was with CACP and later when I was with ACT. Joel Rocamora's *Breaking Through* is a good source book on the mass movement written by somebody watchfully attuned to the fray. I sometimes wonder if writing a book abroad is better than in the immediate backyard of this struggle; Joel R. was in the U.S. between 1976 and 1986. The book focuses more on the NDF high-ranking militants and the historic disagreement that consequently split the country's Left in the early 90s.

To many of us working with the NGOs, the NDF was a guiding light, a trusted political crutch during the faltering days of resistance to Marcos. When direction was lost, the activists merely went back to the Ten-Point Program to get their bearing.[27] This was mixed with trepidation among middle class activists who secretly maintained a desire to be differentiated from what was legal and what was illegal (which the NDF was). Or, what was principally not a communist and what is to be wanted by the authorities as a communist (even if one were not). The ambivalence had persisted to this day where the state, repressive and unsympathetic to the questioning of its authority or the various misuses of its power, is ready to pounce at its perceived enemies. As activists of the period, we could not but feel that we were these "enemies."

---

[27] At one time, it was 12-Point and then 14-Point having gone several revisions due to many consultations with mass organizations, under and above grounds. See box..

against corrupt officials or exposé of U.S. predatory interest in the country was ever launched without the invisible hands of the NDF shaping the affair. The influence was pervasive. This was how many POs saw their role. This was, it seemed, how the open mass movement had linked its umbilical cord to the underground.

There were two ways of looking at this supposed linkage: one looks at the mass movement from the point-of-view of the underground, the other from the point-of-view of the above ground mass movement. I think that the two were the same revolutionary wave with its crest and trough.

12-Point Program of the National Democratic Front (1972)

1. Unite the people for the task of overthrowing the semi-colonial and semi-feudal system through people's war and completing the national democratic revolution.

2. Prepare the way for the establishment of a people's democratic republic and a democratic coalition government.

3. Strengthen the people's army and a people's defense system.

4. Uphold and promote the people's democratic rights.

5. Terminate all unequal relations with the United States and other foreign entities.

6. Implement a genuine agrarian reform program, promote agricultural cooperation, develop rural production and employment through modernization of agriculture and rural industrialization, and ensure agricultural sustainability.

7. Dismantle the dominance of the U.S. and other imperialists and the big comprador-landlords over the economy; implement a program of national industrialization, and ensure an independent and self-reliant economy.

8. Implement a comprehensive and progressive social program.

9. Promote and develop a national, scientific and mass culture.

10. Uphold the rights of the Bangsa Moro people, the Cordillera people and other national minorities to self-determination and democracy.

11. Advance the revolutionary emancipation of women in all spheres.

12. Adopt an active, independent and peaceful foreign policy.

View from Above Ground (AG)

The mantle of dictatorship that covered the country was dreadful and suffocating politically. If political storms at the time of martial law forced one to choose between freedom from fear and the safety of cooperation with President Marcos, the protective cover available then neither gave us lasting security nor at the end guaranteed that we were really free. The NDF in the early 70s openly put up a strong resistance to the dictatorship by organizing the masses of workers in factories against repressive employers, and the peasants in some haciendas in Tarlac and Negros Occidental against exploitative landlords. I witnessed the latter having been from Negros myself.

Earlier, the first sector that responded to the emerging authoritarianism was the student sector. It is the most homogenous, concentrated, idealistic group, vigorously desiring to explore and learn new things. It is eager to throw overboard every other thing that obstructed its nationalist vision for the country. Although many students were unaffected by class antagonism like that of the oppressed farmers vis-à-vis their landlord, or of the exploited urban workers against the owners of factory or business firms, or the government, they were organized, concentrated, carefree, critical and bravely vocal. The militants from this sector had less friction with the UG than those who had not shed their middle class habits.

They grouped themselves under umbrella organizations like the Movement for Democratic Philippines (MDP); Gary Olivar was prominent here. I met him again during the 90s already a corporate lawyer striking a cocksureness in his walk. A lump formed in my throat; I was looking for an idealist but it was not in the swagger. Another group was the militant *Kabataang Makabayan* (KM), and the Samahang Demokratikong Kabataan (SDK) already active as early as the second half of the sixties.

In mass actions of hundreds or thousands, or merely twenty or fifty students, they crossed the thoroughfares of Manila slowing down traffic. In true Maoist fashion, armed with slogans in their placards they marched against "U.S. imperialists," "bureaucrat capitalists," and "feudal landlords," the three embodiments of the country's problem. Many believe this has not changed much even today. Not a few of these youths came from the elite high schools and colleges, and therefore, children of middle class Filipino families.

If the issue against the dictatorship had not yet registered well into the consciousness of the urban population, the student sector was to fire–with inflammatory speeches, slogans, denunciations, graffiti, red flag waving–the opening salvo against Marcos. This is what was meant when these exploding demos and marches were later emblazoned in the consciousness of every militant as the continuation of the "propaganda movement of the Philippine Revolution" that started one hundred years earlier. It was this appeal to history that the youths' political anger resonated to other sectors of society. On the other hand, their elders initially were indifferent, then curious, and finally worried.

The open resistance came in various forms. These addressed various social levels, in languages that pierced class distinction; free verse that when vertically read its first letters spelled the obnoxious role of the dictatorship; ironies, tropes in the local language, caricatures and comic strips, all these mushroomed. It was using the literary power tools of semiotics that language philosopher Charles Pierce or semiotician Umberto Eco had barely imagined in their writings.

A large section of the middle class intelligentsia, church people, politicians and businessmen either became low whispering voices, part-time critics or full time watchers from the sidelines. Those in the newspapers "either lied low or lied", a witticism attributed to former U.P. President S.P. Lopez.

What was the martial law government up to? This was a new experience even to the educated sector of society. Where was it taking the country? When about 7000 of those suspected critics of Marcos were hauled to the military stockades, the nation was dazed with uncertainty and gnawing fear. This was capped with ominous, slow realization that the country was no longer the same overnight.

In the months following the declaration of martial law, the sudden social calm (no killing, no bombing in plazas, no kidnapping, no demos and rallies, no criticisms in the media) that reigned under military rule gave a respite to the nation. There was a semblance of peace and stability. I saw Marcos was no novice in public manipulation. His plan worked.

The first to capitulate to this imagined stability were the businessmen. Then the owners of media, whose offices were earlier raided and closed but later opened under the "guidance" of the military, or sequestered in favour of the cronies. They were followed by the big landlords, the institutional churches, the banks, the movie houses, and the rest of the corporate world especially those with foreign connections. As ideological apparatuses, they all helped to support and advance the dominant values of the dictatorship.

The three big foreign oil firms—Shell, Esso-Mobil and Caltex—never paused increasing their prices. They stood by the regime under the philosophy *"business as usual"* and contributed an impressively false façade that under martial law the country had achieved economic stability. This was about the time that we together with some teachers in St. Scholastica College organized the CACP.

Free Information Took Different Route

The newly hauled prisoners especially coming from urban areas were not lacking in sympathizers who hid during the dawn raids. These people formed info networks running through the academe, the convents, the inner sanctum of their libraries and homes, and vacation houses outside the city. Those who used to be with the media but this time closed or sequestered went underground. Later they became stalwarts in the mass movement directed from below. This was where the late Tony Zumel and now partylist representative Satur Ocampo belonged.[28] Even the ill-lighted *Taboy's Singko Litros* in Mabini Street, a regular watering hole for newsmen after the day's work, was taken over by roaches and rats. The city in darkness turned eerie, quiet, sad and funereal. But many in the shadows prepared to fight back.

---

[28] See letter by this writer in PDI Op-ED, 27 August 2001.

Due to scarcity of political news from the controlled media, the church-supported tabloid-size *Signs* openly came out but with limited circulation and was short-lived. It became the forerunner of the news agency *Philippine News and Features* (PNF) that trained several progressive reporters and later absorbed by the mainstream media.

Mimeo sheets like *Facts and Figures* (FF) associated with Sister Sol Perpiñan, a woman of fierce determination, were circulated in the crannies of Metro Manila. Copies were passed around in homes and campuses by activists hiding from the police. *Facts and Figures* contained news, ideas and analyses about advances made abroad in other revolutions against dictators. Stories from Nicaragua, China and Cuba were regular fare. These transformed the reader's frustration and despair into political hope and brighter view of the social revolution-in-progress in the country.

Middle class sentiment was starting to rise against Marcos and his military regime. (I am using "middle class" not as an income-based concept, nor in the sense of conflict relation between one oppressor against the oppressed, but principally as a cultural concept alluding to people and families often with common western educational background.) These people possessed a Lockean readiness to fight and survive against threat to life and to protect their property, to learn and openly teach others, and to identify themselves with the threatened masses. They developed solidarity with the masses, a strong feeling that the suffering of the poor was equally theirs. They were (and still are) among the middle class that often become the base of organizing and could easily draw them against a targeted "oppressor." The milieu became a fertile ground for mass organizing.

Human Rights on the Agenda for para-Legal Education

Marcos gave his repressive rule the patina of legalism. My lawyer activist friend Greg Fabros used to call it "*parang* legal" ("as if it's legal"). Even as non-lawyers, my companions felt we needed to know some basics. The more intense martial law was linked to more arrests, torturers, confiscations of what was privately owned, more forced evacuation, killings by the military, the more the news of violence affected the wider population. Many of those were the poor and defenceless peasants in the countryside. The middle class (with conscience) felt that their efforts to defend themselves must also involved the defence of others, especially farmers and their families who were often less prepared to defend themselves in the legal arenas. There was a crucial need to know one's legal rights.

This need overtly manifested in the semiotics of activism was central to the fight for human rights. It rapidly became popular. The growth of free legal assistance and related programs for the poor and defenceless were associated with NGOs like the Free Legal Assistance Group (FLAG), MABINI and BONIFACIO.[29]

I observed that in many NGOs that responded to ML reality, the emancipatory replaced the eleemosynary goal for charity. There were lawyers, newspapermen, fictionists, and poets who organized NGOs that extended assistance to the poor. They even helped to draft statements of unity and resistance in fiery prose and engaging verses. Academicians from U.P., PNC, St. Scholastica College held secret meetings, usually addressing human rights and other critical issues in faculty conclaves outside towns. Their common NGO was CACP.

NGOs systematically monitored widespread human rights violation. The annual report of Amnesty International was an unrivalled source for accounts of torture and abuses by the Marcos military. This AI report incorporated gruesome details submitted by Task Force Detainees (TFD).[30]

What role did the NDF play as viewed from the above ground (AG) mass movement? The following is my political summary surrounding NGO responses to NDF guidance:

(1) The human rights issue had broadened the struggle to other sectors including teachers, peasants, wage earners and the urban poor. Earlier it was limited to the middle class in defense of civil liberties and property.

---

[29] The first acronym stands for Movement of Attorneys for Brotherhood, Integrity, Nationalism, Inc or MABINI; BONIFACIO alludes to another Katipunan hero during the revolution against early colonialism.

[30] See *Torture in the Eighties* by Amnesty International, London 1984.

(2) The middle class (often with implicit derision called "the petty bourgeoisie") threatened by bad business or joblessness or arrest had abandoned charity as a mode of helping the poor, and instead pursued "freedom and security for all" both denied by the corrupt Marcos state.

(3) The increasing impoverishment of many was seen as the handiwork of a dubious section of domestic big business (a part of the "national bourgeoisie") in collusion with foreign investors and multinationals. The economy was prostrate vis-à-vis US control and exploitation, and the slogan "US–Marcos Dictatorship" became easily substantiated and validated by much of our experiences. This became a rallying call. The period brought out more NGOs in the sector of the radical Left. Specific issues created more militant sectoral assemblies.

Hubris and Hesitations

Looking back after 22 years, when I have more direct participation in forming these alliances, COGs, NGOs mentioned above or coalition of NGOs; e.g. CACP, ACT, PNF, BUNSO, separate sections will treat them more descriptively. It remained unclear whether the anti-imperialist or anti-fascist mood of the movement was influenced by the NDF Program or that the latter had maintained a correct reading of middle class struggle against the government of Marcos. The period covered the decades of the 70s to the mid-80s.

The dialectics of memory against time does not allow for simple reading of this story. In many of these progressive NGOs, the internal tension that was building between the CPP and the NDF mentioned by Rocamora in his book was ignored, or not felt at all among the middle class militants. This observation makes exception of the very few who integrated with the open legal mass organizations, often acted as political officers giving "ideologically correct lines" in several group discussions.

The intellectual "hubris" of the educated middle class usually did not allow for accepting with readiness this kind of "guidance." The leadership of the open, legal mass movement was usually found in these sectors occupied by the middle forces. He or she would be a college graduate, professional, with safe sources of income, a believer in Christianity if not a devout Catholic, a beneficiary of the American system of education, a secret, academic Marxist if not yet a Leninist or Maoist. Often he or she writes with dedicated passion *describing, or interpreting* Philippine society rather than *changing it*, unlike those militants who have decided that the only option left was the armed struggle.

Leaven or Laggard?

The involvement of the literate class partly explains the rapid spread of the revolution-related information among its ranks. On the level of the abstract and ideal, concrete knowledge helped clarify and advance a commitment. But intellectual commitment alone could not sustain a real change toward the hoped for social revolution. This is part of the romanticism afflicting the educated middle class in the mass movement. Uncorrected, it could be a hindrance to genuine integration with the lower classes, an integral component in the ongoing mass movement.

In any movement the middle class participates in, this commitment could be either a leaven or an obstructing laggard, a hastening factor or a hesitant, delaying element. Correctly, it could be accused, as often it is, of vacillating. There was this kind in the mass movement. He vacillates readily, not sure whether "to take up arms against a sea of troubles" or to wait, hoping the troubles would ebb away or pass to others. How often it came to my mind, whether Hamlet, belongs to a royal family or from a "respectable" middle class like so many of us sick with vacillation.

A Return to Semiotics

One of the missing links in the description of the revolutionary movement that had grown out of this period is the clear importance of semiotics. How language in various levels and forms constituted by signs, signals and significations in varied ways was completely ignored in several analyses. The polysemic reading of texts used in the mass movement could temper political dogma and ideology on rocks of old beliefs of the Left. Marches in the open street are not only people in angry motion. They constitute both messenger and message of social changes. A government is wise that listens, observes and gives these its serious hearing.

I observed for instance that long marches during the Welgang Bayan or people's strike emanating from north of Luzon and other coming from the south generated massive responses not only from those along the highways watching but also from the windows of the high rise dwellings. Even the government had to double its policing or even calling the army to block the marchers, or surround the Palace with tanks and soldiers bristling with machine guns. This made the masses angry and they hated more the national leadership for it.

When both organized crowds converged at Rizal Park, the message was more than what one could see or hear in the public harangues delivered on that manicured expanse of the park. It had proved to be an instrument for policy response, perhaps a call for a reconsideration of the state practice of suppressing public outrage or responding to it with gunfire. This last was a method used by the dictatorship that while it harvested many corpses (remember the Mendiola massacre?) it never succeeded except to damn itself more.

An account of these responses is at present absent in the sociology of politics. This could have enriched the tools for advancing the open mass movement an Umberto Eco or a Paulo Freire, great practitioners of semiotics that they are, could only nod with understanding.

The colourful streamers and banners more than filled the air with fervor and patriotic convictions. They stirred the nation. Every sign, signal or sound delivers a strong unmistakable message to the ruling regime. Could one do a reading of power in more visible, audible and physical way with the presence of warm swinging fast-moving bodies? Had analysis been focused on that? How the organizers of the mass movement could compel a response from an otherwise insensitive state is a lesson rich in political savvy.

If my assumption is right, that the open mass movement was initially energized by the middle class, then some of us find partly the answer why it was difficult for the CPP and the NDF to achieve the longed for unity between the peasants and the workers. The continuing mass movement that embedded the historic EDSA Uno, EDSA Dos plus the failed EDSA Tres illustrated the cases. That elusive link although repeated with tireless logic, free verses, songs and rhetoric in many an agitation tracts of the mass movement in the 60's, 70's, 80's and 90's remained unfulfilled to the end. Is it because the revolutionary movement remained under the leadership of the middleclass intelligentsia? The revolutionary impulse of the Katipuneros in 1898 and the early clergy wanting to separate from Rome and the 1930s communists under the PKP seemed to suggest common political errors attributable to the middle class.

Political analysts often ignore the impact in the mercurial circumstances between 70s and mid 80s of semiotics in the consciousness of the masses. This is one view of the mass movement by those from above ground (AG). Something needs to be explained or described what has happened beyond year 2000.

How Do We Approach a Myth Created by Media?

The response to the death and subsequent burial entourage of Fernando Poe Jr. (a.k.a. FPJ) depicted millions of people joining in the public mourning from church to cemetery. It suggested an emotional upheaval rooted in strong cultural value; that real, living FPJ (the actor-turned-presidential-candidate) as often portrayed in films was a hero who fought for the oppressed or the weak.

The highly partisan turn of the media coverage and of some organized marchers indicated a dangerous political slant. It never portrayed that the death was perhaps a comeuppance for an actor who was unprepared politically to become the Republic's head. Were the masses or the media politically immature? It bothers me no end.

Where the sympathy was supposed to be on the hero portrayed in many FPJ's films that highlighted an important cultural value like defending the defenseless, the message seemed to come from beyond the grave that the country lost a good president. Tell that to the COMELEC or to the Electoral tribunal, two institutions that have been traditional punching bags of electoral losers in this country. In failing to distinguish between entertainment and personal tragedy for FPJ's family, the media failed to educate or open the public eyes.

The View from the Underground (UG)

I saw the mass movement going beyond exposing corruption in the bureaucracy or the cruelty of landlords to their tenants or the imperious arrogance of Americans to their Filipino subalterns. This was how often middle class people *personalized* the problems. When Jose Maria Sison formulated the problem in his now famous essay into "a struggle for national democracy," thousands of students under politically liberal-oriented teachers and elders caught this encapsulation with patriotic readiness. It was a straightforward political guide for the activist students. Some of us attuned to frequent marches started to stalk the corridors of underground politics.

On the other hand, many teachers who were marooned in classroom teaching, but educated in the conventional histories of the country written from perspective of the colonizers, taught Philippine history under the shadows of conservative historians Alip, Zaide and the epigones of U.S. scholarship. From the opposite spectrum Agoncillo, Majul, and the elder Constantino, coming from the unregulated liberal philosophy of the state university were viewing history not from the conquerors' point-of-view but from those of the conquered. I learned at this juncture that the first stage in reversing social relations is in reversing one's thinking about each other.

The contemporary writing of the country's revolutionary history had its roots among these last three historians. No mention of Marx in their pages, but the relationship between the oppressor and the oppressed, the exploiter and the exploited, the powerful foreigners and the hard-working Filipino workers under them were pitted on the level of political domination.

Following this, "Joma" (a moniker of Sison among the young) was moved to re-write Philippine history in his own way. It involved expunging the existing text of all remnants of the conquerors' point-of-view for the last 500 years. From the dregs of the past the new history has raised the revolutionary experience of the exploited people. This kind of romance with history resulted in focusing the semi-feudal, semi-colonial picture of Philippine society. The book, *Philippine Society and Revolution* was the outcome, a much beloved read among the young militants.

A clearer representation of the mass movement as imagined history (not imaginary, mind you) leaped from the pages of Sison's autobiography published in 1989; co-authored by Rainer Werning, a German married to an activist Filipina now living abroad. This was how Sison looked at the rising mass movement: (from an interview by Rainer Werning):[31]

"From the latter part of the 1960's to 1972, the political factions of the exploiting classes were engaged in an increasingly bitter struggle for power and spoils of public office at all levels. Room for mutual accommodation among these factions became constricted. There was a strong trend towards the formation of armed groups as well as the determination to rig elections through fraud and terrorism. The Marcos faction was at the head of the trend.

"In the 1960s legal mass organizations of the various patriotic and progressive classes and strata emerged one after the other to make anti-imperialist and anti-feudal criticisms of the system and demanded for national and democratic reforms. Throughout the 1960s up to 1972 the progressive mass movement developed comprehensively and carried out mass actions....

"Whereas the revolutionary armed struggle had to start from scratch, the urban mass movement made a big leap with the First Quarter Storm of 1970 in the wake of Marcos' re-election as president in late 1969. There were unprecedented mass actions from 1970 to 1972. The basic masses of workers and peasants and the students and other youth were rising up in protest, even as they were increasingly subjected to disruptive police and military attacks during mass actions. The urban petty bourgeoisie and the national bourgeoisie became emboldened and put forward their own progressive views and demands in the mass media and other legal channels.

"As early as 1968 . . . . the CPP declared in a concluding part of its program for a people's democratic revolution that the crisis of the ruling system was so grave that the ruling classes could no longer rule in the old way; that the people wanted to have a revolutionary forces and the entire people to victory over a protracted period of conducting people's war...."

---

[31] *The Philippine Revolution, The Leader's View*, (Crane Russak, New York, 1989,) pp. 26-27.

Marcos, for all his pretensions to be a student of the revolution, seemed not to have learned a lesson that when you suppress a mass movement, it comes out later as highly inflammable material to become a surging revolution from below. This happened when he declared *Kabataang Makabayan* illegal. He also hounded the members of the Movement for the Advancement of Nationalism (MAN), the intelligentsia's call to prioritize Filipino interests. The leaders of the *Pagkakaisa ng mga Mambubukid ng Pilipinas* (PMP) a peasant group in central Luzon were hounded by the military. Pushed to the walls, these peasants later joined the CPP's armed section called the New People's Army.

A joke used to run at that time that Marcos was "the most effective recruiter of the NPA." On the other hand, more facetiously, the corrupt military when pursuing its version of "IGP" (income-generating project) was supplying arms for sale to the underground NPAs. Foot soldiers many of whom sold their guns when in bad need of cash were an underpaid lot (very much like classroom teachers and government rank and file.)

Let me quote extensively for the last time from Sison's autobiographical interview by Werning. It's a summary of NGOs that served directly the UG:

". . . mass organizations proliferated. Among them were Katipunan ng mga Samahang Manggagawa (KASAMA–Federation of Labor Unions) and Pambansang Kilusan ng mga Manggagawa ng Pilipinas (PAKMAK–National Workers Movement of the Philippines) among the workers; Malayang Kilusan ng Bagong Kababaihan (MAKIBAKA–Free Movement of New Women) among women; Samahang Demokratiko ng Kabataan (SDK–Association of Democratic Youth) and Katipunan ng Kabataang Demokratiko (KKD–Federation of Democratic Youth) among the youth. Kapisanan ng mga Gurong Makabayan, (KAGUMA–Association of Patriotic Teachers) among teachers. Christians for National Liberation (CNL); and League of Editors for a Democratic Society; Panulat para sa Kaunlaran ng Sambayanan (PAKSA–Literature for People's Progress); Nagkakaisang Progresibong Artista–Arkitekto (NPA–United Progressive Artists and Architects); and a wide variety of sectoral and community organizations.

"In the urban mass actions . . . KM youth activists from schools and communities predominated and rose . . . to more than twenty thousand . . . a significant increase in worker participants coming from trade unions to which the young worker members of KM belonged . . . (they) took up not only national and international issues but also local issues." (Sison/Werning, p. 27)

The tension between the Marcos government and the mass movement intensified. Many individuals joined the ranks of the CPP. This was the "high" of the revolutionary fever at this time. The hot vocabulary and rhetoric, the tightened feeling that raised the political discourse of the period, all these were enriched by the patina of Left romanticism: for example, "Diliman Commune," "*makibaka huwag matakot*," "surround the city from the countryside," "Armed Revolution, the answer to Martial Law." These were often painted across the dark, moss-covered or stucco-ed concrete walls of the city, in bridges or on roads.

Student Activists Went UG Expecting Martial Law

Sometimes, the naiveté of students or their political artlessness made Marcos look at the restless youth condescendingly. He had his own comeuppance later as the volume of students in a series of mass actions was getting more expansive and their rallies frequent. I was with the teachers and there was hardly a week without mass action or marches. These were disturbingly becoming closer to the next, with more attendance, more students cutting classes to join street marches. The collective temper of thousands of students went beyond conventional "misbehavior" of the young facing their venerable elders with whom many could no longer agree.

The mayhem that ensued during the 1970 opening of Congress where Marcos was supposed to deliver the traditional State of the Nation Address was watershed of a society no longer at peace with itself. Who started the violence in that historic afternoon of January? The controlled media chorused their own answer attuned to the whisperers from the U.S. Embassy, "The communists!"

I remember activists expecting martial law and the massive repression it would entail went underground. Many more decided to integrate with the peasants for organizing work. This was the climate of the growing mass movement. They started to live, work, study and learn with the peasants in the CS and integrate with the workers in factories in urban centers. The first quarter storm (FQS) foreshadowed the rising social and political turbulence of the 80s all the way to the 90s.

I wish to pause for a question that has been hanging fire below the rhetoric of the historic storm called FQS. How big was the movement that it had engendered? Here I depend on Joel Rocamora's *Breaking Through, The Struggle within the Communist Party of the Philippines* (1994). He wrote that ". . . national democrats accounted for probably as much as eighty percent of the organized forces of the Left. Even now after several years of decline, national democratic groups still constitute more than twice the organizational bulk of all the other Left groups put together."(p. 5)

To my knowledge, the NDF maintained 14 underground sectoral organizations. Many of these have counterparts with the aboveground, legal formations, cause-oriented groups, NGOs. The 14 sectors included those identified with the church, youth, teachers, federation of labor groups, peasants, trade unions, artist and writers, health, ethnic groups, lawyers, scientists, women, the CPP and finally the armed NPA.

Before we leave this part of the unsettled friction between the CPP and some personalities of the NDF, let's have a chronology of the organizations and the high points of the democratic mass movement. I am hesitant to characterize it as "national" at this stage. Let us put aside Marcos altogether although he was the biggest contributor to this revolutionary fervor that fired Filipinos against their government. We recall that the decade of the 80s covered a period of surprising coups and solid coalitions; of new attempts at seizure of power by the military officers and foot soldiers; bombing of cities and a nervous search for stability and the elusive peace.

The following are the momentous years of NGOs and POs in the decade of the 1980's:

1980 – **KMU** formally launched with Bert Olalia leading on May 1 in Araneta Coliseum, Quezon City; another witness claimed this was launched in Pope Pius Auditorium in U.N. Avenue, Manila. In the same year, the Health Alliance for Democracy **(HEAD)** was formed with doctors from U.P. in its core, Doctors Romy Quijano, Jojo Carabejo, Sylvia dela Paz, and Nurse Minda Quesada.

1981 – Marcos lifted martial law de jure, but many people did not believe he was sincere. **NFPC** launched addressing the issue raised by the Bataan Nuclear Power Plant.

1982 – The Alliance of Concerned Teachers **(ACT)**, a militant teacher group opened its congress with Jaime Cardinal Sin officiating; cleansed itself incidentally of being a "communist front."

1983 – Justice-for-Aquino-Justice-for-All **(JAJA)** launched a middle class mass movement, mostly Makati-based but energized by UG participation. Amado V. Hernandez Resource Center **(AVHRC)** founded in the service of organized labor; Nationalist Alliance for Justice, Freedom and Democracy **(NAFJD)** launched; August Twenty-One Movement **(ATOM)** organized responding to Senator Aquino's assassination on his return from self-exile.

1984 – **GABRIELA**, an all-women mass organization initiated by middle class forces; **CORD** organized; Katipunan ng mga Katutubong Mamamayan **(KAMP)** launched. Satur Ocampo escaped from his military escorts during a **National Press Club** election where he was allowed to vote but slipped out by the back door.

1985 – **BAYAN** launched to become the largest and most sustained people's organization; **KOMPIL**, a short-lived middle forces initiative opened a congress of NGOs and personalities; massacre by the military during a September rally of several peasants and farm workers in Escalante, Negros.

1986 – Multi-sectoral siege at Gate 6 of the Palace. **COURAGE**, a nation-wide organization of government workers launched. (February 22, 23, 24 and 25) a four-day rising that concentrated in the EDSA highway and later billed as the first People Power in the 20th century.

1987 – Mendiola massacre by Cory Aquino's army killing 16 farmers who tried to cross the bridge together with hundreds of others in their peaceful march to Malacañang.

1988 – Freedom from Debt Coalition **(FDC)** launched addressing the country's debt burden that seemed not to end.

Some Unresolved Issues

The above events, often not recorded by the censored press, had far-reaching impact on the mass movement. Within the UG, issues like the military's deep penetration agents known as DPAs and the paranoid response of the CPP followed by increasing execution of cadres and kidnapping of others working in the legal mass movement was not clearly resolved. Example, we at the CACP "lost" two volunteers but were later "released" to their families who agonized for more than a year looking for them.

Another issue that had unnecessarily embroiled the above ground mass movement and hundreds of legal formations was the ideological quarrel between the hardened "from-the-countryside-surrounding-the-city" Maoist within the Party and some prominent leadership of the NDF in constant contact with urban national democrats. Note that even the approval of the NDF Constitution took seventeen (17) years, and this was not even acceptable to the Party without its emendations until 1992. This could not be glossed over as so much of revolutionary vitality depended on the élan of the mass movement that fed on broad solidarity.

The killing in 1983 of Senator Benigno Aquino, persistent critic of Marcos and potential presidential rival, made visible to all middleclass cause-oriented sympathizers and even "the silent rich" the naked brutal power of the regime. The years of repression, corruption, torture and predatory development fed by the greed of Marcos, his "partner in crimes" and the U.S. government backers of the dictatorship placed the country helpless and completely prostrate. The ways of governing under Martial Law were anything but right and decent, and a social volcano was about to explode.

Chaos that Followed Call to Boycott

Rodolfo Salas (Commander Bilog) following Sison's imprisonment took over as acting chairperson of the CPP (1977-1985). Under his leadership there occurred the disastrous election boycott in 1984. This decision led the progressive NGOs and mass movement into chaotic disorientation.

Later in the 1987 referendum, some called for "critical yes" against the Constitution; this was our position in ACT. Others were for rejection.

Australian Kathleen Weekley mentioned four "tendencies" that carried contradictions among underground leaders during this period (pp.220-221):

(1) "The political military mentality" that believed in increased NPA activities and in the intensification of legal mass movement believing in "partial victory" towards transitional coalition government."

(2) The Manila-Rizal Group of Popoy Lagman, with the ABB his squad directing their "clean methods" against military and corrupt officials, believed the revolutionary forces (including the open mass movement) could gain victories regardless of what's happening in the countryside. Some mass actions like "Welgang Bayan" was considered "adventurist."

(3) The CPP orthodoxy directed by the "Executive Committee of the Central Committee" some of whose members were in Utrecht, Netherlands in exile, including Jose Ma. Sison wanted to go back to "basic principles" and were not interested in partial victories envisioned above.

(4) Others, cadres of the CPP-NDF continued to work outside the formal structures of the Party but neither criticised nor supported it although still considered as part of the "national democratic effort"; the popular democrats or "Popdems" were still groping for the correct position to take vis-à-vis the Cory Aquino government in post-EDSA that had unhappily restored Elite Democracy.

There were internal refinements to these "tendencies" that were based on some ideological interpretations of the objective condition. We in the open legal mass movement were either unaware, or only half-aware, or fully conscious that these disagreements were not good for the unification efforts of various elements of open alliances and coalitions of NGOs. Remember that although many had never seen the face of Popoy Lagman's ABBs, activists in the open mass movement had them at the back of their minds as security blankets against potential military abuses and threats of repression or arrests especially during demonstrations.

The above belief or some version of "Left romanticism" brought a moral boost from time to time. This was further validated by reports of execution of a military or police officer or a corrupt official who had not been brought before the courts of justice but was now meted revolutionary justice. We read this kind of stories in the underground mimeographed press. News of deaths of this kind brought some sense of redemption to the UG and poetic justice.

The open logic behind many ideas traceable to the underground was not always straightforward and clear to several leaders of the mass movement. But "reformism," "surrenderism," "peace without justice," and "landlordism" were anathema to progressive activists seeking a clear future. With the ideological infrastructures in disarray, the 'RJ-RA' cleavage (please see glossary) did affect the unity of the open mass movement. The reason for it was that the NGOs and POs found this to be a distraction. Instead of searching for the right organizational form (alternative social formation, ASF) in response to the new situation that subsequent issues brought by People Power I, their attention digressed to the "correctness" of the roots of their old loyalties. Are they RJs or RAs?

First, there were indeed DPAs in the UG. But nobody for sure knew who among the people we were working with were DPAs. In the sector where I was deeply involved, consumer and teachers, I mentioned earlier, three to five members were lost and possibly executed. After two years of agonizing speculation about their fate, the three surfaced. These three quit the movement for good. One went to the province and became a carpenter. The other became a salesman for children's books; the third got married and raised four children by a former activist who has no permanent job as of this writing.

From the foregoing, we could sense that the mass movement was an implosion, a caving-in that resulted in a social, political chaos. It was definitely not a consequence of a class war as envisioned by Marxists and other enthusiasts of the armed revolution. What happened was that a theory was badly needed but theoreticians disagreed among themselves. What next? A revolution it was not either although a revolutionary situation existed. I thought of the famous line of Lenin, *"A revolution needs a revolutionary theory."*[32]

Unfortunately, the theoreticians of the revolution were at loggerheads at this time. One of the difficulties confronting the underground National democrats (remember there were also legal, above ground NDs) had been their inadequacy in balancing their theorizing bend with actual experiences. This was worse for the exiles both in the U.S. and in Europe. One symptom, observed Rocamora, was the readiness to lean on the Marxist classics to solve a thorny issue on the ground. In connection with this, please see also the chapter on my experiences narrated in *"The International Dimension of the Mass Movement."*

Should the proletariat take leadership in the revolution? Raising this question in the UG was an act of apostasy, the equivalent among Catholics of doubting the virgin birth. This was the nature of the constant friction between the CPP leadership (read: Amado Guerrero) on one hand, and many NDF militants on the other especially those in constant contact with the open, legal mass organizations in Manila. Is the CPP the tail that wags the dog? This was how often Filipinos take their unresolved problem with a funny face. This question persistently surfaced in the movement with middle class tendency to be facetious when un-solvable issues confronted them.

These theoreticians became two-steps removed from the scenes of the *revolution-in-the-making*. First, they were theoretically prone to take the concept "revolution" as a series of direct practices that have to be theoretically controlled or tamed to avoid anarchy. Second, these Marxist theoreticians were living abroad. They looked with a telescope from outside the country but the field was fast changing. One cannot disregard the charges that their practices of theory were dogmatic. I have not heard of a satisfactory explanation of the class of marching militants on the ground who had long instigated the movement since early 70s.

---

[32] Writer Frankie Sionil Jose attributed the break-up of the old PKP in the 1950s to irreconcilable "egos" of the top people, a middleclass weakness. (Interview in his Padre Faura Solidaridad Bookstore, June 9, 2005).

The underground accepts Marxism as a science, and its class analysis as the ultimate scientific tool in disclosing the hidden contradictions of society laced with capitalist greed. The undercurrents in the Left continued to plague the relationship, i.e. between CPP and NDF, and when theorists insist on applying their scientific "laws", common sense practices become a casualty. Often this casualty could include human lives and/or veritable disarray in the mass movement.

While the NDF maintained 14 UG sectoral organizations that were actually responses to perceived social and political issues arising from the ineptness of the dictatorship, these issues were often equally linked to reflect concerns of the legal groups in the open arena.

Active Sectors Uninfluenced by NDF

In the NDF list (from Sison's autobiography and Rocamora's book) we noted the absence of particular sectors like environmentalist, children, nursing mothers, small and medium entrepreneurs (SMEs), veterans, senior citizens. These sectors were amply represented by organizations already active in the days preceding People Power 2, "not yet revolutionaries but no longer reactionaries" to quote the CPP definition of "middle forces."[33]

Added to the above list are Muslims, airline ground workers and flight attendants, government employees. They number by the thousands. I attended a lot of these sectoral meetings and consultation outside conscious NDF influence. All have become participants in sectoral rallies and demos, organizations influenced and led by the "middle forces."

Of what value were these legal or open groups to the CPP-led democratic revolution? *"The CPP has great difficulty dealing with the NDF where the CPP goes outside of itself; where it builds from a secure core to the organizational and theoretical uncertainties on the outside. One of the three 'magic weapons' of the democratic revolution (1) the Party (2) the army, and (3) the United Front—the last has proven to be the most difficult to build,"* opined Rocamora

---

[33] I mention some NGOs and alliances, where I've been involved for the last 24 years.

(p.141). I am inclined to make reservation on the last point mentioned about the United Front. These groups got involved in many legal COG formations.

The difficulty was reflected in the unstable hold of the CPP on a wide range of initiatives especially in the much visible urban-based mass movement. This part of the mass movement came under the control and direction of the upper middle class and the traditional elite like the institutional church under the leadership of the Archbishop of Manila, the well-known landlords of the martial law days, the business tycoons under the aegis of the Makati Business Club. Sison may proclaim his "protracted accommodation" where their interests stay protected.

1986 Aftermath Called "Restoration I"

We have to step back to 1986 or even earlier in order to understand the new stream of alternative formations. They were no longer called cause-oriented-groups but NGOs and POs and coalition of NGOs, etc. They attempted to stabilize the gains of EDSA *Uno*. The floodgate for coalition building opened for entry of new sometimes short-lived NGOs. Many of these were formed against nuclear plants, against multinational oil companies by groups called Coalition Against Oil Price Increase or CAOPI. Others like FDC were against foreign debts; against multilateral agencies re-shaping education in order to produce cheap skills for foreign firms in the country demanded by the ILO Ranis Report.

EDSA *Uno* was supposed to give the Filipinos back their freedom. It turned out to be the restoration of elite democracy.[34] But what was rarely recognized was that the unresolved undercurrents between the CPP and NDF contributed to the development of the new stream of cause-oriented groups and the re-alignment of new formations. A lot of NGOs including personalities behind them, active former militants of the NDF fuelled the creation of many alternative formations, networks and labor centers. But many more were keeping their distance from the political guidance of the UG-influenced national democrats.

---

[34] See Walden Bello's *The Future in the Balance, Essays on Globalization and Resistance*, U.P. Press, 2001.

These formations kept their reservations. A persistent question surfaced among those who knew better: when would the tail stop wagging the dog?

From here, two trends defined the period of the eighties. First, an unhappy estrangement of those who weakened in their political conviction, believing that the Cory Aquino government already took care of what was needed. But the first People Power euphoria was fast slipping. It suggested that many would like to be independent from the ideologically motivated mass movement led by leftist militants with the mass movement from below.

The emerging division in the Left fully developed at the early part of the next decade. This split had produced an entirely different discourse characteristic of all ideological splits in the socialist movements around the world. The rhetoric of nationalism became effectively muted. Everybody in the Left remembered how Cory Aquino used to march with the crowd, but this time she stayed behind when the rallies started to turn to Roxas Boulevard in the direction of the U.S. Embassy. Many of these cause-oriented groups became the nuclei of the emerging socio-economism of the new coalitions of NGOs calling themselves Development NGOs. These new NGOs put aside their previous political agenda (i.e. the emancipatory struggle). This was the first casualty of this massive foreign funding from UNDP, USAID, ADB.

Meanwhile the heated quarrels within the national democratic ranks were beginning to explode, giving rise to the Party exposure of the "renegades." Those militants who outgrew this period look back to it with secret nostalgia as if not to continue the political emancipatory tradition is to deny them their heritage. But many of these activists belonging to the FQS have later become corporate characters, respectable bureaucrats, technocrats in government, or consultants to foreign institutions. The revolution that they were a part of may have faltered after having successfully driven out the dictator in 1986 but for those who continued a tradition, many felt that what was restored when Cory Aquino assumed power was democracy *manqué*.

Letter to the Editor
OP-ED, PDI
August 21, 2001

People Power I Was Not A Picnic but an End to a Long Dark Night

When Amado Doronila starts to call People Power a "counterfeit revolution" (August 17, 2001) I strongly need to explain to myself (and to many others who were also witnesses to the martial law period) how a respected journalist and political analyst could make such blistering blunder.

A recollection is in place here of what former UP President Salvador Lopez noted about the press at the onset of Martial Law: "There are now two kinds of newspapermen, Lopez said, "those who lie low and those who lie." The names Mr. Doronila mentioned like Satur Ocampo and the late Tony Zumel neither did lie between their teeth nor lied low. They went underground to organize the masses.

The 10-year absence of Mr. Doronila from the country between 1975 and 1985 is a period characterized by widespread underground resistance to the rising dictatorship. Filipino exiles abroad like Doronila kept in touch through reading no doubt what one could take hold of in Australia (or in the US) about what was happening in the country.

What he terribly missed was the 24-hour organizing work in the different progressive sectors and the mobilization of the masses resisting Marcos during those 10 years. NGOs and people's organizations gained historically unprecedented unity of thousands of Filipinos under the influence of the National Democratic Front (without being a communist or anti-communist, mind you) that even those in Manila were unaware of the massive organizing in the countryside because they were too focused on EDSA I. They thought that EDSA Uno was the beginning of the People Power revolution when it was actually a culmination of a rising. This manner of viewing of EDSA I triggered by Ninoy Aquino's assassination, as a start instead of as an end, puts aside the manifold socio-economic-political antecedent that made people suffer under the Marcos dictatorship. If Doronila ignores this factor, as he seemed to have done, then he can blame no one but himself as a student of history! Call people Power especially EDSA I "a counterfeit revolution" only if you take it as a start of a new day, when it was actually the end of a long dark night.

A proper tribute for the late Tony Zumel and Ninoy Aquino is to recognize their part in the climax called People Power in 1986, and for Satur Ocampo by recognizing the massive support from the masses (proof of which is his topping the partylist election). Satur's case is a continuing fight in another terrain. And also, let us not forget the hundreds of other journalists today who "neither lie nor lie low" but continue to fight to save democracy from the hands of the elite in all the People Power marches, demos and scores of direct actions thereafter.

(Sgd) Raul E. Segovia,
Development studies professor
(ret.), U.P. Manila

While street marchers may have outlived Marcos, the machinery he left behind was largely intact. The new Constitution of 1987 may have slightly changed the condition but many of the old cronies were back in the high echelons and the foreign predators also came back to continue running, operating, directing the economy.

With the corporate entities in their control, these cronies have become more secure, powerful and the influence far reaching. NEDA came out with its "People-Powered Development Agenda." Outside this rhetoric the corrupt, ineffectual bureaucracy remained unchanged. I look at this as constricting the genuine development of the country. The government was still running under an effete civil service hardened by a political framework that did not allow it to play the dynamic vision of an emancipated people.

Look Again, It's the Economy

The Philippine state can no longer be truly sovereign vis-à-vis the requirements of the international finance institutions mentioned above. The country had become a caboose in the economic direction worldwide that the IMF, World Bank, and recently the WTO had steered like what they have been doing for the rest of the Third World. They restore the health of the capitalist system. The country ultimately had been subjugated by the neo-classical economics steering its market even faster than what its businessmen, agri-corporate leaders, exporters, workers, consumers are prepared for, "safety nets" notwithstanding. (See FTA story.)

The CPP and NDF had every reason to be cynical about the 1986 election participation not because the "*trapos*" had complete control of the election terrain but because the jobless masses still believed that election time is redistributive time—time for money to get around liberally or literally imbedded in sandwiches. It has been the marked character of traditional politics. No democratic mechanism has ever been invented for the rapid distribution of politicians' wealth than is found during elections when money starts to flow into the poor constituents' palms. The system proves the strength of neo-classical economics over political practice. This meant that everything of value (like votes) could be tradable in the market place. This silent cynicism runs panting on two legs from precinct to precinct on election day.

In the old tradition of politics where the poor were supposed to have political rights but no economic security, vote selling encouraged by corrupt politicians is one of the powerful features in a faltering democracy. This is the unchanged reality we still have after People Power I. Dire poverty is found in many parts of the countryside. When President Arroyo in the 2004 elections declared that the problem is mass poverty, she seemed to have prescience very few politicians in power are willing to admit openly. Her campaign style for-re-election reflected this perspective. The name of the game is institutionalized dole in social services. Former Social Welfare Secretary Dinky Soliman who felt "guilty" about the practice later confirmed this was widespread in the department she used to head.

Furthermore, what the president was doing like hugging the poor and the dirty, shaking hands with the downtrodden, visiting them in their waterless hovels, promising one million jobs every year, schools in every village, and a costly "*ad infinitum*" were common knowledge to all. This cynicism in politics is mirrored ironically in empty government coffers every time the old government departs. Was this the reason, as late as 2004, why President Arroyo was headed to changing the 1987 Constitution? Changing the system of governance but not overturning decisively mass poverty is a gamble only politicians play.

The Coming of an End

The issues in the open mass movement remained un-problematized. In spite of Cory Aquino's call "to institutionalize the gains of People Power I revolution," this was unheeded, unfulfilled. An enormous vested interest grabbed power and some ex-activists re-installed themselves in the different echelons of the bureaucracy and the corporate world. Some turned into columnists in mainstream media earning their keep by criticizing the problems and endlessly carping about the solutions.

Historic Weaknesses of the First People Power as Transition

What was expected as a transition from dictatorship to democracy turned out to be a path strewn with old thorns. These were not difficult to remember because many were actually products of unresolved issues coming out again as a veritable *déjà vu*. History has already judged President Corazon Aquino's government when she *failed* to abrogate cronies' debts and behest loans; *failed* to put behind bars crooks and cronies; *failed* to recover the Marcos loot; *failed* to overhaul the corrupt, inefficient bureaucracy; *failed* to stop the big concessionaries-politicians from destroying the forests; *failed* to place the military under her complete control; *failed* to recover the lands previously grabbed by the big landlords; *failed* to raise decent wages of thousands of workers, *failed* to give lands to the landless; *failed* to give a decent life and livelihood to the poor both in cities and the countryside. She *failed* other things her people needed badly when the dictator left huffing into the U.S. helicopter to take him away forever.

These omissions could no longer be excused. While Marcos is judged harshly (and deservedly so) for taking away the people's power and misused it, Cory Aquino had that historic "people power" handed to her but failed to use it to liberate them. Instead, she listened to the adulations of the U.S. Congress and the American businesspersons and thereafter bringing down the future of a self-liberated people crushing. Such judgement will be harsher historically. Even today, we are still picking up the pieces in order to surmount and survive the same old problems.

The weaknesses of the transition did some terrible dynamics for the country. Cory Aquino claimed to be "the opposite of Marcos." Her government did not turn out to be that. Start with the issues of energy, power, oil, tax collection failings and a proneness to foreign exchange reserve shortage, environmental degradation. Since our overdependence on imported oil had been sending the economy into a downward spin, the only question left was "When do we hit the bottom?"

On February 22, 1986, I was in Legazpi City finishing a symposium with the teachers and some student leaders. I was told about Secretary Enrile and General Ramos holed up in Camp Crame "under the protection of the masses." I flew back to Manila the following day. The imagined political turmoil in my mind did not fit the normal appearances of what I saw in the streets. The people I saw in the streets walking seemed to be taking things in stride: no soldiers in battle gear, no tanks roaring to put things in place.

The Siege at Gate 6

I wish to make a concluding vignette of the Eighties as it signalled the termination of the dictatorship. I'll call it "The Siege at Gate 6" because that was where it happened.

Gate 6 of the Presidential Palace is at the end of Arlegui Street and Azcarraga (now Recto). J.P. Laurel passes in front of the gate and snakes all the way to the old San Miguel brewery overlooking the Pasig River. The gate is a high grilled entrance about ten feet tall, made of strong steel a tank would have a hard time ramming against it in order to open it forcibly. There used to be a guard house nearby with soldiers armed to the teeth.

A few days earlier, various EDSA marchers in different groups increased their political crescendo in the different parts of the city. I recall now that there was not a week without marches going on. All seemed to converge in Mendiola about 500 meters from Gate 6.

In the afternoon of February 25, 1986, some of us were folding up our streamers, collecting posters and handbills; they would be handy in the next march. The ACT had just had another symposium that day at the back of the acacia covered building of Mount Carmel church, somewhere in Broadway, Q.C. Over the radio we heard that Marcos and family had fled and were no longer inside Malacañang. It sent shivers in many of us accompanied with a passing disbelief and then to be replaced by indescribable joy. What could happen next?

Three teacher members of ACT joined me in my 1978 old diesel converted Camaro. We roared back to Manila. We passed Laong La-an street avoiding the "Welcome" rotunda that was always heavily policed. My companions got off along the way. I was left alone in the car and hesitant to proceed to Malacañang.

The afternoon caught me along the darkening street of Arlegui where I slowed down and my arms on the wheel a little trembling. There were people running, walking hurriedly against the traffic. On reaching a small bridge I could see a large convergence of people, actually shadows of people, at the end of Arlegui. Instead of a clear horizon I saw heads in constant motion and this started to blur my vision. I parked the car as close to the sidewalk as possible.

"Ratatatat . . . tatat." I heard heavy gun fire. The first man I asked about it said the presidential guards were dispersing the crowd trying to climb the irongate. The people were in constant motion of going and coming, coming, going without end. My romantic imagination connected the rapid moving scene to the fall of the Bastille two hundred years ago.

"Coreee, Coreee, Coreee," the crowd screamed. Then more gun fires that cracked the evening. A few minutes later I saw a short man with a bloodied head trying to wipe his face with his shirt shadowed with blood. No, he was not hit by the bullet but somebody beat him when he was trying to step out of the gate. Maybe he was an employee from inside Malacañang. The rage of people did not distinguish persons trying to escape from the other side of the gate to the outside world. I told the man to cover his face with his shirt and walk naturally and not to run as this would only call attention.

More gun fires. There were people running with pieces of 2" x 2" wood; others were brandishing wire ribs of old umbrellas. More gunfires but they seemed pointed in the air as I could see some sparks in the black night air. I rushed back to take cover behind my car but found the narrow place occupied by three people crouching behind the fender. One of them looked Caucasian, maybe a foreign correspondent, I thought. "Are you not supposed to be there?" I told him pointing with my mouth in the direction of Gate 6.

The evening was turning into a carnival of excited people. When I peered at the side of my Camaro, I could see the vertical grills cutting the shadows of those climbing the tall gate; some fell or jumped back to the ground. This was about 11 o'clock. The melee thickened with no purpose except to go inside the Palace ground. How would this end? There was no answer to that silent worried question. As Arlegui was beginning to clear, and the smoke from gun fires faded into the night I started my car and turned back home emotionally drained. I realized the life of an activist does not end during the last gunfire.

Chapter **7**

Some Progressive Forces in the NGO Community
1980's

THE SEVENTIES AND EIGHTIES were decades of political crises, perhaps the most severe in the country's history. Marcos was a good learner from a Chinese adage that "a crisis offers opportunities." He created the crisis and took most of the opportunities.

On the other hand, the progressive forces where I stayed close most of the decades also seized the opportunity of organizing the sectors in the Left. They built more coalitions; ceaselessly recruited the young into the rank, encouraged them more to join the mass movement. This initiative produced numerous NGOs as each one mobilized the people whose interests Marcos threatened. Many of these groups became dynamic nuclei of the open mass movement.

Every left-oriented NGO above ground has an equivalent NGO in the UG. Many of these legal NGOs strongly made a difference. I discuss some of them in this chapter, describing the socio-economic-political milieu that gave birth to them, some people around the organizing initiative, the issues that triggered their birth, what they had achieved, etc. Among those included here were I believe historic exemplars. In most of these, I was a co-founder or was occupying a leading role.

1. Nuclear –Free Philippine Coalition (NFPC)

2. National Coalition for the Promotion of Breast-feeding, Child Care (NCPB-CC)

3. Alliance of Concerned Teachers (ACT)

4. Council for Health and Development (CHD)

5. Philippine Environmental Action Network (PEAN)

6. Freedom from Debt Coalition (FDC)

1981 – Nuclear Free Philippines Coalition (NFPC)

The critical heat that gave birth to the NFPC was the nation-wide energy crisis. It caused prices of oil-dependent goods and services to rise inexorably. This worsened in late 70s. The oil industry was having a heyday increasing the prices of gasoline and other oil products, with the Marcos government piggy-backing its taxes on their increased prices.

Faced by a looming crisis, the country launched an intensified search for alternative sources. The effort interposed with lot of counter-skullduggery by the cronies ran on until the early part of the next decade. This was the period that a nuclear plant for the country was proposed.

Nuclear energy use was getting popular in the industrial countries. So was the information about the increasing number of nuclear power plant accidents. The Three Mile Island meltdown in Pennsylvania in 1979 was preceded by other serious nuclear plant accidents in other places, mostly in U.S. As early as 1961, there were serious wakeup calls to persons and governments toying with this dangerous alternative. Burning, contamination, radioactive steam exploding, pollution of the environment, leaks and a slew of dangers were linked to the original projects, not to say of the cost in billions of dollars just to entomb one defective plant.

The rationale for all this perverted interest in putting up a nuclear plant in the country technically unprepared and heavily indebted was the dictator's dream of attaining rapid "national development goal."

The two-year old Citizens Alliance for Consumer Protection (CACP) I then chaired raised the issue against a nuclear plant in the country. We called for alternative sources of energy neither harmful to humans, costly to taxpayers, nor environmentally risky. It launched a popular education program on the dangers of the plant and what the citizens could do.

The CACP created a "nuclear desk," a project of its Study and Action Group (SAG) attending to special consumer issues. Former newspaperman Joe Cortez, then CACP board member and head of the "desk," recommended that a separate independent organization be created to address this rising danger. The first target was to stop the building of the multi-million dollar Bataan Nuclear Power Plant (BNPP). Mass mobilization was accompanied by popular education and organizing the communities. I spent large part of my time talking in symposia about alternative energy.

The BNNP was preceded by a series of scandals, scams, suspect deals by the cronies who had dark links with Westinghouse, the American supplier firm. Add the fact that people in Bataan province living in close proximity to the proposed plant site were beginning to be uneasy and fearful for their lives. A cause-oriented group (COG) that could organize, educate, and mobilize them into action was envisioned. This was later broadened in coordination with other groups here and abroad in order to stop the initial work on the BNPP. Thus, the Nuclear-Free Philippines Coalition (NFPC) was born.

This was the géneral soil that surrounded the growth and development of one of the big coalitions of NGOs. It also included personalities (local, national and international), schools and universities, even towns and villages, professional groups, alerted consumers that constituted the early NFPC.

I would hasten to add that this was not one NGO or a single COG initiative but a collective undertaking that affected many branches of the state and the broader community. Even the repression and corruption in the martial law government also contributed in the political dynamics of the people behind the anti-nuclear plant movement.

Focus on the Principal Problems

The *three basic problems* as analytical framework was gaining popularity in the mass movement. It gathered all the loose ends of issues and tightened the rope against the dictatorship. It bundled together disparate issues like health, environment, militarism, corruption, and nuclear waste proliferation. The rapid responses against the BNPP were like prairie fires.

Other emerging issues e.g., environment, health, nuclear waste, lack of capacity to secure the plant against nuclear accidents, the procurement of costly uranium to regularly fuel it, the risks in shipping it, cost over-run, graft and corruption linked to its construction by Westinghouse latched themselves to other issues *ad infinitum*. The BNPP was not a solution but a problem that hatched more and riskier problems. These unresolved challenges were racing ahead of its putative benefits claimed by Marcos cronies and cabinet members who had suspicious vested interests with Westinghouse.

Nationalism Reconstituted

The open mass movement was getting stronger because of the living intellectual élan that fed it guiding its popular education. Included here were the ideas and deeds of past heroes and also those of the political epigones. There were the likes of elder statesmen Recto and Tañada Sr., Salvador Araneta, the younger Diokno; several journalists and political scientists like Renato Constantino; and writers, publicists, young nationalist economists like Larry Henares and Alejandro Lichauco. They were the intellectual circle that forged the ideology against the BNPP. Add also the political clouds that hovered and thickened around the issues of the U.S. military bases as their presence was now closely linked to the BNPP. Nationalism was hitched to the issue whether it was opportune time to renew the U.S. military bases or terminate them.[35]

Nationalism was not a monopoly of the patriotic student activists. The fire that fed it in the streets of the metropolis and the rhetoric that inflamed the nation were further fuelled by the persevering presence and push of the NDF. This was evident in several handbills and underground readings usually distributed during public rallies. The 70s was a fertile decade for the Left under the leadership of Jose Maria Sison. The three basic problems mentioned earlier were enriched by the experiences of "returnees" from Mao Tse Tung's country. Many of them were student activists, academics, newspapermen, ex-priests, mavericks of the Catholic seminaries, etc.

---

[35] In 1991, the Philippine Senate in a historic decision terminated the U.S. military bases in the country, and turned the developed infrastructures into export-processing zone.

It was a much clearer direction for the many nationalists and marching democrats than what Marcos and his technocrats guiding the nation were parroting in press releases. Policy statements embodied in the slogan "National Development Goals" turned out to be echoes of the increasing pressures of the World Bank, IMF and the rest of the multilateral agencies taking hold of the country's economy. It was a period when foreign creditors were demanding payment from the nation under a profligate government, squeezing blood from turnips.

After EDSA

The NFPC in 1987 received its initial victory in the long campaign against the BNPP. The first few proclamations of then newly-elected Cory Aquino was to keep her promise to "mothball" the nuclear plant. This same year the new constitution was ratified and embodied the historic provision that the Philippines remains "nuclear free."

Later the politics and ideology of the legal mass movement took deeper roots, took a different slant. The foreign debts incurred by Marcos and his cronies remained the responsibility of the Filipinos, so was the land under CARP (comprehensive agrarian reform program) since the funds supposed to finance it would come from the till held and controlled by Marcos and his cronies in foreign banks. Many repressive laws that emanated from the presidential decrees of the dictator were still in place. The whole bureaucracy, including police and the military, was still guided by these repressive PDs.

It was then that the NFPC transformed itself into a secretariat for several NGOs that were steered by the anti-U.S. bases movement. The coalition became one of the strongest in the history of the people's movement. Former Senator Pepe Diokno led it and remained its icon until he died. It left behind the issue of what to do with the suspended BNPP infra structures, a secondary problem. More energetically the NFPC rallied beyond coalition in driving out the U.S. military bases from Clark, Subic and scores of other areas in the country.

But all this should not detract us from the historic achievement of closing the dangerous nuclear plant in Bataan and driving out the U.S. military bases from Clark and Olongapo. It was a collective struggle that involved a strong coalition building by nationalists and democrats, young and old, peasants and factory workers. This was an indelible lesson in the formation of strong, principled "people power" movement ripening from the fruit of coalition politics.

Lest we overlook, the Americans left in haste because of the rambling at the backyard of their beautiful houses on the forested hills overlooking Subic Bay, and the continuous pouring of ominous ashes from the evening sky ceaselessly spewed by the almighty volcano Pinatubo. That also helped in precipitating a decision. The social volcano about to erupt turned out to be a real angry mountain dormant for 500 years.

1981 – National Coalition for the Promotion of Breast Feeding & Child-Care (NCPB-CC) or BUNSO

The Citizen's Alliance for Consumer Protection (CACP), one of the many cause-oriented groups that mushroomed under Marcos acted on the report of KMPI, a partner organization, about the lead-laced cans of milk sold by foreign-owned companies. This signalled a need for immediate action to cut down this risk to babies. Later studies confirmed the danger that canned milk posed to the consumers, especially infants and children. The risk deepened when millions of mothers were made the target of commercial ads hyping the goodness of their products. This unwittingly weaned breast-feeding babies from their mothers. The ads mesmerized the misinformed about canned milk as substitute to mother's milk.

The CACP took this as a serious issue affecting a large number of vulnerable consumers, the babies. It passed the subject to its Study-and-Action-Group, a mass action oriented circle of cadres. Ines Fernandez coordinated the core group. She suggested creating an independent NGO separate from CACP so that it could define the terms of its popular education, its programs reaching out to the broad masses. This was a formula follower by CACP in creating other NGOs in the years to follow.

The early formation of BUNSO included several militants from the middle class. These persons were Tina Ebro-Carlos (CACP), Julie Amargo (KMPI), Lita Logarta (KMPI), Sister Pilar Versoza (Pro-Life); Mary Concepcion Bautista (CWP), Remy Rikken (PILIPINA), Leny Miran (PNA), Irene Santiago (Konsumo Dabao), Dr. Mita Pardo de Tavera (AKAP); Linda Senturias (UCCP), Donna Zapa (MABINI), Lita Nery (SAMAKANA), pharmacist Teng Escobar and Raul E. Segovia (CACP). All, one could safely say, belonged to the politically conscious middle forces and anti-Marcos groups. Often they occupied responsible positions in their private or public life. The organization was registered with the SEC in 1982; that much was its official status.

The acronym BUNSO (*Balikatan at Ugnayang Naglalayong Sumagip Sa Sanggol*) was adapted. In local sense, "bunso" refers to the youngest child in the family, culturally the center of loving attention, embodying the values of family warmth, tenderness, protection, and care. The concept "bonding" with the nursing mother starts from here.

In 1982, one year after its formation, the NCPB was publicly launched as one more NGO contributing its forces to the mass movement. What steps did it take? It put to ask the policies of the dictatorship regarding babies and child-care, nursing mothers including government connivance with the manufacturers of artificial milk and junk foods many of which were multinational corporations (MNCs).

The struggle was never easy. It was initially uphill and mostly re-educating consumers, especially mothers. While there was lack of funds, there was no lack of manpower, i.e. eager and dynamic volunteers. While there was a dearth of protective legislation for children, there was a good deal of public calls that children among them babies be also the concern of enlightened legislators. While tradition leaves to the mother solely the responsibility for the child's care, BUNSO turns this around saying in its popular education that the father has a different but equal responsibility for the caring of babies. (This last point was the reason why this writer accepted his election as second National Chairperson after Dr. Mamita Pardo de Tavera joined the Cory Aquino Cabinet.)

Lead in Milk

In the late 70's, the problem called the attention of the public of the presence of lead in canned milk. The toxic lead in the bodies including the child's was a scientific finding. But beyond the lead-in-milk issue the CACP Study-and-Action-Group had discovered that the milk-substitute MNCs had a broader plan to take over control of the food system that was serving children especially in schools. This included marketing their products in places where nursing mothers were most vulnerable, that is, in maternity hospitals, delivery wards and clinics, or in school canteens where children are trapped in consuming carbonated drinks or junk foods, and are prevented from going out of the campus to take snacks.

At this time the CACP with the help of the Philippine Normal College Research Center under its director professor Lorna Z. Segovia launched a separate campaign against junk foods in schools.[36] The food MNCs are still raking profits especially on baby food sales. Sometimes they temper their greed by observing some minor marketing rules like giving directions on how much water to mix with the powdered milk, etc.

But the hype continued unabated. Mothers abandoned developing their natural milk because there was a promise of easy feeding in milk substitutes, and initially (and falsely) cheaper food for babies, forgetting that their natural milk is free. Even maternity rooms were emblazoned with propaganda how important it was to shift from mother's milk to canned milk, added with suspect vitamins. Artificial milk, powdered milk, milk-substitutes, all these have colonized the market for baby foods; portraying of (falsely) smiling mothers and super healthy babies fed on their products.

Nursing mother's milk, a valuable source in breastfeeding has important physiological, mental and emotional support elements for the growing child. Under the leadership of BUNSO a campaign was launched to popularize breastfeeding. This usually preceded the organizing of mothers in poor communities.

---

[36] The initial failure of this campaign was attributed to school administrators receiving gifts from big firms producing carbonated drinks. Many of them including the canteen operator were recipients of doles and gifts from soft-drink firms like providing them with freezers or refs usually for exclusive use of their products. But the campaign was a success. Teachers supported it to protect the children from the ill effects of too much junk food in their diet. But generally administration usually heads of schools, silently opposed this as they themselves were in the "gift list" of corporations supplying the canteens. (See PNU Research Report, 1987.)

The devastation that milk MNCs often wrought on the traditional breastfeeding mother's practices was often irreparable. The enemy was neither small nor powerless. It was well entrenched, heavily financed, deeply embedded in the economy. BUNSO realized it must put into action a plan to organize mothers and concerned allies.

Understanding less, many mothers in the rural areas thought that water diluted with powdered milk and "looking like milk" was good enough if not economical. It was a formula for massive malnutrition and attendant health risks. The early source of immunities found in the mother's milk was destroyed. This observation was supported by case studies after studies by health institutions done in the country and abroad. Examples included are artificial foods, bottled mashed solids for children laced with artificial nutrients, colors and harmful preservatives, vitamins of suspect value, etc. with pictures of nursing mothers stupidly beaming happiness.

Link with International Activists

Since the market was worldwide, the risks were equally and dangerously worldwide. The broad international partnership of NGOs for children's protection pressured two U.N. agencies to address the problem seriously. The U.N. came out with what is known today as the WHO-UNICEF International Code for Marketing of Breast Milk Substitutes and Related Products. The role of BUNSO would be discussed later when it hosted one big international gathering in Manila in 1989 as partner-NGO of International Baby Food Action Network (IBFAN).

A broad link partnership was born among the national and international NGOs, among health workers and urban poor and peasant women, among research entities and scholars, legislators and ordinary concerned citizens, church people and laymen, housewives and young mothers.

The coalition created one of the most enlightened and militant groupings of NGOs supporting children's fundamental rights to health. The protection of these rights or the threats to them united several groups and individuals to form a coalition against milk companies and their suspect products.

Organizing the Mothers

As a consequence of consumer-protection concerns by the CACP, BUNSO grew into a coalition of several NGOs involved in women issues, children's rights, consciousness-raising and organizing. It reached out to urban poor and peasant women mothers. It even involved the trade unions.

Lecture was less important than street theatre when it came to dramatizing the issue, including demonstration in the communities by health caregivers on how to enhance mother's milk. Other methods included putting up mother's clinics, classes and community kitchens demonstrating to nursing mothers the healthful ways of food preparation and how to protect their children from dangers of unsupervised eating. The latter concern linked to CACP campaign against junk foods through street theatre, lectures, pantomimes, and radio programs.

The programs caught the attention of international groups like IBFAN, and the International Organization of Consumer Unions (IOCU). These two were equally involved in the struggle against the milk companies and even first world countries eager to send their surplus dairy products to developing countries as aid. Even multi-lateral agencies like WB or Australian Aid was not above committing this heedlessness that had cost more lives of babies in developing countries than they are willing to admit. What's important to aid agencies was to export these surpluses under U.S. Public law 480 in the guise of low interest credit. While this subsidized their dairy industry, it neglected the concerns on how it should be used by the poor in the Third World.

In 1989, BUNSO as a member of the International Baby Food Action Network (IBFAN) hosted a conference of international, militant groups promoting breastfeeding. It was a historic occasion held in Manila, attended by more than 250 delegates from 16 countries.

Beyond BUNSO

For more than 20 years, all of the above efforts were focused on the babies, young children and the nursing mother sectors. But the movement in the latter years veered away from breast-feeding and the profit-oriented institutional threats. One NGO, ARUGAAN that has maintained the philosophy of BUNSO and many of its practices need separate treatment. Heading this NGO is former activist and first BUNSO executive director Inez Fernandez.

What has BUNSO achieved? It is now 23 years (1982-2004) since BUNSO was officially launched. What has this NGO done to make a difference? Let us enumerate them but bear in mind that BUNSO was a coalition. The term "coalition" implies both plurality and autonomy, a part of the open mass movement guided by people above ground, steered by militants (read: those hounded by the minions of Marcos) and inspired, consciously or unconsciously, by the NDF 12-Point Program.

In the lexicon of activists, BUNSO became a half service program in the community, half political struggle against the well entrenched responsible for the numerous risks nursing mothers were facing. *It was also directly, instantly ameliorative but strategically emancipatory.* There was a dearth of community programs serving nursing mothers. The dilution of original principles by numerous other projects by new groups and new legislations caused the children's issues to spring up but slightly off-focus in many other groups. Several volunteers inside POs, NGOs and even trade unions carried the children's programs assiduously. This is how BUNSO grew and spawned other progressive groups. The professional and health worker groups in the cities and other populated towns reflected the BUNSO mission in their academic lectures. I carried this mission even as a lecturer in U.P. Manila.

The Boycott Call

Media, seeing the international dimension of the campaign, made news out of this otherwise banal activity common to nursing mothers among the poor. Radio, print and TV started to consult BUNSO on issues about breast-feeding practices and about subtle opposition by food MNCs. It raised the issue against transnational firms planning to control the food system, especially baby foods. Dr. "Jaypee" Perez, a former militant from the SDK, was among the last executive officers of BUNSO.

Liv Ullman, a popular movie actress in the 1980s who was in Manila to help the campaign, denounced Nestlé of censorship when her TV program sponsored by the firm was cut off. Her TV appearance promoted breastfeeding. This stirred a row in the public arena on the issues of freedom of information.

Liv Ullman's TV declaration got a lot of public attention. This was one big success for the advocacy work of BUNSO. Nestlé in the months to follow was paid back for its arrogance by a call of boycott for all its products by progressive NGOs.

A medley of militant organizations and groups, here and abroad, became support infrastructures of BUNSO. This made its influence felt widely. Other coalitions like NFPC, labor centers like KMU, people's organizations like the peasant group KMP, church people, science and academic groups and government bureaus made possible the permanent acceptance of a lot of BUNSO's undertakings and principles. The triumph of breastfeeding mothers is now emblazoned in every TV ad selling milk: telling the mother that breast-feeding is best for babies.

1982 – Alliance of Concerned Teachers (ACT)

For most of its gestation period, ACT was not an alliance of teachers in the public and private schools. That came later in 1982. Its forerunner was a union of teachers and non-teaching workers in the Jose Rizal College (JRC). Its early president was Loretta Ann Rosales, one of the founding members and first president of ACT. Mrs. Rosales was later elected to Congress as partylist representative. The elements of ACT's stance were later developed from out of the political genome embedded in the earlier struggle of that private school union. Slowly it broadened its issues beyond the private schools.

Militancy of Organized Teachers

The conservative climate of the period was similar in many other schools, the educational system being an authoritarian hierarchy. The Department of Education, Culture and Sports (DECS) was at the top controlling, supervising and regulating the schools through its various bureaucracies all over the country. This made teacher organizing relatively easy and inevitably radical and vibrant. The rest of the unorganized teachers were either silent or afraid or pursuing some social and socializing chores outside the classroom.

But the crass materialism of many school owners, the lack of respect and often brutality of security guards (the time being the martial law years), the chicaneries of school administration, the openly anti-union management and the labor laws militated against genuine unionism. All these made for fertile ground in organizing teachers into radical fighters for their rights.

Many school officials (then and now) believe that when one is with the government he/she has no right to criticize it, a false belief that worsens public service and shelters it from its own shortcomings. These officials invoked some kind of "code of ethics" for this turtle-like behaviour they wish to cultivate among teachers. ACT members could not accept that because it did not respond to fundamental needs and problems of half-a-million workers in the schools especially during the 1980s. This conservatism in traditional teacher organizing helped to disguise the symptoms and suppressed the root causes of restlessness among teachers. The issues cankered. Even today, this systematic evasion of facing the real problems of education rooted in low pay of teachers' plagues the educational system.

What does it take to be radical in a sector of workers historically known to be very conservative? Teachers usually believe they are propagators of knowledge and preserver of values. This dual role is not supposed to be contradictory. The first is of professional interest; the second of social responsibility concern. Both were undermined during the turbulent martial law period. But more than these two, the core group that later organized ACT saw the government unsympathetic to the ideals of nationalism and the democratic values yearned by the Filipino masses. Hence, the restiveness of teachers against the elitist and authoritarian direction of the country's educational system.

What Kind of Reform Do the Schools Need?

One who does not have the cash is not likely to get a good certificate of education, much less a real education. Every step in the "reform of education" goes nearer to being commercialized because better education has been equated with increased fees, charges and contributions expected from students and parents. This situation has been going on for the last half century.

The crucial provision of Education Act of 1982 worsened this spreading cancer in the education of Filipinos, especially the children of the majority of low-income families. The law allows, nay, encourages school owners to transform education into a commodity sold in the market place. In the heart of this practice, the school owner has found a profitable business in the institution of learning. Look at the "reform law" provision, for instance:

> **"Tuition and Other School Fees**: *Each private school shall determine its rate of tuition and other school fees and charges . . . . shall be collectible, and their application and use authorized by the Department of Education."*

Two elements in that provision—the school owner determines his price and the DECS regulates when to collect—but without the consent of the one who pays (the parent). The ACT saw through this and could not tolerate it—explaining the issue to hapless parents. The latter were furious.

Important to organizing teaohers effectively were their economic and democratic rights; after these, their professional rights. ACT was not just a teacher organization. Its militancy was a function of what were (and still are) wrong with the educational system. Reforms after reforms since World War II have not made a dent on the dire economic conditions of teachers. The authoritarianism of the school system has persisted and its oppressive bureaucrats since Marcos eroded the teacher's democratic values.

"Our demands were basic. We wanted legitimate salary increases (to respond to increasing cost of living). We wanted to receive our wages in full, our allowances on time, our bonuses complete. We wanted the laws we (have) won fully implemented. We wanted a stop to illegal deductions, refunds made for our claims . . . We wanted a decent life, a life of dignity and self-respect. We felt this was not too much to ask as teachers, as public servants," from an ACT handbill titled **"1983: Year of the Teacher, Year of Struggle".**

This ringing rhetoric written by its first chairperson Etta Rosales, then a scourge of private school owners, ignited a prairie fire of radicalism in the sector. The year began with militant protest actions as thousands of teachers spilled into the streets of Manila, Baguio, Pampanga, Iligan, Davao, Zamboanga and Tawi-Tawi. Ms. Etta Rosales declared in the same paper quoted above:

"We were tired of dialogues, empty promises, and government neglect. We decided to assert our collective will in stronger protests, in militant action."

Thousands of classroom teachers joined mass actions; traditionally docile and obedient beyond belief; put aside their lesson plans, pens, chalks, erasers and record books, stepped into the streets in their run-down shoes. They put out hurriedly drawn posters and placards summarizing their plight. They filed leaves-of-absence simultaneously, conducted mass sit-downs and walked around picket lines. They attended lectures and symposia organized by ACT, hauled streamers in street marches denouncing exploitative private school owners, repressive police, and ultimately on one placard screaming: *"The Government is the Greatest Oppressor of Teachers!"* This was only during the first quarter of what ACT organizers called **"The Year of the Teacher"**.

Unknown to many teachers and even to school officials, a parallel development in the education policy was concocted by the international finance technocrats. In April 1980, the World Bank came out with its "Education Sector Policy Paper." This became a sort of vade mecum for technocrats and education reformists.

Reforms for Profit, Not Human Development

What made the whole effort suspect was its early version in the Presidential Commission to Survey Philippine Education (PCSPE) which coincided with the advent of the dictatorship in 1969. The infrastructures for this development in "reforming education" were traced in the Educational Development Decree of 1972 (P.D.6-A), the EDPITAF (1972-82), 2nd WB Edu., Project (1973-78), 3rd WB Edu., Project (1976-81), 4th WB Edu., Project (1977-82), 5th WB Edu., Project (1978), 6th WB Edu., Project (1980-85), etc.[37]

For every aspect of the problem in education, the Education Department, like a typical bureaucracy, had an acronym to solve it: PRODED for decentralizing education, SOUTELE for a study of the outcomes of elementary education, NESC for developing new curriculum in high schools, etc. In many of these "reforms" the USAID, ADB, Ford and Rockefeller foundations, and later some other big name corporations like Toyota joined the profit–inspired reformist fray. Following these "reforms", education was finally ensconced in the bosom of the corporate world.

Everybody was for reform of education except the teachers, students, and millions of parents who were neither consulted during the planning of the program nor participated in the stage of policy formulation. Authoritarianism enshrined itself in the implementation of these reforms. The schools have become virtual factories for the making of skilled, English-speaking, cheap Filipino labor for trading in the marketplace.(See PNC Research Center study series on WB for elementary education, 1984-85; also the Gustav Ranis' ILO Report.)

Nowhere was the triumph of neo-classical economics more evident than in the concept that created a mass of unemployed and/or unemployable coming out of the school system. Its output started to be measured in terms of commodified labor, cheap skills for the market. The social meaning of working with others, for others, recognition of one's contribution to others seems nullified because there was no immediate money equivalent for it. This state of "educational reforms" introduced into the country hastened the degradation of labor. The latter started to lose its educational humanistic meaning. In its campaign for genuine reforms, ACT continued to expose these changes directed to serve the economics of corporate interests, both here and abroad.

ACT and the Mass Movement

What has ACT achieved in the legal mass movement? Towards the second half of the 1980s, I became its second national chairperson. Its founding chairperson joined and was absorbed with new responsibility by BAYAN, a larger umbrella of NGOs and People's Organizations (POs). The militant spirit of organizing was continued. Expansion was broadened. Historically, one in every three teachers was an ACT member; the rest were non-teaching workers in the schools. Members came from more than 100 organizational affiliates from all the regions of the country.

---

[37] See *"What's Behind the Education Act of 1982?"* a booklet published by the Nationalist Resource Center, an ACT supported NGO.

ACT was an alliance of other teachers' groups like the State Colleges and Universities Faculty Alliance (SCUFA) which it also helped organize. This was based in the country's oldest teacher-training school, the Philippine Normal University. Another was the Teacher Center-Philipppines (TCP) that used to be chaired by the late Enrique Torres.

TCP was a training ground for militant unionism of teachers especially in the private schools. ACT also was once chaired by National Artists for Literature Bien Lumbera from the state university. It has more than a hundred affiliate member organizations throughout the big towns and cities in all levels.

It was about this time that ACT joined the World Confederation of Organizations of the Teaching Profession (WCOTP) based in Morge, Switzerland. At present, it is known as Educational International (EI). The group gained a consultative status with the United Nations.

Under my term, ACT extended its reach to other countries like Australia with whom it developed progressive relations, with Japan teachers groups, (then) West Germany, Netherlands, France, U.K., Ireland, Canada, Greece, Hong Kong, South Pacific region including New Zealand, India, Malaysia, etc. These working contacts strengthened international solidarity work. These further enabled ACT to relate the issues of repressions, professional degradation, and teachers' low pay.

With international and funding support expanded, ACT was able to increase organizing programs for teacher affiliates. One was the Human Rights Program for teachers. It was the first teacher group and alliance that submitted a human rights module to the post-dictatorship government to become part of teacher re-training. It was addressed to hundreds of teachers who were passively witnessing their violations in the Marcos period. Secretary Lourdes Quisumbing of the Education Department adopted it under DECS Memo 36, s.1987. ACT submitted the first Human Rights module for official adoption in schools after the fall of Marcos.

The module allowed ACT to reach widely and to expand organizing inside the schools, a new thrust that gave a breath of freedom in teacher organizing. It was also an effective tool empowering the teacher vis-à-vis the administrator. This new legitimacy caused ACT to expand membership.

A Women's Desk for women teachers was formed under the leadership of its Secretary General Melba de Guzman; Melba remains active in organizing work in Australia. A co-worker in ACT secretariat was the indefatigable Susan V. Siar. Dr. Siar is now with the FAO in Rome. The Secretariat's concern was extended beyond the women teachers to mothers, factory/office women workers and women peasants in the countryside. These militants were political dynamos in organizing rallies, mass actions, marches, television and radio talk shows and print media interviews. ACT's hyperactive secretariat that included Enrique Villanueva, a physics scholar from PNU, served as the nucleus that organized most activities related to the broader mass movement.

While libertarian and democratic principles gained by ACT were embedded in the 1987 Constitution like the right to organize independently, the right to be consulted and to participate in decision-making and the teaching of critical and creative thinking, many remained un-enforced or unenforceable. The reason for it is the absence of enabling laws that Congress habitually failed to enact.

Even today militant teachers have a deep grievance against their lawmakers. The problem remained closely tied to the authoritarianism of the educational system. School administrators are leery and wary of teachers' demands and militant organizing. Many ACT leaders are no strangers to school repression.

The field for teacher militancy has remained wide open. Many teacher groups are still active and defiant even if they were no longer under the tutelage of the 12-Point Program. So much of teachers' objective problems remained ignored, bypassed, unresolved by the state in spite of the ringing call of the Constitution that *"education should have the highest budgetary priority."* (Article XIV, Section 5)

By 2000 ACT had more than 200,000 active members. Its influence extended beyond the school system thus interlocking with other NGOs catering to researchers, teacher-aides, non-academic employees and school janitors and security guards.

1978 – Council for Health & Development (CHD)

In a handbook written 26 years after it became an NGO, CHD explained how it started as a community-based health program focused on important health values for Filipinos. These values included the health workers' dedication to their work, skills to meet health emergencies, thrust in the community problems, and awareness of the interrelationship of diseases and "the country as a whole." Not the least of these was the recognition of the importance of organizing the people.

The above paragraph describes the common, typical path progressive, militant NGOs follow from gestation to birth. A health NGO like the CHD could not come from the brains of health workers or health-care students educated in the arena of making money. Although many recognized the value of the cash nexus in their work, they were (and still are) confronted by an immense number of people with less cash to pay for the health services these needed. Meanwhile, the nation they have opted to serve is not only low on cash. It is also high in needless casualties.

Sometime ago in U.P.-Manila College of Medicine and the Philippine General Hospital these skills and values were functionally a part of their academic preparation. In the early 90s, these institutions turned the health complex in U.P. Manila from being "Hospital of the People" into "the hospital sponsored by the drug multinationals" and their medical epigones.

Generally, market economics had taken over the health especially the medical colleges. When the practices of many doctors and their personal needs started to be laced with perks, many have cohabited with the foreign drug companies. Graduates of medical schools currently eschewed the rural areas. Worse, they leave the country with dispatch, some to study further but many to chase the green bucks. (There are always exceptions.) This was (and still is) a part of the growing pains undergone by many health activists in the profession and those about to enter it.

Pathologies and Politics

Health workers including nurses and midwives dedicated to serving the masses are confronted by additional problems in the countryside: not strange pathologies but old politics of the local variety. They find that the poor farmers are bound to their landlords, their benighted elders, their superstition-oriented local leaders, the untrained shaman-like medical quack, last but not least, the effete priest just too glad to continue the modern version of shamanistic practices at the expense of scientific solutions. The last one like a bad shepherd to his flocks usually utters the spiritual words of comfort to them in their suffering, "God loves you all because you are poor." Without revealing the bigger, nastier truth that God loves the rich more. Otherwise, why does He make them richer and the gap with the poor wider?

The overweening fatalism of the rural poor is a higher hurdle to the activist doctors. The problem is directly linked to feudalism, an old system that keeps on renewing its grip on the poor, often semi-literate land tillers. The solution to malnutrition is embedded in the people's political struggle. This was what the interlocutors were told in Tandag, Surigao community seminar, where I found myself years back. Several people in the audience received this with big eyes of baffled wonderment.

It was my turn to speak and I tried to answer the question raised during a forum on nutrition among mothers, "What has landlessness to do with malnutrition?" The audience, mostly peasants, was told that the products of their effort in the land they do not own often did not go to them. More than half of the children in the community usually die before they reach 15, less visibly, not because "the Lord loves them" but more because of widespread malnourishment and its attendant diseases.

Feudalism is a century old problem in the country. Even today, the gradual process of acquiring land of one's own is a low, agonizing process made more difficult by government rules and petty grafts by people involved in it.

The failed land reform programs of previous governments since the Commonwealth period have exacerbated the people's loss of faith in their government. Meanwhile, the suffering is great and widespread, the solution slow so that the underground preachers of "armed struggle" make the goal of land-for-the-landless program look as easy as saying the rosary.

For some, the immediate problem is not necessarily land. A local people's organization called KAMAS, which translates for United Peasants of Surigao Sur set up health committees in communities smaller than the villages in the far away "*puroks*" or sitios. Organizers discussed issues with the mother and elder daughters doing their laundry or when doing their cooking while in the kitchen or mixing "health stories" with other domestic chores. Education does not demand for a four-walled classroom to advance its emancipatory pedagogy. When the organizer integrates with the people, the learner will find every occasion to learn more from the experience.

From my experience, groups of between four to seven families (20 to 35 people)got together and held discussions in study sessions on health. Here pathologies and politics mixed but serious social changes and feudalism were like water and oil. One is always on top of the other.

Hundreds of NGOs like the CHD put up by progressive health militants, usually students from nursing and medical schools in Manila and other urban canters were guided by a political philosophy inculcated from years of practice during and after the dictatorship. This was Maoist in origin but easily confirmed and strengthened by their own experiences with the masses and the repressive character of the Marcos government.

Distant communities reached by health activists were organized to see the problems of official opportunism, a.k.a. "bureaucrat capitalism", why government services were seldom adequate or even visible. These affected health services for the poor and increased morbidity and death in rural areas. Common causes were usually tuberculosis, diarrhoea, respiratory diseases and a bunch of preventable infections. Hope for government assistance increasingly began to dim.

It was about this time that communities started to organize themselves for alternative solutions. This was the advent of the Community Based Health Program (CBHP). As usual other health-related NGOs preceded these health programs. What is important was that this paved the way to the broader alternative social formation (ASF) that was reaching out to the whole country's health sector. A number were found especially in the countryside. NGOs like CACP helped create many more.

Health was not Government Priority

People's health was perceived to be in the back burner of the nation's priorities, with other social services receiving less than the need to pay foreign debts or to boost the military budget. More and more NGOs realized that organizing meant direct people's participation in solving their problems.

Activists in health sector saw the immediate problems needing amelioration. They opened their eyes to the usefulness of herbal medicines, the effectiveness of the hilot (the traditional medicine man) if he were trained to the scientific aspects of his practices. These included acupuncture and understanding the objective condition of his environment.

Many medical graduates turned activists did not only teach the peasants but also learned from exposure to the peasants' way of life. This experience was an enriching process that helped advance his knowledge before it acquires a corporate bias. This bias includes the belief that largesse and donations from drug companies can immensely improve health services. The College of Medicine, U.P. used to send medical students to communities to introduce them to the reality of the countryside. It showed them how the majority of their would-be patients live. Several medical schools, hospitals and nursing colleges under progressive administrators echoed this practice.

Hippocrates vs. the Health Officials & Drug MNCs

Investors and profit mavens did not leave this trend to the activists and die-hard votaries of Hippocrates with their alternative medicines but otherwise science-supported rural pharmacology. The health issue engendered by the neglected countryside became a target for massive procurement program of the health bureaucracy. The attendant budget increase followed. With more funds in regional officials' hands but no record of health advances to show, NGO activists were hard put to disbelieve that the clever grisly hands of the bureaucracy were no longer on the budget till. They are still there.

The medicines that were being sent to the rural areas were either expired or samples from drug companies introducing expensive new brands. The others were surplus procurement by thieving bureaucrats in health agencies.

This practice was rampant during the Marcos years but not eradicated totally in the decades that follow.

The drug multinationals were (and still are) in control of the drug market. More than 95 % of branded and therefore expensive medicines in the retail outlets are products of the drug MNCs. The medical profession has become a strong infrastructure for the propagation of branded, expensive drugs produced by these foreign-owned firms.

NGOs in the health sector find it difficult to cooperate with the government health agencies. For every problem the NGO health volunteers encounter, they feel the roots were hidden deep and often linked to practices of bureaucrats caving in before these drug MNCs. The latter poured into the lap of health professionals a cornucopia of gifts, cash and other favors.

I see how the recent commitment to globalization through WTO worsened the problems. The country is already open wide to the entry of foreign goods competing unfairly with lots of low-priced but tested generics Filipinos themselves can and do produce. The economic pressure threatens to close local pharmaceutical industries.

What's wrong with the medical and health education? Why have many medical graduates parted from their Hippocratic Oath of principally attending to the sick and the suffering? They still do but only if the sick are prepared to pay for the cost of being ill. And the masses are short of cash. And what's happening to the nurses? Do they still serve with caring energy and sacrifice like their model Florence Nightingale? They immediately file their applications for immigrants' visa to the rich countries even before graduation.

But health NGOs many of which I was closely associated with remained undaunted with these problems. Other health related NGOs, POs and coalition of several other groups formed themselves to resist the rising malaise within the sector not to say of the continuous taunting by the drug multinational industry. Among these are the Medical Action Group (MAG), the Health Alliance for Democracy (HEAD) the Health Action international Network (HAIN) and many others existing independently but in solidarity with their country badly in need of their services or some alternative sources of low priced medicines.

1990 – Philippine Environmental Action Network (PEAN)

PEAN was composed of several NGOs, cause-oriented groups, church people, research groups, labor unions, teachers and students, consumer militants and personalities who were dedicated to protect, promote and develop alternative ways in restoring an endangered ecosystem. They did these through the handmaiden of activists' life: by educating, organizing and mobilizing the masses. It had a nationalist democratic awareness-raising agenda. As with NGOs in the 70s-80s, the core steering PEAN kept close behind the NDF.

This broad alliance was founded in the early 1990. In one year's time it reached out to more than 140 other groups, mostly mass based. There were more than a quarter of a million members. It was a political response long needed. There were environmental groups significantly present in the scene in earlier years. None seemed to have consciously pursued a political line warning the people, getting them together, putting into their hands the power to stop the continuing environmental destruction. Education for the masses was as important as organizing them. I felt that in making them open their eyes, they alone could make a difference in the current environmental protection effort.

Solutions after solutions were brought forth many of which gave rise to crucial issues.[38] That example of how or by whom the denuded hills should be replanted was one of them. The Green Forum in 1989 put out a "sustainable development philosophy" articulated then by its chairman ex-banker Sixto Roxas. It focused its concerns on various ecosystems in the communities. This was one of the broadest coalitions in the sector but seemed to fail in making explicit whether the masses of Filipinos would be benefited principally from this effort, and that the emancipatory services addressed to thousands of displaced mountain settlers and indigenous people should take precedence.

---

[38] A research study by the writer sponsored by and was submitted to U.P.-Manila, 1994, describes during that time these so-called solutions and the concomitant problems they generated.

The Forests We Lay Bare

The problem of the environment was described starkly as in a "disastrous state." The ecosystems like the forest, cropland, freshwater, coastal and marine, urban environs, etc. were experiencing alarming rate of degradation or destruction. Either natural or man-made this was seen as leading to the final dissolution of these otherwise mutually re-enforcing systems in nature.

A government neglectful in protecting most of these ecosystems was guided by a predatory policy. Its destructive effects on the country's forest condition, often hastened by economic pressures, would not be experienced until years later. The massive flooding and landslides that ensued in 2004 like the ones in General Nakar and Infanta towns were prophetic and tragic; they compel one to go back to biblical comparison. The most recent (February 2006) was in Saint Bernard, Southern Leyte where a mudslide after heavy rains covered one village tragically together with its 1,800 residents.

The reckoning comes late in the day. This includes seasonal floods, soil erosion, sedimentation in public reservoirs and dams, scarcity of water supplying irrigation systems, reduced production on irrigated lands, rice shortage, etc. The train of disasters leaves in its wake not only property destroyed but lives lost.

According to an assessment by PEAN, the loss of forest cover whose ideal proportion should have been 54 % of the lands to maintain an ecological balance had already been surpassed since 1992. But still sadder was the fact that government had not stopped issuing permits to loggers. Until 1993, we were denuding our forests at the rate of 200,000 hectares annually. Coming home to the point, before you finish reading this sentence another dipterocarp falls down by the mountain.

Members of PEAN believed that to continue cutting trees in our forests is criminal enough. This has given tragic signals to a lot of native fauna and flora. For example it is reported that 16 out of the 1,075 birds and animal life forms have been declared endangered. Unless we reverse destruction of these species we will lose them forever.

Even the government conducts a massive re-planting program but does not arrest the criminal log concessionaires; or launches school-wide education on the uses of trees but does not mention those who are abusing the forests, deterioration will go on. Even if it organizes a tree planting in the communities but the people do not see the direct benefits to them, the activity becomes futile. What can be expected? All these efforts are water in a sieve.

The Ecosystem is Losing Breath

Siltation of water bodies like rivers, irrigation canals, reservoirs caused by mining upstream could also diminish the value of these productive water systems. I visited Marinduque. Its coastline has stretched more than 11 kilometers to the sea due to massive flow of silts from the mines; also due to massive extraction of ground water for industrial, commercial and even for aquaculture uses as have occurred in Cebu and Negros islands. About half a million hectares of fresh water areas are affected by salt intrusion. Laguna de Bay with 21 tributaries, except Pagsanjan River, is significantly polluted.

Out of 59 watersheds in the country where millions of people depend for their productive uses of waters at the time of PEAN formation 19 were already destroyed. The area covered about 854,000 hectares. Even the Department of Agriculture and Natural Resources (DANR), now defunct, reported then that not a single river in the country passed the test of being safe to drink in its natural flowing condition. More than 10 % of the 384 major river systems are biologically dead including those in Metro Manila and five in Cebu.

Even the usual source of Metro-Manila's potable water—the Guadalupe aquifier—was being over-pumped five times its capacity, how much of this is known to the people in the metropolis?

The PEAN as a coalition was short of funds but strong in the network. As with other progressive NGOs, PEAN is peopled with politically driven activists. I was elected head of this more than 140-member network sometimes in early 90s. It was not all environment protection oriented. But the environment issue was equally important for trade unions, students, priests, housewives, their children, etc.

Under such a medley of members what political harmony could one achieve? The united front principle works best here. Unite them on what is most common to their interest; educate them on the risks they take if they don't get together in an organized way. Seize the moment and mobilize them, a formula right at the fingertips of militants I was working with.

NGOs in the environment sector were many, mostly dedicated to Joyce Kilmer's poem about trees, with God making the latter; praise and prayer making them bloom. Few took to the streets to dramatize the political message of their vision until PEAN took that cudgel guided by a generalized political line of protecting one ecosystem—the Philippines—and by empowering the masses.

Twelve years ago, the country was about 70 million. By 2004, the population increased by 85 million—about the time that PEAN member organizations thrived. It was noted then that 75 % of the people about this time lived below poverty line. They do not have enough food nor adequate shelter and clothes to cover and warm themselves. About 30 % of the people in the country lived in the cities then increasing social pressures and creating more jobless urban poor.

This economic aspect of the crisis was not lost to PEAN. The popular education has included awareness of the increasing burden of foreign debts then where more than 40 % of the national budget goes to interest payments alone, all this at the expense of basic services direly needed by the masses.

How to Disband an Alliance

PEAN's "*People's Environmental Agenda*" a 36-page manifesto concluded after surveying the landscape of what remained of the ecosystems:

> "*Massive poverty and increasing cases of justice . . . lead to social unrest particularly in the countryside. But the government prefers to treat the situation as "a police problem" necessitating counter-actions and violent military response. This purblind approach when used too often could legitimize the formation of para-military groups only to be followed with escalation of human rights violation. Reports were spreading of forests being set on fire, or communal ponds being poisoned, or agricultural lands destroyed by the military all as part of its counter-insurgency operation.*"

This was PEAN's parthian shot before its 140-member organization disbanded to become independent from each other and to carry more effectively the environmental agenda peculiar to their sectors. It did not die; it multiplied into various forms as varied as the problems of the environment.

PEAN was a short-lived coalition as its individual NGO components broke up into independent groups, pursuing different agenda but not abandoning the environmental protection, care and restoration objectives. Many militants worked inside government agencies monitoring, helping to plan and implementing the programs when practicable. Others continued to march, lobby for new laws, or call for resignation of bureaucrats who blatantly failed to enforce pro-environment laws.

1988 – Freedom from Debt Coalition (FDC)

The Debt System

The FDC was formally launched in 1988 although organizing work started earlier. Like many NGOs of this period, many of its members were increasingly appalled to see the country's debts developing, spreading roots to something already systemic, cancer-like. It started long before the Marcos years.

Then Marcos and cronies borrowed and borrowed until the economy could no longer sustain paying even its interests. To describe the country's deteriorating terrain, the language changed into a hemorrhagic metaphor: it was "undergoing profuse bleeding."

Among the organized masses, the people behind FDC started to look at the country's debt not only in terms of money borrowed but also in terms of its impact on the lives of the many.

To Pay or Not to Pay

Starting in years of the late President Diosdado Macapagal, the government had initially entwined the country's debt policy with the "conditionalities" of IMF and the World Bank. This worsened during the Marcos years and was continued by Cory Aquino's administration but did not turn out any better. In 1986 when positive conditions ushered in by historic first People Power became ripe for the asking, i.e., to cut clean from unjust debts, this did not happen. The opportunity went away like a mist in history.

The foreign creditors at that time and probably the rest of the world were in a state of wonder: how did Filipinos depose the dictator in such nice bloodless way? The world was listening to what we badly needed but President Cory Aquino looked somewhere else.

One of these calls was to repudiate all Marcos-tainted debts massively incurred by his cronies through several behest and suspect loans. Cory, lacking the basic instinct of a housewife beseeched by increasing debts, listened instead to the advice of her economic advisers who encouraged and introduced the idea of borrowing more.

Then the total debt was a whopping $25.26 billion. This was equal to 80 % of the country's gross national product according to Jeck Cantos, an economist at the Action for Economic Reform, an NGO think tank.[39] That's like, if you are a farmer paying your debt, giving away your eight cavans of palay out of 10 you're producing to feed a family already starving.

The Core of Early FDC

The core members who constituted the early activists of FDC were from the school of economics and college of public administration, U.P., the Makati business circle and assorted NGOs. If I remember right there were Butch Montes, Maitet Diokno, Boy Tripon, Bong Mendoza, Men Sta. Ana, Jeck Cantos, Lidy Nacpil, the latter then representing Bagong Alyansang Makabayan (or BAYAN). The large part of the original hand-work was Bayan's. Perhaps one or two are missing in this list. Liling Briones, who later became National Treasurer under the scandal-wracked Estrada government, played almost like the spokesperson for the group being in front of the TV camera during street marches.

Earlier these people were mostly businessmen, academics, liberal, militant, nationalist Filipinos. It was a mix of progressive thinkers and tinkerers of neo-economics. Some were in-and-out of the influence of the NDF's 12-Point Program until the early 1990's when the split in the Left started to be publicly embarrassing.

---

[39] Interview, 8 July 2004; see also *IBON Facts and Figures* 1988.

The attempt to place the FDC under conscious NDF direction did not succeed. Aside from being independent-minded and highly individualistic, many of these people were incorrigible "Marxist-liberals," an aporic combination.

Losing Battle with Corporate Capital

The mass movement was zeroing in on debts that finally tied even the generation of unborn Filipinos to this obligation. The issue was hotly debated. It was between those who claimed that these debts did not benefit the people and demanded for their complete abrogation. And those others who looked at the IFIs like IMF, WB, etc. as the source of development funds needed by a bankrupt government inherited by the housewife-turned-president. If I remember right, the FDC was pushing for selective debt repudiation, its early position.

What was not evident at that time was the mass movement had no visible alternative economic mechanisms to replace the corporate cronies running the economy. They continued to control big businesses and profitably licking clean the boots of the new government. In short, cronyism did not die under Cory Aquino. It gained a new shine.

What was the alternative? FDC supported Joker Arroyo and Edcel Lagman who were then in Congress working for the repeal of R.A. 1177. This is the law guaranteeing automatic appropriation for the country's debt payment. Cory Aquino vetoed the Arroyo-Lagman bill. Solita Monsod, then a member of the Aquino cabinet had a solution but considered radical at that time: put a cap on debt payment. This slow bleeding process recommended by her did not get Aquino's approval either. Monsod, a woman of strong common sense, quit the Cabinet.

Obviously the president had ears for other a Western-educated, corporate-loving advisers who not unlike her were scared to displease the foreign creditors and less concerned with thousands of Filipinos who hew wood and carry water to their homes.

The ameliorative NGOs—those that pursued socio-economic programs, income-generating projects, etc. were either too weak or too enamored with various foreign assistance and doles to continue fighting the resurgent power of corporate capital.

The NDF had a program of government but this lacked concrete mechanisms to be put into instant operation. Its socio-economic programs like its politics depended on the direct participation of the masses. When the country was in critical transition only a number of people could be relied on to carry these effectively. The political books that guided many of us militants were devoted to organizing people not re-organizing the economy.

A Call for Political Blitz Was Unheeded

The Aquino government or at most the people constituting the cordon sanitaire around the president were walking along the Palace corridor worried about multifarious threats; like another coup? This was 1989. When would the uncontrolled military faction strike next? Obviously the foreign debt obligation was there like an old clock's pendulum ticking, a reminder that the creditors would be coming again next year, telling us of interest due.

A time for launching another coup perhaps? Army officer Greg Honasan was lurking in the shadows. Why was Aquino passively reacting to a political solution, drastic and effective, to the country's foreign debt and perversely sticking it out with the IFIs? Possible answer: she had no faith in the masses that placed her in Malacañang Palace. Is the Marcos law requiring automatic appropriation to pay debts an impregnable legal fortress protecting rich creditor countries? Even today (2005) congressmen hide and cover behind their collective stand; their people bribed and silenced by ignorance of what's behind their various perks and pork, the scandalous so-called "countryside development fund."

Did the government insist as the masses did that it washed away these debts? We were not lacking of examples for this kind of solution. A few countries like Brazil and Argentina and much earlier Poland brandishing the mass mobilization of militant *Solidarity* got their moratorium on their massive debts. These countries were not punished for demanding debt erasures as the Aquino advisers were scared the Philippines would be when taking such path.

A long line of financial negotiators behind Cory Aquino, Fidel Ramos, Joseph Estrada maintained paying these debts as their priority. Now President Gloria Macapagal Arroyo with a new mandate to continue the presidency for six more years apparently knows better her economics than all previous presidents although this kind chortles the country in the short run. When will real change come? The foreign debt system has become apart of the nation's life, a veritable albatross around the masses' collective neck.

When a political blitz was called for, i.e., more concerted actions, more pressures and marches by organized masses under the progressive banners, a new stream of NGOs had a different thing in mind. The ameliorative NGOs egged by opportunism and purblind goals opted to organize to form a coalition of NGOs hunting for funds. I look at them as secret partners of corporate capital as their ways have become like an acquisitive corporation.

The notorious example was the group called Code-NGO in the late 1980s. The group practically captured almost all the influential funding agencies (local and foreign) to rally behind its dubious ameliorative enterprises, community programs which were mostly undisguised doles.

Meanwhile, in the countryside, land occupation was popular. Landless farmers started to apportion marginal lands as their own, ahead of land reform. In cities organized resistance to cronies taking back their stolen wealth and other forms of properties, mass opposition to government appointments by President Corazon Aquino of known Marcos people, etc. These were weapons in the hands of the politically strong organized masses that Cory Aquino now had wished had not grown stronger, and should be quiet instead.

Was corporate take-over an option? How about re-writing the rules of engagement with foreign creditors? The FDC seemed to lack a good re-conceptualization on how to deal with past debts and the deepening foreign indebtedness. Its tendency to fall back on abstract econometrics instead of focusing on the political economy was alienating a lot of mass followings.

Superseding the issue of foreign debt write-off was the recurring crisis brought by the oil price increases. The demand from several workers' groups and transport drivers to roll back oil prices rose like a thunderclap. A new short-lived group called Coalition against Oil Price Increase (CAOPI) was launched with the militant KMU, a jeepney drivers' group called PISTON, CACP and other consumer organizations. This was the persistent climate that strengthened the need for the FDC to re-conceptualize its programs and strategies.

The objective condition developing in the nation's contemporary crisis worsened especially for the middle and lower classes, the fixed salaried and daily wage earners. All of them were being hammered twenty-four hours by the increasing costs of utilities. These included electricity, water services, transport, cooking gas, etc. The government's answer to its massive debts was to privatize government owned and controlled corporations or GOCCs. They are groaning as milking cows of politicians, corrupt bureaucrats and cheating contractors and suppliers.

GOCCs were created precisely to service the needs of the people at affordable cost. This was no longer the case. Many were heavily indebted beyond reckoning especially the biggest electricity producer-supplier NAPOCOR whose foreign debts shaped the direction of the rest of the economy. The government this time aimed to pass the immense debts to the users of these services (read: Filipinos consumers). But we are going fast forward to the fiscal crisis that was beginning to unravel during the year 2000 and beyond.

Other economic issues that had engaged the FDC activists in the late 80s and the 90s included the introduction of value added tax or VAT, oil taxes, budget deficits, etc. The present decade of the new millennium presents the ramification of what could happen with the government's deadly triune started by FVR: *deregulation, privatization and liberalization* in an economy unable to feed, shelter, educate adequately millions of its citizens who are pushed to the margins of subsistence living.

Future of FDC as an Emancipatory NGO

What did the FDC miss? An explanation came from some of its ex-members. Sometime ago the FDC liked to bill itself as a coalition to accommodate all sorts of political blocs. It went into coalition activities with these blocs. It embraced NGOs and people's organizations like BAYAN, socialist–oriented militants of BISIG, and assorted old-timer communists group called CONFREEDEM, etc. in a grand coalition that lasted a little beyond the day.

"It involved different personalities and political blocs. It was impossible to create order. How do you traffic such a mess?" asked Rene Raya now with Action for Economic Reform (AER).[40]

Some FDC officials rationalized this by saying that the group believed that no one force could change the Philippine condition, a conviction that doomed any solidarity work. RC Constantino, one time member of the FDC board, was a meticulous analyst of assumptions like his late father around whose circle we activists often sat intently listening. His method at first was tolerated but eventually it exasperated RC's colleagues at FDC no end.

Liling Briones, often seen by the public on TV, although conscientious in mass education about debt issues, was short of interest in mass organizing. It is an important ingredient in the mass movement that had been placed unfortunately by the early FDC in the backburner. This put FDC lagging behind even before the 1990s split had occurred in the Left.

Lately, FDC has been catching up again with new issues. it is taking center stage in current advocacy under its new leadership. It is focusing on the lobby work in Congress assuming the politicians would listen and act. Or, is FDC underestimating the politicians' risibility?

The last I heard about it was that FDC was organizing in the communities like rallying the urban poor against increasing cost of utilities like water, electricity, cooking gas. Better late than never.

These issues were made for FDC. The new FDC is working to make consumers equity owners of corporations whose services millions of consumers pay and, therefore, it is calling for rights of representation in the boards of

---

[40] Interview at AER office, Q.C. 9 July 2004.

utility firms like Meralco and Maynilad, the electricity and water corporations respectively. These firms are regularly soaking thousands of consumers with monthly bills they could hardly afford.

Again, FDC should not fail to look hard at thousands of electric cooperatives in the provinces and study if there is another democracy manqué in their decision-making and choices of officials elected. It is called tuning-up for legislative entrance through the Party List system. Is it worth it?

Chapter 8

International Dimension of the Mass Movement

SOLIDARITY work between peoples reflects understanding of issues that affect them. The search for justice for the oppressed people continues, prevails. This has a unifying impact on the consciousness of everyone involved. My foreign contacts advance the mass movement at home.

Part I

Before closing the 1980s, I would like to go back and focus on networking of NGOs especially with those outside the country. Churches, human rights groups, here and abroad, were immensely responsible for funding the travels that made possible direct contacts with various socio-political groups especially in Europe and the U.S. These formations and the people behind them were attuned similarly to the struggles that were political, economic and cultural in the Third World; in some there was special concern for the Philippines. Their continuing interest was the basis for the funding infrastructure we built among these partners. They made possible rich contacts with other social movements. There were problems but we learned to resolve them as they came.

*The focus was in the late 1980s. These observations were personal. The following excerpts quoted from a **Journal** would give neither beginning nor end of the account except in the airport or train station or bus terminal where a friend usually waited to pick this traveller-activist.*

10th September '87 (*Waiting in Dublin Airport*)

This diary will be going backward for three days, that is, September 10, 9, and 8. This seemed to be the only way (and the only time) I could take a breather and recall what had gone by the last three days in the course of my trip here before taking off again. It's 10:25 a.m. at the airport waiting for my flight back to London.

It's good to start with my guide who is a young ex-Columban priest. He stayed in Negros Occidental, it's almost 10 years and because we speak common Ilongo dialect, a quick warm affinity grew between us like water seeking its own level.

He had been a great help to me and to the movement. He was equally interesting, articulate and well informed. Our last minutes on the way to the airport was spent by him giving me the "political structures" (his phrase) of his work in Ireland. He cautioned me about certain Trotskyites (pls. see Glossary) in Dublin who have been working closely with the Irish teachers' group. He seemed to have the same apprehension that verged on a healthy phobia of the hidden agenda of these ideologues inhabiting usually in the French capital. This was not the first time I heard of this and I didn't think it was the last. My going to Paris was an invitation to more of these precautionary tales against the "Trots."

Jimmy Martin, ex-priest, is a very conscientious host and a bad cook. He narrated to me his pampered life in Negros.

"Raul," he told me, "I was spoiled as a priest. I've never been able to do things for myself. In Negros somebody washes for you, serves you food before the table, cleans the dishes, makes your bed and attends to your other needs. Everything was done by others from morning till night mostly by hard-working helpers in the house."

I was myself born in Negros and grew up a few miles from the foot of Kanlaon volcano where I spent the most formative years of my life during the Second World War. This was early 1942 up to 1944 under its rain forests when there were still tall hardy woods before they were ravished by big loggers.

Jimmy questioned me this morning if boiled mongo needs to have crushed "loy-a" (ginger). He met an equal in the cooking "art." I told him that onions, tomatoes and garlic in boiled mongo are ok but not ginger; a personal taste. Breakfast was fried eggs, banana, orange juice, and an Irish version of oatmeal with milk.

We lived in a house, a duplex, its back facing the railroad tracks right at the other side of the shrubby fence with vines clambering. The weather was very cold by comparison with Baguio (the only place I can compare with in foreign countries I find myself shivering.) Jimmy lent me his thick sweater and layers of blankets. Below my sheet was an electric blanket that was reinforced by an electric heater flaming red.

We visited last **9th September** two major teacher groups: primary teachers and higher education teachers. We were met by a bureaucratic visage. The primary teacher federation being especially under right-of-centre kind of leadership. The higher education General Secretary was sympathetic and mentioned the common anti-imperialist sentiment of both the Filipinos and the Irish. The primary school federation is also a member of the WCOTP, the worldwide teacher group that ACT was affiliated with. I was about to draw up some cooperation when I invited him to work out a more specific program on human rights for teachers which we could present to the WCOTP that the people in Morge, Switzerland seem interested. He promised.

Last night I met the teachers' committee of the Philippine Support Group (PSG). There were five of us, and we spent the evening synthesizing the results of my day's visits with the Irish teachers' unions. We recalled some funny incident when the day before we found ourselves (three of us) in a meeting of do-gooders who seemed to have a lot of funds for third world projects, etc. Cookies were served; also tea and coffee. The problem of the "Trots" came up again which made Jimmy observe when we were alone that "some of these people in the teacher committee seemed devastatingly naive."

This is the day **8th September** following my arrival the previous night. It is my first Dublin in daytime. The city has the patina of tradition; streets are clean and wide. We ate for lunch in a pub, a favourite place for the Dubliners with bourgeois inclination. Another Dubliner, Michael, a college teacher, was introduced to me. He was in RP about nine months ago. While he does not belong to the Philippine-Irish Group, he expressed willingness to contribute some efforts to the movement. I noted that he is a good contact in higher education teacher groups.

Jimmy drove me home one evening. Earlier we toured the city, passed the exclusive school (Belvedere) where James Joyce used to study. I felt romantic when we crossed the river Liffy (full of history and literary links in my mind, all of which were coming from what I could remember of Joyce's works): *another instance of literature defining my experience.* This has always been the case in these travels. It is not what you derive from your ephemeral experience of monuments and bridges, parks and exotic streets. The walls of the buildings are dark bricks and city ordinances require the maintenance of this old look in their facades for new buildings and renovated ones, also ornate steel lamp posts, and yes, prostitutes leaning against them at night according to Michael. (I did not see one myself.) Michael drove a car with a remote control anti-theft gadget to ward off "joy riders". This was "popular" here several months back. (I thought of "carnapping" back home.) Dublin is a sparsely populated city and I did not think the ordinary Dubliner thinks or acts or behaves any different from the way Dubliners of James Joyce that I know so well from his fiction. Jimmy Martin and Michael seem to have jumped out from his pages.

I met on this day a woman teacher from the Teacher Union of Ireland (TUI). Her name was Anne whom Ding Q. had met several months back. It seemed that Ding Q. was remiss in writing to the TUI about the fate of an arrangement with local teachers in RP. This was supposed to facilitate the flow of (modest) funds, etc. I've to take over from here and assume the responsibility of nagging people back home with my teacher group (ACT) to immediately acknowledge future assistance. I've even had to write a thank you note for the funds I've not received, etc. just to mollify some union members who were anxious to know what had happened to teacher organizers they sent money back home. This was called "repair work in international solidarity!" I hope I would not be doing more of the same in the future.

I'll end these notes here. They suggest how I usually spend my time waiting in airports for the next flight. Now, it's about time to get back to real life in real time that started this looking backward as reverie about what had transpired since three days ago.

3:05 11 Sept '87 (London)

The train left Victoria station. It reached Dover port two hrs later. In 1985, I passed the same place except that I look the ferry to Amsterdam and saw the white cliffs of Dover made immortal by Mathew Arnold's poem.[41] This time the train took me through the tunnel and could see only the backside of the famous cliff or at least the narrow side of it as the train careened along the coast. Nothing exceptional could happen in a train except a collage of images in the mind as one remembers sensationalized news stories about collisions. These of course added spike to an unresolved anxiety that always accompanied me.

The Hovercraft looked festive at a distance. It is usually a propelled sea monster that could leap and speed through waves with ease as this hardly plowed deep into the water. Less resistance, more speed. We arrived at the other side of the channel at Boulonge and from here took another train to Paris. The trip was supposed to take two hrs and should therefore arrive by 9 p.m. (add 1 hr from London time). The French train was smoother than the one in London reaching Dover.

A few more things I wrote down on my crowded notebook: duty-free shops at Dover allowed me to unload my English money. I bought soap, a carton of biscuits (Nona, my sister-in-law running the London office for DFA prepared me a sandwich and a left-over salad from last night's dinner) and these should re-enforce the continental spirit of a hungry traveller like me. I bought a book by Suskind, a young German writer who has been a rave in Europe recently according to the blurb. Then I sidled to the perfumery where the woman was dispensing samples. I borrowed one bottle of perfume, inspected it with interest and care and this being a sample bottle sprayed myself liberally. That

---

[41] It runs like this: *"Ah, love, let us be true /To one another/ for the world, which seems /To lie before us like a land of dreams. . . /Hath really neither joy, nor love, nor light, /Nor certitude, nor peace, nor help for pain; /And we are here as on a darkling plain /Swept with confused alarums of struggle and flight, /Where ignorant armies clash by night."*.

should take care, I thought, of the need to take a bath immediately upon arrival. The fragrance had now accompanied me.

I arrived in Paris Nord train station; was tired, anxious and groping in my mind whether I should take a taxi (and how much this will fleece me) or to call Marianne first. (Marianne needs a separate story and how she has been assisting Third World activists like me yenning for revolution when they're in Paris.) The only telephone that operated in coins was in use where to get one. A long line of travellers who just disembarked from the other trains signalled a long and late evening.

The night waited for me and darkness seemed slow. This kind of anxiety was not new to me but the tension was not mentally comforting. The language problem was an uneasy hump as Frenchmen usually refused to understand my two-semester worth of French.

I arrived in Marianne's place near Sorbonne before 11 o'clock, the rooftops of Paris giving me an outline indescribably eerie. A Frenchman who is in RP recently was also there. I arrived after dragging myself up the fifth floor. He tried to show off some Filipino menu he tried that evening. This would remind me of home. Marianne served boiled balatong, (I don't know what they call this in Paris), cheese, red wine (which I refused thinking of my uric acid level) and a hurriedly cooked water-drenched rice; it was half-way porridge, this way was one disastrous thing French friends in solidarity work could do. Marianne prepared dinner when she knew I was already at the station. She was expecting me two hours earlier.

The following day, Saturday I left for Lyon by train; 450 km south of Paris in two hours; first class accommodation on my Eurorail pass which cost me $550 in London, a wrong place to buy it. I was advised next time to get a Eurorail from my country of origin (Manila) because it's cheaper there.

I reached Lyon after a beautiful, comfortable ride and I was still too tired to enjoy continuously the scenery. As usual with most countryside I've seen in some parts of Europe, it was pastoral and always deeply moving. One's critical mind is set at rest, waiting to be seduced more. When one gets too tired and things get embroiled with creeping monotony, falling asleep is a sweet seduction.

Yvette together with another girl met me at the station. Yvette is the woman with Pascal when the latter stayed at the house in Manila when I left for Dhaka. She spoke English well, being a teacher in English. She also served as being Pascal's companion-translator, a good cover as I later discovered Pascal himself was fluent in English. They lived together on weekends. One time I passed by the office room and caught a glimpse of the two necking. I was not sure who was embarrassed among us. Pascal looked consumptive and pale and I suspected this had connection with his work in the chemical company, the biggest in France: Rone-Poulenc.

The two historic rivers, Roance and Soane, embraced the town. Lyon itself had a great history associated with these twin water bodies. There was a mountain range in the margin of the city and ancient buildings, yes, and churches on its cliff. This cliff cut across a kilometre long tunnel, built after the Algerian war. It connected the new suburbs with the old city. My hosts took me around the part of the city where people converged to eat on a Sunday evening. Streets were cobbled and paved with stones of ancient vintage. The brick walls looked ancient and the architecture paid homage to the 16th century tradition. I was told the merchants of Lyon used to transact businesses in the hidden caverns of these old-looking buildings each of which was connected by narrow passages. People (ancient capitalists that they were) used them to move around, away from public view, not in the open street to transact business.

There were five of us and we seated ourselves around a small table with awning overhead. It was outside in the street and the evening was young, light and pleasant. Everyone poured wine into his glass. This was a national pastime and a way of giving homage to a native product, the French way of patronizing their own wine, I suppose. I was conscious of my uric acid and spared myself developing the habit; nothing anti-French to it.

From my companions' explanations of the menu, the foods without seeing them, sounded good. Later, came a huge sausage-looking roll that was filled with shredded intestines and liver. I ordered one that in the translation sounded "eggs and cheese and sauce" by somebody who was reading the menu for me. (My two semesters of French in Diliman did not help much to guide my gustatory bent.) In a few minutes, actually cut short by ceaseless talking, the plates arrived with the usual vegetable mixed salad, bread, cheese and glasses of water. Each one had a different order and an exchange of pieces from one's own plate to another took place. It was international camaraderie thru the stomach.

13 September (Sunday)

It was a full day. I met with members of the three networks of BAM (Brothers for All Men). A network is composed of one town plus the activist members of the local organization. People from four towns came: Lyon, Avignon, Aurilac and Marseille. I gave a "natsit" (our own slang for "national situation" presentation peppered with overtone of agitation in support of the mass movement back home.) I delivered this with a lot of flourish as my English was either too fast or too "Spanish-sounding" for the interpreter. In the afternoon, I as coordinator for Asia gave again a sectoral presentation of the eight BAM partners in Asia. The purpose of my coming to Lyon actually was to stir up the interest of members in supporting financially, morally, materially and militantly the programs of their partners back in the country. The mass movement could have been less lively without this foreign support. To some extent, I succeeded and they asked me to help them concretize their assistance.

14 September (Monday)

Philippe Blancher, a Frenchman whom I met in Dhaka with his wife a few years back, picked me up at the place in rue d'Ecole. Philippe worked in an organization that did research and consultancy. His group publishes every two months a political/economic critique. A priest founded it sometime 1942. Today, a Dominican priest, Jean Claude heads it. I talked to Philippe to encourage him to come to RP. This was sometime in January '88. His group made studies about urban housing in Indonesia, commissioned by the French government.

In the afternoon, Pascal and Guy took me to a local radio station where we had a 20-minute interview, mostly in French. My conclusion consisted of about ten sentences, translated freely by Pascal. Bayan Ko was background music from a tape, with the interviewer signalling with his two arms when to have the volume high and gradually low. More talk in French followed: about Cory, child prostitution, NPA, military operations, etc.

In the evening, I met with the gathering of pupils coming from different organizations friendly to BAM; another "natsit" followed by questions. We went home midnight followed by a long distance call to Pasay.

15 September Tuesday

We visited a consumer coop selling mostly what they call "biologic" food: natural food, no preservative, no artificial coloring, no chemical, etc. They showed me re-cycled papers turned into pads, envelopes, calendars, etc. These were more expensive than the commercially mass-produced notebooks. The political economy of recycling is not to produce cheaper consumer items but to stop/minimize pollution, promote direct conservation by the consumers. The translator (who said he was formerly a member of the French CP) told me people to patronize the store not for economic but for political reasons. Things were a little more expensive in the store.

The sales girl, actually a store volunteer gave her sale's pitch, "You're not buying a notebook. You're supporting a movement." Her group wanted to stop the MNCs from further poisoning the environment with chemicals and destroying the forests. The translator was interesting but ·convoluted. I left behind an ISAT brochure[42] and an invitation to come to RP. This volunteer comes to Lyon as part time worker in the cooperative where he is planning to put up and expand new buildings for the store. He serves as "technical and user consultant" to the Algerian government.

"I don't serve the French government," he emphatically told me. He sports a moustache, exhibits a huge bay window and wears faded jeans.

After lunch at BAM today, I met a staff member of BAM and a translator named Marielle. She was a native of Madagascar who was studying in a university in Lyon. She accompanied me to the train station for Avignon. I am writing these notes on a first class couch to Avignon leaving at 2 p.m. This is a 2-hr trip to the south of France.

A few more observations on French life: the French drink their coffee at home in a round bowl, which back in the Philippines we use usually for porridge.

---

[42] International Solidarity Affairs of Teachers was an ACT program inviting foreign groups to come to the Philippines to support the mass movement against dictatorship.

The toilet is located in a part of the house separate from the bathroom. One pulls down a chain and a huge gurgling sound of water comes rushing with finality to clean up. There is an elongated bread across the table the size of one's arm; this is carried unwrapped like one carries a small log: sometimes under one's armpit, sometimes swinging it in the air when one walks away from the grocery.

Avignon is about two hours away south of Lyon. I spent exactly 15 hours there, half of it sleeping. Since I arrived hours ahead of the meeting with the teachers in CFST, my guide brought me instead to a tower of the walled city. One is reminded of Intramuros in old Manila, stonewalls, moss growing in their crevices, seeds sprouting in-between adobes. One sees the Pope's residence or tall cathedral, and various types of dwellings including business houses, doctors', tourists' offices, etc. It is a mixture of Catholicism and capitalism, history and leisure. This is a reconstructed site made close to its 13th century originals. Five popes used to live here in the walled city, I was told. (I wondered why they were not in Rome.)

I met nine team members; again "natsit," then sectoral organizations and the campaign for food and freedom. Philippe, my host (another Philippe) told me that slides would be useful during campaigns. These would be shown to children in schools. When I get back to RP, I should learn how to use the camera better and perhaps buy the auto-focus video.

16 September

It is 9:25 a.m. Am on the train back to Lyon where I've an appointment with three teacher groups in the afternoon. (One teacher was interested to join ISAT and wished the school or ACT could work out an official authorization with the (RP) government for her trip. She would pay for it. She was from CFST and another two teachers who were there from FEN. (CFST is progressive: FEN has the most number of members belonging to right-of-center).

When I started from Avignon, the fog was thick. Then after three stops, the sun shone again and 20 minutes from Lyon the fog descended with grey heaviness over the wheat fields and orchards. I could see only the margin of these lands as mirrored on the other side of my train window moving faster along with me. Was this what a James Joyce's character called a parallax?

18 September, 7:00 pm., Paris

Am writing this behind the 20-foot statue of Charlemagne riding a huge horse covered in gloss green moss fronting the immense Notre Dame. It was still bright and the dark brown façade of the cathedral with numerous statues of churchmen lining stood stiff and majestic. The middle storey where more statues stood over the heads of other churchmen lining were carved on the arches of its three major entrances. It was a reminder of the massive waste of labor dedicated to the feudal values of the church. Up there in the highest end of this tall edifice kissing the sky of Paris were gargoyles. They, holy men and mythical creatures, immortalized the religious and pious oppressors of the period.

I had just finished a long sandwich stuffed with hot vegetables and sliced grilled beef. This is an old habit just to avoid going home early where my host would have to fuss preparing dinner for me.

In the morning I visited the UNESCO again; this time the education department headed by a Thai lady who spoke English (worth noting when one encounters a person speaking a language one understands.)

Yesterday I visited an old acquaintance in the Human Rights department. Senator Pepe Diokno once mentioned to me this person whom I should see when in Paris again. I met her first time in 1985. This time I handed her a note from Ka Pepe.

The Thai lady (she was petite, frail but steel-nerved and fair-skinned, possibly a Catholic as she was wearing a cross pendant) promised she would help me or ACT on a project proposal on street-theatre a la PETA. She said she would come to R.P. sometime December as soon as she could act on the project proposal I planned to submit soon enough. It was about a tool for non-formal education teaching (dramatizing) through street-theatre human rights issues. The second proposal she made was that she would invite a representative from ACT to come to Indonesia on a seminar she planned to organize sometime July-August 1988.

She suggested that the proposal for the support of ACT should be submitted directly to the Director General and preferably to be accompanied by recommendation of the National Commission of UNESCO in RP or that I should ask WCOTP for such recommendation. This could be done under a non-regular program under Programme XIII.3 "Education for Peace and Respect for Human Rights and the Rights of People."

An invitation could also be made for the UNESCO representative from the "Education for International Cooperation and Peace" section addressed to the D.G. without mentioning her name. This forewarned me to learn the ropes of the bureaucracy with international organizations.

The proposal on street theatre would have to be directly sent to her. A proposal could also be made on research on H.R. This could be addressed to Ms Yamane of H.R. division. This is the lady Ka Pepe Diokno wrote a note to. I brought this with me. I was thinking of revising the fact-finding report ACT made about the militarization of areas affecting children. I wrote it before I left Manila.

At two in the afternoon, I went to visit the FEN, the biggest education sector federation in France with half a million members. There would be a separate note for this. I had lunch (by myself) in an Italian-looking restaurant where, not knowing how to order in French much less understanding the menu, would cost me 62 francs for a lousy pizza that of course I did not finish!

1 October, 10:00 a.m.

From Bruxelles where I left early this a.m., Paul Jourez, chair of the board of BAM-Belgium, drove me to the train station. Paul was a Belgian pilot. I stayed with him in his suburban house. His wife Agnes seemed always at home preparing for his arrival from work in the early evening. They've three children and two grandchildren but were not living with them. All these from the pictures that hang on the room I occupied. I met P.J in Bangladesh in the last ACC meeting in Dhaka.

This train was supposed to reach Milan after 12 hrs from Bruxelles. There was plenty of time to write and to organize myself for the next 12 days. I noticed there was a wide gap (in the journal) since Paris. Holland was entirely unwritten. Usually this happened either because I was always pressed for time or because some discomfort in my leg had recurred during my stay in Holland. Now I've recovered and I should note down that Marianne even had to mail my Ponstan capsules from Paris. I received them four days later after the pain had left.

Someday I'm going to write an exhaustive thesis on the view of the world from the train window. While the sceneries from here were varied enough, there were some periods that framed the experiences in great monotony. This was where I took off and wrote other things, e.g. about my "official meetings."

There were two Italian-speaking passengers with me in the train compartment. Their talks distracted me sometimes and this partly explained the rambling notes in these pages. At 4 p.m., the train left Lucerne, Switzerland. The view of the lake from the mountainside where the railroad tracks ran on its edge was breathtaking. The houses were far apart but in some parts, houses were closer. Immediately below the train window was a narrow cliff lined with fruit trees. In parts that were not steep, there were little meadows. Parallel roads run encircling the edge of the lake just like the rail tracks and the eyes would fall glidingly to rest on the still dark green lake.

I recalled what a Swiss friend Jurge told me: "In Switzerland, the cows graze on the hills, the capitalists make more money on the lowlands." He said this in a form of the Swiss "nasit."

This was about 20 minutes out of Lucerne, separated by dark green trees covering the promontory. The sun sparkled against the waters in dazzling brilliance. Across a grey, imperceptible shadow was another tall mountain range, the sharp light on its edges gave out an ominous shape against the sky. This was Switzerland or part of her, not as impressive and sharp-clean as the images in the postcards but touchingly real to me from the train window.

One entered a new town and the first sight invariably was a train depot. Then another one and the dark steel beams endlessly crisscrossed one after the other, a cobweb of iron bars one finds in every industrial town in Europe. There was permanence of sameness and an infinite variety in-between that engaged without end a tired mind. It was thus that philosophy keeps one awake.

Meanwhile, the abstracting mind takes off in wonderment about humanity, nature, cruelty, love and terror. These are also real in another dimension back in the country where democracy without mercy was raped by the dictatorship.

Before lunch, the restaurant-train coach was detached and left behind. I have been subsisting on chocolate bars that I bought in Brussels yesterday. There was no water to drink in the coach where I was. I'll have to wait for Milan three hours away.

At 8 P.M. the train entered the terminal. Somebody representing my host at the end of the gangway was holding the logo of his organization. This had now become familiar to me every time I arrived in a strange city. After the brief greetings he brought me out, walking along the shaded station. We walked hurriedly to the center of a cavernous train main building where six other companions were waiting for us.

We Enter Milan

This was my first and possibly the only view of Milan for that evening. The place was inundated with lights, incandescent against the night except that this huge place gave a visitor no more than what advertising billboards could engage a mind ready to take in as much as possible in so brief a time. Following this was the ride in the car, the group having separated into two. For almost one hour we went round-and-round looking for the hotel where I was supposed to check-in.

"Now this is Milan at night," said the driver-host, Gen. Sec. of BAM in Italy. I saw nothing but burning lamps and shadows and blank walls passing past my eyes and of course the streets ahead of me and lots and lots of cars parked along the road.

"Milan in chiaroscuro" I mumbled but nobody responded. It was my first non-statement since arrival. I could hear my own words fall and stumble against the evening, shredding over the cobbled streets of this new city. My eyes wandered among the flickering darkness against the hazy horizon. Or what a horizon looks like through the windshield of the car.

We reached the hotel, registered, and climbed on the sixth floor, pushing No.3 button inside the old-fashioned glassed grilled elevator. By the look of it, this hotel was a sort of YMCA—clean, severe in its facilities, cozy enough. The bed sheets were angel-white and there was a wooden carved crucifix hung on the wall just above my headboard. It reminded me that this was not only a

Christian country but an old civilization. If accounts of travels were written from inside the hotels, there would not be much to remember worth keeping within crumpled notebooks.

I woke up with a good hot bath, the view from the window looked to be an entirely different world. Or maybe because this was a new day. I told myself this was the time to fall into temptation by straying out of the perimeter of my accustomed hotel block. I usually go round the block where my hotel is located as my first exploration of any strange city. All these after I've done washing of my socks, undershirt, shaved and did a little push-ups as if now I was ready to "conquer" Milan. I was hoping I could get back to my hotel on time for a roundtable talk at 4:00 p.m.

Before Milan, I always believed that Paris is the center of fashion and fashionable women. The Milanese is an artist in dresses. Sandro my guide exuded the spirit of living in the order of clothes as an expression of discrimination and correct judgement. Maria, maybe Sandro's girlfriend, kept the purse for the organization on matters of food, transport and miscellaneous expenses. She was a young, attractive and a warm person whose dresses (new every day in the last three days) were a blend of beauty and color, neatness and care. If I singled out this couple for these notes on fashion it was because I found them the types of many common people I met in Milan. A newly attired and expensively dressed woman in Manila, by comparison, is a female ragamuffin to the Milanese.

I arrived in the city with streets emblazoned with streamers announcing the publication of a new fashion magazine. A Congress of Designers was going on in the city. This climate of fashion, with the sky colored with buntings promoting this important Milanese industry perked me up.

Part II

There is another level of experience, still on the growth and advances of the mass movement as shared by one Filipino activist. This is gleaned from the interview with a friend Nado who used to host me in Paris, circa the eighties. My notes were taken sometime early

2002 after an interview with Nado (not his real name). He is a Filipino resident in the French capital.

Nado was again in Manila briefly. I knew about his coming from Lu B when I asked her I wanted to see somebody who is or was an old hand in the PSG in Europe. She mentioned his name and told me he'd be in Manila. I was glad about it because of the suggestion that Nado is still sympathetic to the Left. One never knows when the political pirouetting could happen. A month later, when Nado returned to Paris after my interview I asked Lu if she had seen him. She said no; he did not appear in some pre-arranged meeting. I knew right away that Nado was avoiding something and was I glad I caught up with him earlier.

27 September 2003

Over lunch with his folding aluminum cane that shortens and that also serves as a seat when he's tired, Nado opened the interview by giving me a long background of his involvement in Europe. More or less of what he knew of the movement, where he became an active part.

Nado's sister (or wife?) was my guide in my sojourn in Paris in early 80's. It was my second time to miss the real Paris. It was Paris I so often watch in wonderment in many travel posters.

I was not particularly enamored with the real Paris (that came later when I left the City and was back in Manila). I did not show interest in the great Louvre or the Eiffel Tower or the Opera House or the Notre Dame, all of which I told my host I could enjoy seeing in post cards or in reading literate travel books. I find this mental frame useful in order to focus on what it was I was going to foreign lands for. I don't carry an image of myself travelling comfortably like a well-heeled tourist.

If I were a stranger with a purpose in the Philippines, I'd abhor to be taken to the Rizal Monument, the Intramuros, to a ride in a Kalesa or drive to Banaue or Pagsanjan to see the "wonders of the country." This would only divert me away from the real spirit of the people's way of life, their hospitality, friendliness, kindness to those who need help, and miss listening to their heart crying on top of a garbage heap in Smokey Mountain trying hard to survive poverty and oppression. In brief, no activist would like to exchange the real experiences with sanitized tourism.

I had missed the tourist spots but in return had been rewarded richly with something Filipinos in Europe and the Dutch, French and German friends could gladly gain and share. They were the ones who hosted me in the Philippine Support Groups all over the continent.

Sometimes, one met other strangers. In Paris, I became close to a Vietnamese exile running away from the Saigon government. She was not a PSG. I met her in the plane when I had a stopover in Bangkok. We were together in the flight to Paris. She had been in Paris for years now she told me in her almost incomprehensible English. I tried hard to interface her shaken English with my tourist book French, and no doubt with the atrocity of my pronunciation of that otherwise beautiful language. We became close friends and developed in the brief 24 hrs together sitting beside each other in a sort of les liaisons dangereuse. Was this a distraction from one's purpose? Such meeting relieved me of the anxiety inherent in political travel.

Now, my interview with my informant from Europe: Nado started his narration with the 1960s when he was with a study group in which he actively participated. The Filipinos in the U.S. were nationalistic to start with. He mentioned Carlos Bulosan during this period. Sonny San Juan's study of Bulosan surfaced in my thoughts. His criticisms of CB's early works brought out the conditions of Filipinos in the "States" picking grapes on dirt wages.

In the early 70's Nado said the KDP prospered. The name "Bruce" and "Melinda" came up. I don't know them personally but lately these became familiar. Bruce was said to be KM. He did organizing in the West Coast when martial law was declared. The KDP developed into cadre organization as a leading core group within a larger mass movement on anti-war in Vietnam and FQS issues in RP. The martial law regime drove several Filipino political activists to the U.S. Their groups coalesced with the KDP then active in San Francisco. This later expanded the anti-ML coalition to the East Coast and finally became one U.S.wide movement, I was told.

This Anti-Martial Law Coalition (AMLC) in the U.S. created a political stirring but eventually split. Some persons in the movement especially in the

KDP had "identity problem." Some of them advocated for a framework useful for an American revolution and the Philippine revolution because a group called "The line of March" planned to set up a new U.S. party. Other persons strongly believed the group should support specifically the Philippine revolution-in-the-making, the anti dictatorship mass movement. They organized exposure programs by sending young Filipinos and Americans to the Philippines. They encouraged them to bring cash to aid the mass movement in the country. An undetermined amount flowed into the Philippine movement in the late 70's. This assistance included attempts to purchase some hard wares in the U.S. for the underground struggle in the countryside and urban centers. Left romanticism and reality started to get mixed up at this stage. All these occurred under the milieu of the anti-war movement in the U.S.

Meanwhile both Catholics and Protestant groups from Europe especially from West Germany, Poland and the Netherlands were expressing sympathy for the workers in the La Tondeña strike sometime early 70's. The news reached them about the worker's historic struggle under the repressive climate of martial rule. This was the basis for the broadening of European contacts.

Several European volunteers and church people became active members in the mass movement supporting Filipino striking workers. This sympathy developed and expanded to other neighboring European states. While the CPP was scouring for arms, what it got abroad was more volunteers desiring to join people's organizations and supporting these in terms of funds, logistics, organizing campaigns, prop materials, etc. This followed on the heels of Eljay's (not his real name) making the rounds among friendly Europeans.

Nado told me that it was the Dutch and the (West) Germans especially from Bonn and Stuttgart who were eager to support the mass movement on issues affecting the urban poor. Eljay was hampered not because he had less contact but because he was sent to look for arms. What he generated instead were more volunteers and various logistics minus the firepower hardware. To reduce meetings with these eager volunteers, mostly church people, Eljay moved himself to Italy sometime 1979-1980.

The problem of the CPP deepened temporarily. While scouring for arms it was harvesting more warm bodies to join the mass movement. It was not exactly a success story for those dreaming of AS. Many of these volunteers after a brief immersion in Metro Manila and some selected towns in the countryside returned to Holland and some to Germany. They carried a better picture of the mass movement they were supporting. But the problem did not resolve itself.

The burning enthusiasm for the mass movement in the 80's continued to heighten the spirit of the strategists in Utrecht. They decided to project the National Democratic Front (NDF) as part of the Permanent People's Tribunal. The PPT was a multinational gathering of intellectuals, lawyers, writers and libertarians that aimed to form a public court to try state leaders who have committed grave crimes against other people. Marcos was one target. It was organized to try the dictator before the eyes if not of the world at least before the eyes of the Europeans. Nado told me the PPT was a sort of "Civil Society" of the period.[43]

PPT while Europe-based included prestigious personalities coming from Africa and Latin America. PPT was also a reaction to the United Nations which has been inadequately equipped in protecting oppressed people. One important work was to highlight the struggle in East Timor, an issue the activist believed was neglected by the U.N.

The preparation for the PPT was done in the Philippines in constant consultation with Eljay who was then in Italy. The group in RP prepared for the main projects, passport papers ("including pants and shirts"), testimonies, money, people to be deployed who were all going under the looming shadows of martial law repression.

The PPT played a more pressing role to Eljay by causing the latter to shift his activities to being NDF's spokesperson. Instead of seeking arms for the New People's Army at home his role is now to project the NDF abroad. His frequent travels in Europe opened a number of diplomatic relations with new contacts with foreign governments and funding groups. He was received by several European leaders like Mitterand of France, Papadopolous of Greece, Khadafy of Libya. The Front surfaced as a legal organization in Europe and almost like "a government in exile" as Nado put it.

---

[43] Nado was using the expression "civil society" when he was describing to me the formation in Europe and was unaware that the phrase has gained a bad reputation among the ND's locally. The expression is now connected with the EDSA II people who helped, among many others in the Left and Right, put to power then Vice President Gloria Macapagal Arroyo to the presidency. Many of these people then were waiting on the wings to be appointed to juicy positions. This was how the tag "Civil Society" attached itself to this group and gained a bad taste in the mouth..

Meanwhile the KDP expanded in North America like Canada and in the south in Mexico in the late 70s. In 1979, a real conflict surfaced between the NDF and the KDP. In 1981, NDF-CPP set up a new structure and leadership in the U.S. The conflict was rooted in the issue of "the line of march," who followed who?

A vertical split in the U.S. front happened. Most KDP people were U.S. citizens, many were formerly Filipinos who got a clean documentation against those who were in temporary exile or continued to be undocumented, conscious of their hiding from the law; "tago-ng-tago." They were called TNT in local argot.

The rapid recognition of the NDF in Europe caused a problem. To adapt to expanding needs, Eljay started recruiting Europeans to become part not only of the Philippine Support Group (PSG) but also as members of the NDF. Then something unexpected turned out. Europeans would outnumber Filipinos inside NDF Europe and hampered the NDF in such work as embassy-type of representation and organizing of such overseas Filipinos in Europe. It would also hamper the work of such support groups and make them more "exclusive" (read: European-dominated).

Demonizing the Trotskyites

Pierre Rousset, a French activist and writer with knowledgeable experience on Vietnam, supported the movement in Europe. Pierre was married to a Filipina, a close friend of Sister Mary John of St. Scholastica College in Manila. Pierre was strongly influential in the French support group for the Philippines mass movement. He was a well-known Trotskyite, and this group of activists seemed to be anathema to Filipinos in the core of the NDF. As early as 1980 CPP decided to exclude the Trotskyite "1000 percent" using Nado's over-arching expression.

For purely ideological reason the CPP cannot accept the Trotskyite although many agree (especially those who had direct contact with Pierre) that he was an amiable and accommodating personality. I, myself, got into the warm personality of this Frenchman. The acquaintance was preceded by a "travel re-orientation" from somebody in Utrecht before my train ride to Paris.

This "warm nice character" and his group were thoroughly demonized by the NDF in Holland.

The role of Nado was to implement the decision of the party, i.e., cleansing the European contacts from the "virus of Trotskyism" in all levels wherever the NDF had gained support in Europe. He believed this was his major task. On the other hand, Eljay and wife called around a number of European friends. Of course, this was no overnight work. The European support groups were easier to get around, but Filipinos living in Europe were difficult to recruit according to Nado. Many of these Filipinos were apolitical. The NDF was to "import" more Filipino volunteers from RP and bring them to Europe. Most of them were wanted by Marcos. Their names lined up the hit list of the military minions of the dictator. They applied for political asylum in Holland. Holland had a great tradition in housing peoples from countries that were oppressive and their leaders tyrannical.

Nado initiated putting up the international version of NDF's *Liberation*, a magazine of interest to activists and military in Holland. Jun Tosong (a moniker), another political exile, assisted him to set up the CPP structure within the NDF. This included a CPP department based in Europe. The reaching out to Filipinos in Europe had to take a serious turn with many Filipino migrant workers.

Another dilemma surfaced. To concentrate on Europeans or Filipinos since the PSG composition was both? This was a simple organizational problem but what further weighed it down were the ideological dregs. You stir hard enough and Marxism whirls on the surface in a rainbow of political persuasions that could thicken academic books whenever you try to write about them. Nado concentrated on organizing the Filipino migrant workers. His meeting me at the railway station one morning sometime early 1980s was one of these chores. This arrangement would allow the European host to take me around to meet new "friends" from the Mauritius Islands, Bangladesh, Brazil, Peru and others. They were a slew of romantic revolutionaries that could pepper any memoir of the mass movement.

The European component of the PSG was principally responsible for broadening contacts interested in sending assistance to support nationalist and democratic Cause-oriented Groups (COGs). Funds were funnelled to the Philippine COGs through foreign assistance of governments, the churches in

Europe and human rights groups. Many of these were responsible for hosting Filipinos abroad, especially those visitors who were active in or sympathetic to the mass movement.

In the 80s, the CPP-NDF formed the international department on RP to handle liaison work and supervision of different groups based abroad. There were three major groupings: North America, Europe-Africa and Asia Pacific. It was in 1980 that Nado formed the Europe-African and North American groups. According to Nado, Alex formed the Asia-Pacific group; later run by Rusty (not his real name). Nado left for Europe in 1983.

Beginning 1983, Nado stayed in Germany for two months, in France for one year, and Holland for two years. One of the difficulties in organizing in the international arena was identifying your friends and enemies. What is the role of the support group and Filipino migrants? Was USSR a friend or foe? There were no clear-cut answers. One resolved these questions along the way. The experience glowed with opportunities, like possessing a refugee passport or document issued by the U.N. Often these were genuine passports with *nom de guere*.[44]

With regard to the U.S.S.R. earlier and up to 1977, the comrades in Europe were still quoting the USSR ideologues. Joe Sison looked forward to an invitation to the 100th anniversary of the October Revolution in Moscow.

Unluckily he did not get this longed for invitation. The CP in Russia and its allies were warmer to the old PKP, many of whose members since the end of the 1950s were already serving time in military stockades or out in the cold lying low or doing odd jobs. Algiers, France, Czechoslovakia and Cuba were all pro-USSR. The Philippine founder of the new CPP was not welcomed it seemed in these places. This unholy political snub had adverse repercussions in our international relations with the mass movement of other socialist countries.

During the period that the NDF was strong especially between 1981-1985, the CPP comrades were close to several European socialist parties, loosely affiliated with the Socialist International. Which of these were real

---

[44] Militants used genuine Philippine passports but with disguised names. Upon arrival in Europe, Filipinos would apply for asylum. If granted they were issued genuine U.N. refugee passports with their real names. When Ninoy Aquino came home from exile, he used the name "Marcial Bonifacio."

friends or putative enemies? It was a perpetual problem to our peripatetic diplomat without portfolio. He said that such role required a study of the histories of these different socialist groups and generally of mass movements in other countries.

"It was a complex problem," my interviewee confessed helplessly. He looked like a diplomat who left his portfolio in a taxi ride to the airport. He revealed however that the most reliable friends were other liberation movement activists, those who have travelled similar paths and whose countries have similar colonial history, tyrannical feudal lords and rabid imperialists. Among these were mass movements in Sahraweh (occupied by Moroco) led by the *Polisario*, another in East Timor, the Eritrean Liberation movement, and the one led by Mandela's ANC (African National Congress). Most of these have their own migrant groups actively working in Europe.

Nado had gained exceptional acquaintance with many of them, he attended their group study sessions. He also attended many of their public activities. Although some language problems existed, many of these have multilingual structures one could easily navigate to mutual understanding. My own experience, especially in Paris, was a little different. It was easier to get an answer from a Third World man for information when one was lost reading a pocket tourist guide. It would not be the case asking a tall policeman with an aquiline nose who is likely to talk to you in a language that flowed over your head like water over the duck's back.

There were three principal movements abroad supporting our domestic national struggle. One was the movement of Europeans or Americans supporting Philippine national-democratic thrusts. The second was a movement of overseas Filipinos, mostly migrant workers (see story on MIGRANTE), fighting for their rights in their own country like their right to vote in communities abroad where they are living. The third was the diplomatic movement of the NDF in building bridges with different people and putting up links with different sympathetic governments.

Along the way, these three movements got mixed up according to Nado. They posed dynamic problems. As one solves one problem at a time, they begin to unravel the political skein both for oneself and for others. They also open up novel opportunities. Often, new and more sources of support would beckon. I found Nado an incorrigible optimist.

Looking back, (this is still Nado in a short stint in Manila when I caught him for an interview) he found that the complex factors even outside the Philippines could be made to effectively serve the aims of the mass movement inside the country. This is a truism when one continues to have his feet close to the ground with the numerous COGs, NGOs, POs, "civil society" groups, etc.

Friends of Filipino People (FFP)

Networking with supporters in other countries requires one to distinguish between the country's government policy and its people. This is true in dealing with the United States where some Americans were sympathetic to the Philippine struggle in the 70s and 80s. The policy of the U.S. government was to support the dictatorship as long as President Marcos protected its military bases in the country. This kind of quid pro quo was responsible for prolonging the dictatorship. One U.S.–based American organization called Friends of the Filipino People (FFP) was a solidarity group that made more affirmative history than all the pretense of diplomatese by the country's foreign office.

One prominent member of the group is the historian-activist Daniel Boone Schirmer. His well-researched studies on R.P.–U.S. relations have become the basis of several political critiques of American vested interests in the country and how these subverted Filipino sovereignty. His short essay on Fidel V. Ramos as the "Pentagon's Friend" between, 1992 and 1997 was an eye opener on how the Ramos government practically handed over the Filipinos to their putative protectors. The role of the C.I.A. and the threat to the Philippine Constitution were grist to Schirmer's critical mill. It exposed the deepening neo-colonialism under President Ramos.[45]

---

[45] When the Senate booted out U.S. military bases in 1992, FVR came to the secret rescue through the U.S.—R.P. Defense Board established in 1958 by allowing Automatic Access under the guise of "port visits, aircrafts transits, and small unit exercises." See Boone Schirmer's *"Fidel V. Ramos, The Pentagon's Friend 1992-1997"* (p.10) printed by FFP, 1997. If you wish to know the roots of Visiting Forces Agreement (VFA) it is behind the skirt of the said Defense Board that the country inherited since the cold war days between the U.S. and the U.S.S.R.

Synthesis

FFP solidarity work was not confined to printed analyses. In some instances, FFP would send delegations to participate in several mass actions. Similar groups came from France, Germany, the Netherlands, Spain and Japan. This kind of foreign presence in street marches enriched the iconic significance of solidarity work. International participation signalled that the U.S. foreign policy was not necessarily supported by the Americans themselves. This was a strong way by which the mass movement disclosed the strength of support from international sources.

Personally I saw the issues of state repression, under-development, injustice, dictatorship, and foreign exploitation indelibly mirrored in the character of the modern state. As these were (and still are) found in other countries, their respective peoples easily located themselves in the identities of the struggles. They aspire for genuine solidarity with each other. Mass movements are branches of the same emancipatory goal of the oppressed peoples. Travels to other countries whose peoples have similar sympathies increase the effectiveness of solidarity. Exchange of militants, mass leaders and organizers as observers and/or participants in marches hugely increase understanding among peoples.

Chapter 9

Historic Split in the Left
1990s

THE IDEOLOGICAL differences among left militants slowed down the mass movement. These occurred between the advocates of MTT and the votaries of other varieties of Marxism. More sectoral groups rallied behind the NDF 12-Point Program undergoing changes. FVR repealed the anti-subversion law. Coalition politics pushed BAYAN to become the leading group among P.O.s A bombing event in New York, U.S.A. with more than a thousand deaths opened to a new discourse about to unfold: terrorism.

Repeal of Anti-Subversion Law

The NDF is one organization that surfaces or submerges at the call of the times. It gained a legal character from the recognition of it by several states in Europe. It was in the decade of the 90s when the CPP, one of the organizations under its broad political umbrella, had a chance of being recognized as a legal organization. Under Fidel V. Ramos, the anti-subversion law R.A. 1700, was repealed. This technically allowed the CPP to put out candidates for elections. It was one political party that was understood then as part of the NDF. There were nine or ten other UG member groups, independent from each other except by a common agenda as explained in the 12-Point Program of the 1970s. These included militantly organized groups like teachers, students, workers, peasants, church people, women, children, consumers, urban poor, government workers, overseas Filipino workers, etc.

In the previous decade, their acronyms were often painted in public walls with messages and epithets on the evils of the government. One example I remember clearly when I was with ACT, and enshrined in the awareness of underpaid and overworked teachers was this: "The government is the greatest oppressor of teachers!" The other was obviously coming from the paintbrush of some frustrated poet-turned-ad maker: "Muck you Farcos!" These texts etched against the city wall or placard made for lively reading during street marches.

In the 1992 presidential election and the closing of Cory Aquino's administration, several candidates vied to fit themselves into the politically worn down shoes of the hapless widow. The festive climate of national elections had returned. The NGOs responded differently. They forged broader alliances with other organizations and personalities.

Coalition Politics

Coalition politics started as early as mid 80s, especially intensifying after 1986. At the end of the decade, the real skulduggery of coalition politics emerged between four people's organizations led by BAYAN. The path was neither paved with roses nor the struggle for unity was a walk in the park. It turned out to be thornier than desired by mass movement handlers.

I had a close watch of this new development. I was with the teachers' group that hewed near the broad people's organization, Bayan.

The 1990s seemed to be the decade that the forces of the Left started to intensify their campaigns to gain further legitimacy. The aim was to participate in the open electoral processes. Block formation increased and alliance work intensified both with Left forces and traditional political parties like LP-PDP. The main problem in coalition work was how to get consensus on issues affecting divergent groups.

BAYAN's line was self-correcting as it brought the greatest number of people agreeing after free open deliberation. The largest number of its constituency, National Democrats that they were, was guided by collective decision-making. The bottom line has always been **class analysis** of a wide range of social problems: who is the class oppressor, who is the oppressed?

Bukluran sa Ikauunlad ng Sosyalistang Isip at Gawa (BISIG) was formed in 1986, a year after BAYAN. It was originally an assembly of Christian democrats, Marxist catechists, academic enthusiasts and a slew of independent-minded socialists aiming to promote their programs. The people within the group created composite currents of multidirectional ideas. It was a formula that created its own problem. The dynamics within could be harmonized not on the level of principles but be saved by tolerance and mutual forgiveness. The un-euphemistic name of this process was accommodation. Since BISIG believed that no one force could change society, the organization decided to enter into coalition politics. With that decision, the fun had begun.

There is an article in Conjuncture of March-April 1990, published by the Institute of Popular Democracy explaining the thrusts of these major groups that decided to join the legal electoral fray. That part about BISIG could have been better explained by its ideologue Ronald Llamas who promised this writer to do an explaining but nothing came out of it.

Another group was the Demokratiko Sosyalistang Kowalisyon (DSK) formed in 1988. Its members included Partido Demokratiko Sosyalista ng Pilipinas (PDSP), Kapulong ng mga Sandigan ng Pilipinas (KASAPI) and Pandayan para Sosyalistang Pilipinas (PANDAYAN). The group hoped to "integrate" multi-sectoral issues. It had an ambition to "reconcile" traditions within the social democratic movement. Frankly I am not certain what these "traditions" were or are. This perhaps explains why there is a smorgasbord of factions within the group.[46]

The last of these politically ambitious seekers of the votes in an open arena was the Council for Freedom and Democratic Rights (CONFREEDEM) that was formed in 1982. It is said there are 12 multi-sectoral organizations under it, some tracing roots to Crisanto Evangelista, a hero of sorts among the organized workers of the 1920s to the 1940s. Evangelista was co-founder

---

[46] In one diagram downloaded from the Internet, supposedly made by Filipinos in Utrecht, the position of BISIG surprisingly was isolated. There was no line linking it with other groups. Either this was just inadvertence or that the people in Utrecht were uninformed about this PO's current activities. This socialist group appeared unconnected to any and accused of being "reformists and reactionaries". The Internet diagram stirred a hornet's nest in the country's open Left early 2005 as it poured vinegar into old political wounds.

of the old PKP, the party that Jose Maria Sison loves to denigrate. According to Pete Baguisa, CONFREEDEM chairperson sometime in the 90s, their peasants and women were most interested in coalition politics in spite of the group's inexperience with coalition work.

All these groupings intensified the building of coalitions after 1986. Problems of increasing of numbers and tightening of the ranks characterize coalition politics. Most of the problems generated were problems of leadership; problems among leaders, many or all were familiar with Marxist doctrinal readings. This last element is the philosophical brotherhood that binds them into one political terrain. The rest is ambition, personality differences, and lastly sheer middle class pettiness that every one wanted to avoid but found it hard to shake off.

As one writer observes, "The promotion and practice of coalition politics have to reach the community level where competition over turfs between tendencies is most intense.[47] It would take years before *Bayan Muna*, springing out from the womb of BAYAN, that this victorious party-list gained a leading role among the NGOs/POs that turned into political parties, thus becoming a strong progressive part of the national electoral contest. Its militant grassroots cadres have paid with their lives more than any political party in the country's regularly violent elections. They were mostly the victims of militarization (killing, harassment and surveillance) in the areas under their influence.

Problems of the Left

The Left has the numbers, but why is it not decisively winning the electoral struggle? The explanations are many but not conclusive for the protean organizations. Among these are internal reason (subjectivism); the problems of opinionated difference among political blocs; suspicion that the people one sees leading openly are different from the ones behind. The external obstacles were the military and the CIA funding red scare; suspect linkage with the CPP; educational, i. e., awareness-raising aspect of the campaigns not given focus.

---

[47] See *"One More for Coalition Building"* by Genevieve Cacho, *Conjuncture*, March-April 1990.

At a glance, the problems were traceable to the lack of consistent theory to guide practice.

The other ideological blocs mentioned above were naturally suspicious of the National Democrats. While these others were commonly united in their electoral orientation, they were never sure of the ND position. This suspicion would subsequently be confirmed by the disjointed voices from the ND forces with *Partido ng Bayan* calling for "active participation," BAYAN-Metro-Manila Region calling for "revolution hindi (not) election" and BAYAN-National asserting "walang ilusyon sa eleksyon" (no illusion with election). I gathered these summary calls from a small book *Grassroots Electoral Politics* by Etta Rosales.[48]

Here Etta at the acme of her ND role when she was still an unblemished ND: "In assessing *Partido ng Bayan's* alliance effort, PnB limited its initiative to practically one camp of the mainstream forces, for this reason, it failed to gain political concessions . . . it otherwise would have gotten if it had opened itself to other fields of alliance work . (p. 54)

"The presence of progressive forces was not limited to the Salonga-Pimentel camp but to other parties as well. In retrospect, PnB could have taken advantage of building relations with them if it had planned this early enough.

"On the other hand there is criticism of LP-PDP in its wishy-washy attitude towards the Left. A few members asserted that if the LP-PDP had taken a more decisive stand in aligning with the Left it could have gained some victories beyond one senator and fifteen congressmen, while (*Partido Ng Bayan*) dismal performance had put it as a tail ender in the day's mainstream politics." (p. 55)

Division between RAs and RJs

In the early days of the UG split, the open mass movement weakened. There was confusion among the ranks of the activists. Many militants shied away from public life. "They are lying low," observed Satur Ocampo during an

---

[48] See P. 54, published by *Patido Ng Bayan*, April 1993.

interview in 2003. The occasion, not without a dash of historic irony, was June 12, the country's Independence Day.

What interested me when I interviewed Satur in 2003 was the growing difference between the RAs and the RJs. He glossed over the subject and focused instead on the convergence of the two highly politicized non-party formations. He said that more NGOs were naturally formed after the rift. Although the differences remained especially in the organizational forms, the two converged in their position especially on major questions of human rights and national sovereignty.

Both ranks RAs and RJs realized they needed to harness their forces against the abuses of the state agents and the continuing threat of foreign military forces (read: U.S.), the commitment to the welfare of the poor, resistance to MNC exploitation of workers and the physical resources, the control of the economy by foreign interests. All these engaged the divided Left. Included are consumer concerns, environment, women and children, the exploited condition of the urban and rural workers, the landlessness of peasants, foreign debts. All nationalist themes are sometimes echoed in both their programs whether RAs or RJs.

Other Consequences of the Split

The split in the Left weakened the mass movement, observed Angelito Mendoza. "Lito" is today a core member of the new anti-WTO group. (See FTA Story). He was one of the unheralded few who assisted on the pre-formation of the KMU in the early days of forming militant responses to the coming repression under Marcos.

The Re-affirmist documents on the split were obviously limited to cadres who had contact with the immediate circles of the CPP. The documents contained a load of indigestible stuff from both sides of the ideological track. They must have given a lot, I suspect, of headaches to the military analysts. Many mass leaders did not have copies of these documents. Those who attempted to do their own exegesis were booted out. They were called not "Rejectionists" but "the Rejected." Those who hewed and re-affirmed their MTT conviction stayed loyal to the cause of the national democratic revolution.

Others, who only heard about the controversy, picked up what they could from the grapevine. Not a few of these bits were military disinformation. They would hear that so and so, a well-known NDF activist or mass leader, had been branded "traitor" by the UG. This hurt or confused many organizers in the open mass movement. The overwhelming responses caused many to distance from the underground or take a breather from active mass organizing work.

The RJs "consolidated" their ranks. But watch the linguistic twist here. The term "*consolidation*" was used when there was a fast increase/expansion of members and the movement attain its tactical ends. This time "*consolidation*" has its opposite: the members are decreasing, the end seems farther after the split. The movement had to pause and take a new head count of what remained. Underneath what was going on was a sort of "loyalty" check, *consolidate* the few remaining members, i.e., tighten the hold on them.

In analyzing a situation whether old concepts retained old meanings or they've gained new implications, one had to be alert to the changing vocabulary used. Is being a National Democrat still one that adheres to the idea of "encircling the cities from the country side"? or, that the "protracted struggle" still retains its old sense or not anymore? The ramification is protean, unstable, often goes beyond the metaphoric.

The RJs facetiously referred to themselves as "Rejoice" slowly distancing from the mass movement but cynically edging to the marketplace or slowly surveying the government for juicy positions. Many degenerated to "liberalism" believing that being open to all sorts of ideas is just as good if not better than getting stuck to one held with nationalist or socialist conviction. They foreshadowed the "civil society" groups of the new millennium.

The plan to get in touch and keep close to people who have the same enemy as you have is good political gimmickry: it could increase votes. People Power II that made Vice President Gloria Macapagal Arroyo (GMA) president brought together strange bedfellows. I saw with secret embarrassment several BAYAN people regaling themselves between champagne toasts with the denizens of Makati business circles who love to call themselves "civil society."

As it was, the BAYAN leadership was seen celebrating "victory" among the epigones of the "civil society groups" supporting the new government. This celebration rite followed the downfall of Erap Estrada, the most popularly elected president in the history of the Republic, former movie actor, an icon of the masses.

The Semiotics in People Power III

The unfinished agenda of the millions of urban poor manifested itself in the May 1, 2001 mayhem by Manila's *descamisados*. They were the shirtless poor who angrily rose in thousands and crashed against the steel gates of the presidential palace. Presidential guards armed to the teeth immediately repulsed them. Police/military forces were even called from the province to block them pouring across the historic Mendiola. It could have been a classic class war of the poor in rubber-slippers against the rich and propertied middle class that have just seized the presidency for GMA. This followed dramatically the failed Senate impeachment and the arrest of President Joseph Estrada.

The powerful semiotics of the call "*Erap Para sa Mahirap*" lingers even today in the frustration and anger of the urban poor and the rest of them throughout the nation. Many still hope and live in the world of movie-heroism of their toppled icon.

Meanwhile, President Gloria Macapagal Arroyo was quick to reverse this hidden crisis through the weapons of doles and personal visits to their hovels and cardboard villages. Then she followed it by more shaking of hands and hugging of the poor with TV cameras on her heels. These were dramatized further (and the real structural causes temporarily hidden) by the business-controlled mainstream media focusing not on objective facts but on the poor's abject sufferings. Thus briefly, the history of the rise and fall of the aborted People Power III.

The history of the Left in this country could stand another re-writing in semiotic narrative. The symbol is in the human person of a drinking-prone movie-actor turned president who had toyed with governing in theatrical plumes as hero of the masses. He did it in less clever ways than Marcos with the latter's rich legal and military medal lores. Even when Erap was too powerful an image as "Defender of the People" to be easily uprooted in the consciousness of the poor, the same marginalized masses (whom Marxists love to call "lumpen proletariat") attempted to re-muscle their marches but failed to pull themselves from their bootstraps.

Another way of narrating this failed story of the city's teeming poor is placed on the shoulder of the organized Left. There was not adequate vocabulary of radical change to rally the "lumpen" out of their wretched situation. The Left was recently in quandary whether it should speak for the masses among the urban poor living at the city's dumpsite, or celebrate with the new powers of the Makati-based "civil society" elite. Is this a temporary aberration of the national democratic movement?

One has to stay close to the semiotics in the analysis. After all nobody denies that the role of mass media in all People Power risings was crucially incendiary as it nearly lighted a candle on a dry grassland. It took 16 years for People Power I to create a successful resistance and oust the dictator. It took only 16 months to get wind over a grand theatre, sometimes called Senate Court, in an inconclusive judgment of a suspect jueting lord occupying the presidency. Ronald Lumbao's "People's Movement Against Poverty" almost prevented the ouster. His PMAP marchers failed against the combined forces of local and "imported" soldiers from Pampanga. The rubber-slippered and horde of *descamisados* were stopped from crossing that historic bridge spanning an estero that smelled to high heavens only 500 meters from the Palace.

At the end, what was useful was not the role played by class analysis. It was semiotics in the skilled hands of the middle forces that focused their political vocabulary on the level of the social class it rallied and wanted to manipulate. GMA played on it but while she was not exactly an expert, she controlled vast resources after succeeding to the presidency. Her media mavens had to find an effective weapon to put down the rising anger of the organized urban poor. Until recently when the grounds surrounding Malacañang started to shake with tremors from stamping feet of thousands of unhappy people marching, she went around giving doles and came back lovingly hugging the shirtless poor.

As summary, the Political Calendar for the 1990s reads like this:

1990 – NDF Program, Constitution and other documents approved in the July Congress, 17 years after its founding.

1991 – Co-development NGO (Code-NGO) organized; one salient activity of this organization which became the envy of many others was how it made P1.8 billion out of "laway" (saliva) and string pulling supposedly for poverty alleviation. It authored a multi-billion bond the government was compelled to guarantee and pay P10 billion a year for the next ten years. The scandal it created during its heyday illustrated what economists call rent seeking. (see Glossary)

1992 – the NDF concept was "corrected" by CPP Chairman Liwanag and a few other officials "to prevent the proletarian elements in the federation from being outvoted within the federation;" and henceforth the above-ground and under-ground groups within it will have relations with each other described as "consultative, consensual, coordinative."

1994 – The Philippine joined **WTO**

1996 – Action for Economic Reform **(AER)** organized.

1998 – **AKBAYAN** founded; entered Congress as Party List.

The New Anxiety

In late 90s, members of Jemah Islamiyah **(JI)**, a Muslim group with birthplace in Indonesia started to penetrate the Moro Islamic Liberation Front **(MILF)** in the South, trained some of MILF's people for terrorist bombing and sabotage work. At the end of the decade, some of these went to Manila on a bombing spree. First target was the mass transit LRT on Rizal Day, with more than a dozen innocent passengers killed and scores injured. This brought the urban population taking public mass transport into an endless knawing anxiety in an otherwise cheap, fast, mass transit system.

Thereafter, the country entered a new political vocabulary, terrorism. Political and economic decisions including our foreign relations especially with the U.S. were colored by it. It was just a breath ahead of the World Trade Center suicide bombing on 11th September by a few Arab militants with an axe to grind against western civilizations's capitalist wing.

Chapter **10**

People's Organizations after Year *2000*

THERE WERE NEW POs at the advent of the new millennium. It was period of new challenges that required new responses. The three groups in this chapter relate themselves to problems that may not be new but their collectivity posed new solutions. The CACP where I was and still head was one that joined the convenors of this formation. Others grew and developed out of the new political climate much as what the rain does to mushrooms: it multiplies them, pushed them to expand into broad formations often serving as spreading umbrellas to other NGOs. Some features were different from previous people's organizations. They became mass organizations not in the sense of BAYAN being a political organization. These three new big formations serve as an organized response to critical problems of the new millennium.

Fair Trade Alliance (FTA)

The FTA sought to consolidate social classes that were traditionally like oil and water. Now this group has for members' wageworkers and business bosses, landless tillers and landowners, consumers and merchants-traders. Others are environmentalists and corporate people. At a glance, it is a novel organizational expression surmounting cultural, social and economic differences. Will it succeed in its new politics? A more apt question: can it survive in a recovered, re-conceptualized political economy?

The FTA is not a political party although its leadership and some prominent individuals inside the organization were veteran, political personalities. Many of them are friends, and my former associates in the street struggle. FTA is principally an economic organization, a response to WTO or its perceived threats. It was believed that government almost sold Filipino business down the unprotected, tariff-less highway with foreign goods coming into the market economy like avalanches.

Its birth in 2001 was the year the World Trade Center, symbol of capitalism in the heartland of America, was crushed by a few determined suicide bombers (illustrating perverse political will). Angelito Mendoza and wife Mars, Steve Quiambao and a few others came out with an idea of pulling together multi-sectoral groups with focus in those in the social margins of the productive process. Many of these were little capitalists who wanted to become big. The explicit aim was to have a voice resisting, decrying the merciless impact of globalization on the sector they represent. Many wave small and medium enterprises banners. That was the original dream.

After a year, FTA membership included the productive sectors in agriculture like onion and carrot producers, ginger, cabbage, pepper, garlic and a host of other vegetable growers looking forward to make good money in a market of 84 million consumers. The country was importing large amount of the same agricultural products that were sufficiently produced locally. They saw that the more real threat was the laxity (or is it corruption?) at the Bureau of Customs when it allowed the same agricultural products to enter the ports in massive quantities. What was equally dangerous to this small community of producers was technical smuggling slipping through BOC officials with closed eyes and grease in their hands.

This was a warning signal that while consumers benefitted from products in large number in the market, we at CACP saw that the eventual closures of local domestic production of the same products would also cause local producers to raise their prices. Simultaneously, the issue equally awakened many Filipino owners of industries like cement, ceramics, glass, etc. facing threats through dumping of foreign products at reduced or no tariffs. The problem escalated, enlarged, and broadened as to effect closures of many more productive economic sectors. This potential economic powder keg was about to ignite and explode in the early years of the new millennium.

Calibrate or Kill?

Members of FTA are owners of capital (big and small), trade unions, federations, consumer groups, and trade union workers numbering about 200,000 as of 2004. The complete dismantling of tariffs, following a precipitate commitment by the government to WTO when not slowed down or place on reverse gear, would find these workers out in the cold. Their families numbering about one million could become a part of a greater social problem beyond mere need of jobs or livelihood.

FTA also pulled to its ranks academics, consumer militants, newspaper columnists, development theoreticians. The organization is a bouillabaisse of critics and big capitalists wanting to find an alternative to WTO requirements without losing its potential benefits.

The Organized Workers Behind FTA

The threat to workers and owners of medium-size capital had a history that goes back to the Philippine Senate approval of the General Agreements on Trade and Tariff in 1995. The Senate committee chair, then Senator Bobby Tañada, was outvoted by other members. "Ka Bobby", as he is known in this group, is now Fair Trade Alliance's chief convenor.

Early FTA initiators were a mix of personalities. Aside from "Commander Teban," a former guerrilla from the underground, there were lawyer Ernie Arellano of the National Confederation of Labor (NCL), general secretary Dave Diwa of the National Labor Union (NLU) and others who helped hatch FTA from the cocoon of their dreams. This was in 2001. The group was obviously unprepared for the dismantling of tariff protection that WTO expected the country. But behind this was what the WTO government negotiators, mostly bureaucrats with no business sense, agreed to.

"Mura Na, Imported Pa", the Bane in Consumerism

The country's economy was responding to the strong export orientation taking off during FVR's presidency in early 1990s. The manufacturers, exporters, industrialists and labor were threatened by imports. Were these not good for the Filipino consumers? This question re-awakened neo-colonial thinking that fed on silly, thoughtless consumerism. The 26-year old Citizens' Alliance for Consumer Protection (CACP) strongly fought against it. It decided to join FTA as co-convenor.

According to FTA, the opening up of the economy as dictated by external forces like the IMF and WB had caused the collapse of industries "and the consequent massive loss of jobs all over the country."[49]

CACP could not support the conventional belief that with foreign goods flooding the market, things would be cheap. I strongly shared with workers and nationalist manufacturers the belief that the problems of the economy would be aggravated not solved as against the optimism of technocrats committed to globalization. CACP within FTA foresees closures of local industries and manufacturing sector like a dark night descending before an ominous storm sets in. Consequently, there will be mass layoffs. Jobless workers who do not have income are disempowered consumers. This depressing scenario is what we tried to prevent. Remember FVR's neo-classical economics waving the triune of "deregulation, liberalization and privatization"? The reaction was immediate. The owners of factories and industries, SMEs rallied behind the economic flag against unregulated foreign competition.

Mass Action Against Government, MNCs and WTO

The organized workers, many of them belonging to trade unions with histories of massive mass mobilization, launched a huge rally calling attention to the department of trade especially its Board of Industries. The BOI has been encouraging foreign investments while down playing the threat these posed on fledgling industries.

It was the Holy Week of 2003. The FTA in the approaching days created caricatures of government officials with suspect commitment to defend Filipino entrepreneurs. They paraded representing the Filipino industry as crucified. Workers from the automotive industry, chemical firms and the agricultural sector donned their mournful black. The street theatre dramatically signalled a determined opposition to the WTO-inspired government policy.

---

[49] p. 13 *Fair Trade, Not Free Trade*, Quezon City, 2003

Five thousand assembled in front of the BOI in Buendia Avenue, Makati condemning the heedless policy. FTA countered the massive importation generated by this policy with "calibrated tariff reduction." *"Hinay hinay lang."* boomed one speaker with a bullhorn standing on top of the open truck. Aside form exposing their factories to virtual closures, the massive lay-offs foretell widespread hardship.

Meanwhile, a delegation presented the DTI secretary a paper outlining FTA's position. The subalterns at the Board of Industries listened, explained their side but most of the time prevaricating. It was not a pleasant dialogue between FTA activists and DTI bureaucrats.

FTA's call for fair trade echoed and re-echoed in several Third World economies about to enter into WTO and other intermediate agreements like APEC and AFTA. They all fought against massive reduction or downright abolition of tariffs in their country.

Is the Economy Unprepared or the Producers Overprotected?

When people ask for protection of the fledgling industries, they are admonished not to use the word "protection" because this has become a curse to the ears of the economic technocrats of the neo-liberal school in the NEDA, the super agency defining the direction of the country's economy. For one closely vetting, we have departed far from the Constitutional provision of "the economy being placed in the hands of the Filipinos."[50]

FTA maintained there were not adequate support structures for Philippine business to be competitive, unlike the other emerging economies of South Korea, Taiwan, Malaysia or even China with which we are always invidiously compared by those who wanted to denigrate Filipino efforts. These support structures include affordable cost of capital, credit facilities, R & D institutions, sufficient funds, and inter-agency linkages. Their inadequacies amount to "the very high cost of doing business in the Philippines" as told me by one worried businessman.

---

[50] See Philippine Constitution, Article XII, Section 1, Paragraph 2.

The FTA observed that "the situation is aggravated by the failure of the government to implement the anti-dumping law (R.A. 8752), countervail duties law (R.A. 8751), safeguard measures act (R.A. 8800), and to prosecute big time smugglers who are neither paying taxes nor creating any meaningful jobs in the country." (p.14 ditto). When these laws are there but no effective enforcement follows, is Congress prepared to make better laws or not? Why are many of these laws unenforced or unenforceable?

Under Regime of Joyful Technocrats, Is Their re-Education Possible?

A broad swath of the economic landscape was seen in the hyperbolic language of FTA, "with the carcasses of enterprises and industries that have collapsed." These include textile, shoe, ceramic and steel. Those "in the brink of its terminal existence" were the cement, battery, garments, rubber, etc. Fast disappearing are traditional commercial value crops like coconut, sugar, onion, garlic, cassava and coffee.

FTA sneezed at the one million jobs created in a year (July 2000 to July 2001) as constituted by half-a-million "unpaid family workers" (like one's mother, sister and niece) and one-half million "self-employed" most of whom were marginal and irregular. (p.10 ditto)

Ask the technocrats defending their decisions and their ready answer is that these industries are "inefficient, wasteful, backward, and uncompetitive." Obviously, these people belonged to the top rung of the bureaucracy receiving high salaries and enjoying perks. Were they purblind because they lead comfortable, privileged life and authority of their positions? One is made to feel these technocrats badly need that kind of re-education after going through Wharton and other fancy business schools abroad.

While they were abreast with the latest economic theory, they seem narrow-eyed to what actually is happening in their country's arrested development. We mentioned these sectors earlier. Many of the government negotiators speaking for Filipino business were neither businessmen nor have they sympathy for business. These were the kind of sapient characters that, in China in early 50s, were sent to the countryside "to learn from the masses" on Mao's program of re-education. Or, made to stand against the wall.

If Not in the Economy, Try Looking at Political Economy

Where is the solution? While the symptoms of the crisis are in the economy or in the policies adapted to resolve its problems, the real solutions are beyond the economy. Total figures adversely affected could reach more than half of the country's population of breadwinners (the other half being minors and other dependents). These are the real and immediate causes of current instability in the actively paying consumer sector that perks up the domestic economy. What we have is actually a hidden crisis carrying economic and political message to President Arroyo's putatively "Strong Republic".

What are cheap prices for when one's income sources are threatened by unemployment, by unstable work, or by inflation-eroded pay? The implication of this problem is beyond economics, beyond creating temporary jobs, beyond managing the economy that had been the victim of bad economic decisions. The unresolved situation presages political dynamite.[51]

The total estimate of Filipinos adversely affected is 32 million. They are consumers who were initially capable of paying for what they need. The capacity is increasingly eroded. We ignore their plight brought by inflation (8.5% in mid 2005). These are the same people who cannot enjoy the so-called cheap imports the government is pursuing as palliatives.

This is the immediate economic meaning of heedless massive imports. Instead of sustaining the sectors that supply them consumers' needs, mostly basics like food and medicine, housing materials and clothing, the government pursues a policy of protection for foreign-controlled industries at the expense of domestic producers. This only undermines an economy due to absence of sustainable consumer-oriented and Filipino-controlled agro-industrial policy. Such policy is enshrined and fixed in the Constitution, but not followed.

---

[51] Read Joseph Stiglitz's *Globalization and Its Discontents* and also the 2004 essays of Paul Krugman in *The Great Unraveling* for what is fundamentally wrong with the direction called "the Washington Consensus" our economy is taking . Also, see Paul Krugman's recent article "The Ugly American Bank," *International Herald Tribune*, March 19-20, 2005.

What is to be Done? A Calibrated Policy

What should be the meat of a calibrated policy? (1) It should strive for 100% Filipino labor; this should solve the problem of highly skilled 'returnees' among OFWs. (2) At least 50% of Filipino capital reigns except foreign direct investments in new industries. (3) Exports are allowed only after Filipino consumer needs are certified as adequately met. (4) Tariff-free for technology needed to open new areas or upgrade existing ones. (5) Strict control of natural resource uses preferably monitored by independent NGOs, i.e. independent from government and fleeting commercial interests.

In a recent FTA conference of rice and corn farmers and some coop people with FTA technocrats and government officials, the mention alone of money or sources of funds stirred the passion of rice and corn producers. The reaction typified one kind of rent seeking economics. It is how to take advantage of proximity to political power, a variant of crony capitalism. "How do we get that money? How much are available and Why not more?" At the end, that kind of politics would not work much less easy to sustain.

The reverse is a call for economic nationalism. Thus, FTA is tasked by its constituency to reverse a policy that has placed profit ahead of empowered people. The thrust of economic development becomes sustainable because Filipino producers are in control of the economic infrastructures mentioned above.

The Filipino consumers are not only the end-market of domestically produced goods and services. They are potentially the largest biggest, strongest resource for a mobilization in the economy.

The partnership of CACP with the Fair Trade Alliance hangs on an important concept of "sustainable consumption." Implied in that concept is the idea of "sustainable industry, agriculture, and workers' income." Often the concept is equated with self-sufficiency of the sector concerned where no one goes hungry or pushed to penury. How does one do it?

Our experience in the CACP made us pursue a position that will maintain sovereignty over the country's resources. The Filipino consumers, should be in complete control of these resources: material, technological, social. While there are other ways of improving and expanding these resources, the consumer-worker-producer promotes sustainability especially when he strives to put the economy in his control. This is also what is meant by the adage "the economy should never part from political economy." We see this as the correct response against the reigning economic philosophy which aims to accumulate wealth without limit and place the same in the control of foreign entities.

To quote one capitalist FTA member, Mr. Meneleo Carlos of the Federation of Philippine Industry (FPI) why we should protect our biggest resource and what is that but "the 84 million Filipinos as our market."

Prospects and Problems

When you have 84 million consumers and you are producing a national staple like rice, look back at how to improve productivity. If the problem is the government, organizing the sector is one more solution in changing bad policy. This is a real challenge to FTA if it wants to be more viable to its community of threatened agricultural producers and other SMEs. CACP's role in the FTA is minor but it learned a lot why Filipino business failed to defend itself from the onslaught of WTO.

The Party List

One historic advantage of the party list system is that it has created the bases for legitimizing groups unjustly perceived as subversive. They now have gained voices within Congress even if that institution remains dominated by family dynasties and controlled by *trapos*.[52] I have noted that progressive party-list representatives do not confine their vision of good government to legislation. They are aware that having good laws is incomplete if these laws are unenforceable. One example is when the law is implemented by those whose values do not support the interests of the marginalized. The marginalized masses are the rationale for the existence of the party list.

The system gives legitimization to the voice of the progressive left which otherwise stays at the gunsight of the military as "communist fronts." Since they represent a wide, critical population this point seems to increase the attention

---

[52] See The Economist in the article *"The Philippines Limping Forward"* (March 19, 2005) which cited that political relatives dominated 61% of elective offices, and still rising.

of congressmen atuned to pro-people proposals. More progressive groups recently have won seats in Congress. That's good news.

What has the partylist system to do with this problem of legitimization? There is a general belief that being an NGO or people's organization massing across the street makes for a loud political voice. True enough, but this does not make legally acceptable or lawful the hoarsest verbal shots or longest streamer or biggest crowd causing traffic jam. This non-conventional procedure of shaping public opinion does not directly refer to the legislative equivalence of People Power. We owe the latter to organized people rising.

The partylist is another vehicle of the POs for developing a stronger presence in the law-making body. Whether or not the group could introduce changes from inside, by breaking through the formidable carapace of a highly conservative institution like the Congress would depend on what further social sectors equally marginalized they could mobilize and influence. The effort at least could add strength to their re-ordained status as a minority within Congress.

People Power Re-confirmed

We remember that another forcible ouster of a president capped the country's political history of the last fifty years in 2001. This was the second time around in 15 years. What we have in that year is a re-confirmation of people's power after *EDSA Uno* Rising. It was an apt answer to the question raised due to the disappointing effects of restoration after 1986: *Can Filipinos do it again?* They did.

A political re-confirmation it was and not a new birth. The explanation for it is that the insurrectionary impulse has always been in the heart of Filipinos. Given a new mechanism to ride on, such collective impulse will further develop and be harnessed for patriotic ends. The mass movement is its vehicle. It could move the country again into a cleansing process.

The partylist system could be one institution serving as a vehicle for the collective expressions of the marginalized and unrepresented masses. That's what Congress intended when it passed R.A. 7941. For the time being, taking into account how the *tradpols* view the electorate, the partylist cannot replace the mass movement as a pre-eminent, power-packed political tool. In an interview, partylist representative Satur Ocampo observed that the partylist he leads "continues serving the mass movement; not the other way around."

The Party List System, What Can It Do?

R.A. 7941 as its enabling statute is inadequate and defective. It allows the COMELEC to come out with rules as to how NGOs that were not political parties could become now a part of the electoral system. It would be like other political parties but not quite equal to these.

This happens when the NGO (not a person) now recognized as a political party gets onto congress supposedly representing a marginalized or underrepresented sector through nation-wide elections. By this step (a pittance to being legitimized as lawmaker) the masses of peasants, workers, women, youths, disabled, senior citizens, etc. are now represented in the business of making laws. That is if their organizations get sufficient votes within the Congress supporting their proposals.

In short, the people sent to represent the NGO in the legislature can now join the fray legally with the traditional politicians. Sometimes they form blocs with those having kindred political agenda. They enjoy their favors and perks, public symbols of being a privileged class and, lest we forget, the risk of being swept altogether with other condemnable practices of the traditional politicians. Being a member of Congress is a moral risk. This explains to myself partly why some priests don't want to be elected to it.

The party list system drew into mainstream politics a large number of big groups. The system provides a vehicle for legal participation with perks and immunities into the electoral theatre. Although it is politically incorrect, the proper name of this process is "cooptation."

There is a belief strong among political analysts of IPER like optimist Ramon Casiple that the party list system possesses "a potential for broadening Democracy."[53] But the Center for People Empowerment and Governance (CenPEG) another think-tank enumerates the following as grave defects of the law:

"Firstly, the provision in R.A. 7149 that limits winning party list candidates to a maximum of three seats virtually reduces party list groups to a small and powerless minority in Congress and stunts the development of the party list system. It is imperative that the 3-seat cap be removed from RA 7941 to allow full play for the Constitution's intention of setting up a truly proportional system of representation.

"Secondly, another problem is the lack of transparency in the process with which the Commission of Election accredits party list candidates. The Supreme Court's Bayan Muna Doctrine, reserving the party list system for the marginalized and underrepresented must be institutionalized.

"Thirdly, the law does not clearly set the rules on recall of representatives. Theoretically, it is the party or organization that gets elected into Congress, not the nominee. There is therefore a presumption that a party list organization may withdraw its support for a nominee, paving the way for the recall of its representative. However, there no defined set of rules on a recall procedure and this may lead to complication where the nominee remains in Congress even without the support of his or her party.

"Fourthly, the COMELEC decision to lower the base figure every time a party list organization is disqualified is also anathema to the unity and stability of the party list system. This renders top party list groups to a barrage of malicious disqualification cases filed by losing party list groups attempting to get a congressional seat with a lower base figure. . ." (Summarized 4-point defects from the CenPEG paper).

Is it wrong for Congress to limit the number of partylists getting elected by the minimum votes requirements of the law? Congress can do that and whatever it chooses absurdly to legislate to protect the interest of the *trapos*. There are instances when what should only affect the congressman's district affects the whole country. This is patently unfair.

---

[53] From *"The Party List Path to a Broadened Philippine Democracy"*, Institute for Political and Electoral Reform (IPER).

Abolish Congress?

The usefulness of Congress has reached a stage when abolishing that kind of law making body might be the next best thing. For example, until now it has not come out with an enabling law that prohibits political dynasties in the electoral system. This proviso has been in the Constitution since 1987. Other parts similarly ignored by Congress include a proviso about the economy should be under the control of Filipinos, about not selling the country's patrimony. This Congress as an institution tolerated by the organized masses shows very little respect for the 1987 Constitution and thereby undercuts its own credibility as an institution for Filipinos.

One of the most organized party list groups with the broadest national reach that received the highest number of votes for the political party is BAYAN MUNA. It spawned three other satellite party list groups that cover the sectors for women, workers, and youth. The first two were able to send representatives to Congress. The last one was short of the votes needed.

Wake up Call or Requiem?

One day in September, after the 13th Congress recess, I visited party list representative Satur Ocampo in his modest residence to clarify some points. *Bayan Muna* after all garnered consistently the highest number of votes in the preceding elections.

"Building people power is the number one goal of Bayan Muna," he told me. That sounded to my ears like another kind of Congress outside the Philippine Congress. In the election of 2004 seven members of *Bayan Muna* in the provinces lost their lives in the election-related killings where the military was number one suspect; a high price to pay for one's striving for legitimacy.

The "broadened democracy" according to the irrepressible wish of IPER is potentially realizable. But how could it be done when the incumbent Congress blocks the legitimate aspirations of the NGOs, POs behind the party list? What is happening is that the *trapos* are denying them their full representation. The combined strength of the *trapos* in Congress persists in making the system a mere venue for this political minority to stay a minority (and maybe not make troubles in the streets that frighten foreign capital).

Until such time that the UG and the Above Ground (AG) will roar again in city streets and the countryside and awaken the nation from its somnolence, I see the agenda for launching EDSA IV stays on hold. The next EDSA needs the mobilization of more unhappy people.

MIGRANTE International

The third example of a novel people's organization is one whose growth and development was dictated by the circumstances of an economy unable to make its own people stay and work in the country. What otherwise was an emergency measure (remember the Emergency Employment Administration or EEA?) during President Diosdado Macapagal's administration became in the years ahead a profitable policy direction on how to solve the fiscal problem of the government. The solution included the export of cheap, English-speaking labor to the industrial countries and currently in oil-rich Middle East. We are still feeling the impact of that policy as Filipinos (about 12 million of them and increasing) go on looking for jobs in foreign lands.

The overseas Filipino workers (OFWs) are products of an economy that cannot sustain creating jobs for the increasing number of people who need them. Thus, they see opportunities abroad more than what the domestic economy could provide.

In year 2004, there were about 8 million of these forced migrants working in 182 countries for lack of alternatives at home. Others who followed their steps left, especially the professionals, more for reasons of national security than for economic reasons.

Where Are They Going?

Migrante International (MI) is one NGO that has a worldwide network of alliances whose principal functions is to organize Filipinos in foreign lands as they converge for reasons of job security, political, social, cultural, and mutual help. It also organizes the OFW families left in the country. It started with activities that included education, especially on the human rights issues that often plague Filipino workers and families here and abroad. Many of them led lives of ceaseless struggle to keep spirit and body whole.

Many OFWs locate themselves in Saudi Arabia, Hong Kong, Japan, United Arab Emirates, Taiwan, Kuwait, Singapore, Italy, United Kingdom, Qatar and Brunei. This last country was popular among labor exporters in the heyday of ill-clad entertainers and sweating domestics. The health professionals like nurses, doctors, and caregivers go to U.S., U.K., Canada, Japan, New Zealand, Australia, and South Korea.

What Is To Be Done?

With this massive diaspora of the cream of productive Filipinos, one wonders who are left behind to tend the domestic front. Alternatively, what is the government planning to do in order to keep track of some who left without even a by your leave from the official agency concerned like the POEA? Are they safe in unaccustomed places, secure from danger and risks in foreign clime? Are there protection of and respect for their rights by the countries where they work? These kinds of questions surround the concern of MI and the nature of campaigns it has been launching among OFWs.

The OFWs are the immediate targets for such MI's educational activities through lectures, readings, symposia and newsletters. Many of them are in constant threat from (1) repressive governments, (2) tyrannical, exploitative employers and (3) negligence of their own government. Of the first type, these include deportations, raids, racial profiling, unexpected state exactions and stranded workers. Of the second, these include wage cuts, maltreatment, inhuman working conditions, physical violence especially of women, unpaid wages, unimplemented non-wage benefits and other forms of contract violations. The last covers ignorance, arrogance and indifference of foreign office officials. The risks like war, criminal prosecution and hostage taking are immense, perilous, often surprising if not heart-rending to families left behind.

All the above have been illustrated by three OFWs in the cases of Angelo dela Cruz (hostaged by Iraqi), Flor Contemplacion (executed by the Singapore government) and Sarah Balabagan (abused by an Arab employer). The three cases moved the nation to a tumultuous reckoning of its foreign relations. Many OFWs get killed in wars not their country's own; also as crossfire casualty in terrorist bombings as in Iraq or Lebanon. These were situations that also called for a strong alliance work inherent in an NGO like Migrante International.

Migrante Workers NGOs and Nation-to-Nation Networking

MI is an NGO that has achieved an extraordinary level of networking among Filipinos working abroad. An important function is working for solidarity with other migrants' NGOs. It has a strong linkage with women's organizations abroad. In its early years, it covered only Asia-Pacific area and the Middle East. At this writing (2005), MI has 95 member organizations in 22 countries.

When called by circumstances, MI mobilizes the families on issues directly affecting the members here and abroad. The access to information technology has facilitated this collective effort with unprecedented reach. (See "IT and the Mass Movement") an important part of this working relation is one with the host government, the U.N. agency, human rights groups like Amnesty International and, last but not least, with other migrant groups. Example of this last is the NGO *Tenaganita* in Kuala Lampur, Malaysia.

Its active link worldwide reaches out to Migrante-Europe and BAYAN International. It keeps the members abroad politically alerted even on local issues like increased taxes, VAT and oil price increase or the impact of precipitate globalization linked to our country's commitment to WTO. Issues like soldiers and officers in mutiny and corruption in the military could singe the Internet that connects each MI chapter in many countries. This keeps members in other countries abreast with national issues. By this means, they take part or express a position on burning questions affecting their country.

Active Participants in Local and Host Country Issues

As one of the progressive NGOs that trace their roots in the anti-dictatorship years, MI is sensitive to issues of the day like malfeasances of local and national bureaucrats, U.S. military forces in the country, the massacre of peasants and workers in Hacienda Luisita, and terrorist bombings.

In middle of 2003, the MI exposed wide discrimination against Filipino nurses working as domestics in spite of the critical local shortage. This kind of de-skilling classifies, pushes the Filipino nurses to the underclass of cheap labor. This made them vulnerable to exploitation and abuse as they hold only temporary status in Canada. As lowly workers, many Filipinos in Canada are paid below their professional training. To illustrate the claim: the Filipino Nurses

Support Group (FNSG) in Vancouver has 500 member nurses. Only 150 are practicing their skills and training according to their profession. The other work as nannies and domestic supports in employers' homes and earn rock-bottom wages.[54]

Filipino nurses today have the Live-In Caregiver Program (LCP) as the option to enter Canada. The work of nannies of home support workers for example entails a 24-hour duty. This kind of modern "slave labor" is worse in other countries less civilized than the North Americans or, whose culture reduces respect for women workers outside the homes. Unfortunately, the Philippine government turns around with eyes and ears averted on these effects on the exports of the country's professionals. Yet, these workers bring in the needed foreign exchange like blood to a haemorrhaging patient.

How Much Foreign Money Is Brought In, and To What End?

The picture of dollar remittances by OFWs is one of the brightest spots like a star surrounded by the cruel night. It's there amidst contradictory policies by government trying to survive chaotic market forces thriving under a flawed economic theory.

The foreign exchange figure runs like USD8.5 billion annually (WB Report, 2004) and that's only the amount through legal channels. The informal channels e.g. friends, co-workers coming home and other means could easily double that figure (ADB estimate, 2004).

A more appropriate question is "How important are these dollars to the economy?" Here we are talking of increasing reserve that will perk up foreign investments. This collective remittance serves as rudder to an economy that aims to sail in globalized waters.

---

[54] Data re Filipino nurses in Canada were downloaded from *"Strengthen Unity among Filipinos Overseas"* September 16, 2004.

Quo Vadis, Educated Filipinos

Because working abroad means honing the English language skill, this could mis-educate further the so-called educated by making them believe better education means ultimately selling one's labor abroad and earning dollars. Before we know it, the school system will be developing hordes of cash-oriented philistines and consumerism as the standard of high living.

Wherefore is this kind of economy heading? One ancient myth from India tells of a practice by people who worship an incarnation of a god by putting themselves and getting crushed across a huge wheeled contraption called the Juggernaut. This crashes everyone underneath.

Symbolically speaking, this is not different from the fate of our people whose lives are spent worshipping gold or dollar. They are ruled by a dominant theory that foist the market as the place where all else is valued according to how much it is worth in money. This belief in neo-classical economics has been on the road since late 1960s.

Who controls this powerful currency controls the economy. When the dollar devalues due to many wars the U.S. is waging or massive spending to save its people from a natural disaster like the typhoon Katrina, our OFWs' earning and worth devalues. The dollar the Filipino workers bring home melts slowly in their palms. While the income is sure, the changing value of that income brings a fluctuating sense of security for our OFWs. This is the common perception of many OFWs I've met in Europe in the 1990s. Today, that dollar could buy less than what it was worth ten years ago.

Chapter **11**

Mass Movement Enters the New Millennium

Envoi

Since formal independence in 1946, the country has struggled against neocolonialism with the masses marking time to create a nationalist agenda. But what turned out was a dictatorship whose long aftermath is still with us today. The organized people have become sensitive to the State as a sovereign instrument in the hands of a dictator. The "New Society" it turned out was a failed experiment.

Between 1972 and 1986, the nation-state experienced the longest nightmarish period in its political life but the Filipinos shaped a powerful tool called People Power. In the next 15 years or so, People Power ousted again another president.

When I was abroad, exploring international alliances, I saw that the mass movement has found solidarity with other peoples sympathetic to its cause. With other nations, especially in Eastern Europe it shared the political experiment as the new millennium unfolded. Thereafter, many more peoples fought against their oppressors to liberate themselves. The continuing people-powered political processes held fast under the leaders many of whom were socialist-minded. Several factors explained this political phenomenon: education in the country increased to politicize the middle class fast. The other is the ready access to IT that made organizing the masses faster. I thought of it as the coming of the Cultural Revolution that signaled a hopeful future.

More Conclusions

No claim is made that this is a complete story of the mass movement. This is a personal account of my political development and the consciousness of the circumstances that surrounded the period. I as writer happened to be there in the places and times described. I've been marcher and organizer.

Within that 50-year span, the mass movement that I've seen as observer and participant has shown symptoms of Philippine society in a state of ill health.

My general recall of the mass movement is that it is amorphous, protean, and border-less. It's exhortatory and hortatory; it pleads and guides, shouts and commands its messages. Often directing and distant, but seldom distortionary while relentlessly seeking to fulfill its search for justice.

While it makes history, the mass movement cannot completely recover the past notwithstanding what it teaches, i.e. *The true account of the mass movements fructjfies with various visions, voices and avowals. Would Philippine Society be less sick because it coughs and hiccups and convulses politically?* As this is a symptomatic reading of what has happened in the country 50 years or so ago, others no doubt will have another interpretation. This is one parti pris, a view.

At any given year, mass protests against the power that rules, perceived or symbolic, can burst out like thunder heralding inclement political weather be this modern state, unstable monarchy, emerging empire, or dictatorship. As these are all possible roots of democracy, the masses experience an awakening like mushrooms after the rain. They begin to possess a new consciousness inspired by struggles and the uses of a new medium they come to possess. This last point secures a speed that even traditional mode of changing society can neither slow down nor stop.

What is this new consciousness? It is a product of a modern mode of communication that makes possible sea change visible for all exposed to the Internet, the radio, the TV, generally a free mass media. Below are a few illustrations readily seen or heard or read about. These are different social movements that have their origins in different places, issues, roots, personalities, and grievances. We witness them less as news but more as simultaneity of events that society has not experienced since the dawn of history.

The Mass Movement Sweeps the Town, Cities Worldwide

With the new millennium, I became more sensitive to happenings that have a hearing on people rising against their governments. In democratic U.S., from San Francisco across the land to New York City, 3 million workers marched against President Bush's policy on immigration. In Nepal, especially Kathmandu, 250 professionals called for the ousting of their king. They were arrested for violating curfew. Following an anti-youth legislation by the French government, horrendous destruction went about in Paris against the government; the law was later withdrawn on the heels of widespread burning of cars. In Thailand where people are known for being peaceful citizens, the masses especially in Bangkok rose against their prime minister on suspicion he profited from untaxed multi-million sales by his business. All these happened during the first half of 2006 with hundreds of Filipinos abroad participating. One feels there's no end in sight and that more is to come to shake monarchies, republics, and even fledgling democracies.

The IT is a revolutionary tool especially in the hands of the masses in bad need of a revolution. Under what circumstances can any of the above happen again? Let's count some possibilities: when institutions can no longer hold back forces seeking expressions outside the parameter of tradition, it can happen. When orthodoxy of changing leaders by elections break up because the masses have lost faith in them. When law-making bodies continue to be dominated by class interest of the exploiting elite. When the exploiters though a numerical minority continue to take advantage over the majority and the latter turns to organizing itself into a collective force, it can inevitably happen.

---

[54] Data re Filipino nurses in Canada were downloaded from *"Strengthen Unity among Filipinos Overseas"* September 16, 2004.

EDSA Uno, Dos, Tres and Growing

By the time the mass movement entered the new millennium, it has had three historic records to its name, including the one mass political rising equally memorable for its failure. Why remember EDSA Tres? What political moral could it teach us? My interview with Ronald Lumbao, its early publicly recognized leader and mass organizer, explained this. The focus is on its failure to defend a president from being ousted by a middle class-led rising.

It was a strong reminder that large sections of the country's marginalized especially in Metro-Manila did not remain passive to any government that continued to be deaf to economic pleadings from the poor. Their being lumpen does not mean that they are un-organizable and un-politicized, harboring a festering issue to their class. I look at them as a bundle of political kegs waiting for an organizing agenda.

People Power I (a.k.a. EDSA Uno rising) was responsible for projecting worldwide the new political concept of power generated by the masses resisting an oppressive government. Its aftermath was responsible for re-installing what I describe in the piece "Restoration," a period of missed opportunities by President Aquino's administration.

People Power II (a.k.a. EDSA Dos rising) stopped from becoming bigger the dimension of government corruption and cronyism. Strictly speaking, these two economic dysfunctions fall under the rubric of rent seeking. They were original neither to Estrada nor to Marcos government. They could not be understood when taken out of their capitalist context featuring a condition of rabid wealth accumulation by other means. In 2001, Joseph Estrada compounded his presidential problem by flaunting his mistresses in a predominantly Christian country.

Growth of People Power; Birth of Democracy

Significantly, people power both as concept and practice did not stay within our national border. Media, especially print and tv, projected it to the world. The event was replicated in many countries like China during the episode in Beijing's Tiananmen Square mass gathering, in the break-up of the U.S.S.R. that resulted in several independent republics, thus gaining political freedom for many Eastern European states. All these occurred circa 1989, three years after EDSA Uno.[55]

Why is it important that our discussion of the 21st century should go this far, often antipodal to or about other nations? The immediate reason is simple. The emerging nation-states from the examples of political upheaval cited clearly described to us the major features of today's polity. It is organized in mass, readily occupies public space (a plaza, a highway, the major avenue of the city. around historical monuments, official buildings like parliaments, etc.) highly articulate, excitable, politically critical and closely attuned to the ways of mass media. The countries that drew out from their respective Constitutions the strength of the masses recognize the role of organized people in running their lives. How often was this against the will of their deposed national leaders?

This was not the case in monarchies before the 18th and even after the 19th century. Successive revolutions (in France 1789, in Russia 1905, and 1917 and in China 1911) created several mechanisms that allow civil society (the true polis in Aristotle's day) to guide its emergent communities under agreed social/political conduct where the masses formed new structures. Earlier I called this Alternative Social Formation or ASF. The French revolutionaries that put up the short-lived Paris Commune illustrated one form of self-government put up by liberated citizens. Another was the rebellion of the 13 colonies in U.S. rebelling against the British.

There is also the election of people's representatives as in a republic like the Philippines with all its blunders and lessons not yet fully learned. Democracy was never the case as taught us in high school that pointed to the Greek city-

---

[55] Western media especially CNN and BBC have legitimized the expression "people power" in describing the ousting of three heads of state in Ukraine, Georgia, Syrgykistian and most recently (April 2005) one from Urbikystan. All these are republics in Central Asia that gained their independence from U.S.S.R. since 1989 through the same political process of unarmed mass risings.

states as source and inspiration. Such "democracy" stood on the shoulders of slaves while the examples we have mentioned stood on the shoulders of emancipated masses.

The Philippine experience that has enriched the semiotics of the mass movement ranges from the time of Emilio Aguinaldo when he declared independence in 1898 up to the succeeding 50 years of the colonial period of the Commonwealth. And then followed by the not-so-genuine "independence" of 1946 handed over by the U.S. which only strengthened neo-colonialism in the country. Finally, when the Republic agonized under the dictatorship for the next 21 years. Not until then did the political imagination of People Power liberated us from repression of the dictatorship.

I believe that the 1986 nationalist-democratic open mass movement gave birth to highly politicized constituencies, repeating the same rising in 2001.Until then, organized masses from almost all social sectors ousted two duly elected Philippine presidents outside the constitutional rule on how to end their term of office. And with *history marking its calendars subsequently*, the Supreme Court legtimized the two EDSA risings by supporting in its jurisprudence the pre-termination of the duly elected. This placed the mass movement as exemplary political weapon for changing elected heads of states. Thereafter, I do not see any elected president holding on to the presidency after a slight misstep against the interest of the awakened masses.

Uses of IT in the Mass Movement

The spread of the modern information technology has indeed revolutionized the mass movement. The benefits of IT arch over our modem life like a rainbow. It paints a broad canvas of uses and reaches out just as broadly to users living apart no matter how antipodal. This includes, sadly enough, the frightening view of the efficiency of modern warfare one could see in several print media and TV news. The abattoir that the American forces and the "coalition of the willing" have made of Iraq is daily fare in cable TV, the same with a ravished Third World country like Afghanistan; along with the terrifying vision of suicide bombings in Baghdad, ceaseless rockets destroying indiscriminately lives and property in Lebanon, etc.

My interest where IT is concerned lies in the historically crucial turn of political events in our country. More particularly, I focus on its role in the mass movement where every other participating militant owns a cell phone, less to get news than to make one. I have not come across a tool more instantly adept in millions of people's hands where the need for fast information is urgent, especially in mobilizing the masses.

Mobile Phones are Bane of Dictators

One can foresee how cell phones will become the bane of future dictators. Marcos was lucky cell phones came later, one reason why he lasted long. People with secret grievance against their rulers love to communicate secretly. Incompetent national officials, bureaucrats, corrupt military and police are favorite targets. Even taxis in Manila are now required to paint the mobile number of the government office approving their franchise to operate. This will facilitate rapid transmission of complaints by passengers against errant drivers. The mobile phone in the public hands serves polyphonic uses.

On the other hand, the users of the personal computers (PC) have made access to sources of information found in the Internet infinitely richer source than ever dreamed of in the past. We are now re-entering the world of Marshall MacLuhan with improved tools for public discourse. It is not only as if everyone lives in a neighboring village but also that our villages, language and tenor of urgency are one and instantaneous. What modern ruler can stop the threat of such potential for mobilizing the masses?

Things Move Swiftly with IT, So Do the Masses

I am conscious of the coils of these challenging clichés of current communication. The prexils move in milliseconds faster than shooting stars. This feature of modern information transmission could trigger a transitory society into a mood of change, for better or worse, no repressive ruler could stop for long. How many of our people have their fingers on this tool? More than half of Metro Manila's population, about eight million and counting.

While it took 21 years (1965-1986) to oust Ferdinand Marcos, it took less than two years to boot out former actor-turned-president Joseph Ejercito Estrada. During the earlier period of the *EDSA Uno* rising, the IT did not reach the masses broadly. In the *EDSA Dos* rising, the IT was in the hands of the mass organizers and participants.

Politics as Entertainment

Let us not mistake the cause(s) of Estrada's ouster from what hastened the masses to realizing that they had elected an irresponsible leader who was beginning to sound as if his publicly admitted womanizing and the corrupt cronies around him were presidential perks. Any lesson from this?

Lesson Number One: There was a long process of popular education, building of beliefs and politically stirred perception of what public service ought to be. The public anger did not sprout like mongo beans after a night's moisture. It was the handiwork of the critical mass media and in many study circles of relentless critics from the Left including the "civil society groups" waiting for new jobs in the government coming in. An instance had arrived when the **medium, message and messenger** (the ex-crony of a governor turned whistle-blower) packaged himself into a historic keg that triggered the explosion of People Power II.

Lesson Number Two: the mass movement that culminated in the second EDSA rising was immensely abetted by the rapid exchanges of information by the restless fingers of unhappy people mainly in Manila and suburbs. They eventually decided it was time to put a stop to the theatrical trials in the Senate floor through TV or popular radio.

When President Estrada the following day after a failed Senate trial for plunder still refused to quit the Palace, thousands of marchers the next day went to the president's residence and to force the beleaguered leader to quit. We saw him finally take the Philippine Navy boat bringing him and family to his private home in San Juan, 10 minutes away. Many people inside the Malacañang ground who witnessed this historic departure were crying over the fate of their folk hero turned president as they saw him limping (he was suffering from arthritis) along the plank by the Pasig River.

Outside, in the streets of Manila and in thousands of homes through out the nation, a thousand viewers watched the same scene on TV and screamed with joy, many of whom elected him to office. They all witnessed a once popular movie hero departing into the sunset.

What happened next has become a part of the unfinished history of the present. It was a tragi-comedy watched by TV viewers during early evening news, perhaps unaware that the public trial of their popular president was equally a symbolic trial of a political system they were or are a part of.

The impact of IT on the mass movement could be summarized this way. The IT caused the mobilizations of thousands when simultaneity became a part of the info-sharing process. It provided an occasion to millions to act according to common information received, heard, read in avenues that made the whole world its common info highway.

Without singly attributing to IT the rapid unraveling of the political process during those riotous EDSA II days and nights, one has to recognize that the spontaneous reaction of people in general contributed much to the historic event. Even on recollection, I could feel this strongly as a witness to that unraveling process.

IT and the Breakup of International Barriers

The spread of cell phones even in closed societies like China and North Korea could signal the breaking down of political walls. The introduction of this kind of product in North Korea, for example, passes the market; the Chinese having such closer relation with its hermetic neighbor than with any trading capitalist from the west. Recently the emergent Chinese entrepreneurs have been distributing their products right into the possession of the middle class. Even defectors from North Korea who are now living in the South are getting in touch with relatives there. Not to mention the consumerist amenity that South Korean business massively provides to the wage-earning friends, siblings and the rest of the family that escaped to the South. Communication becomes officially uncontrollable although state censorship is not entirely absent. This kind of freedom makes the military elite protecting Kim Jong IL uncomfortable.[56]

Another impact that IT could produce happens when it becomes vehicle for globalizing popular issues. It directly connects deeper causes of local problems to their structural roots in dominant economies of the west. The Filipino activist who reads and plays with his PC is expert in linking with foreign sources.

The strength of local organizations like NGOs, COGs, POs increases qualitatively knowing through the use of IT that other peoples in other countries are affected by the same problems. In all the above, IT breaks through political walls or locates the starting point of national issues outside local politics and economics.

It is usually the young militant activist who is nimble in the use of the IT in the service of the mass movement more than his carping, captious elders who only could dream recklessly of the revolution when angered by the government. While the youth sends his political text his elders could only wonder: what will happen next?

---

[56] Read "Cellphones Spawn an Information Boom in North Korea" by Rebecca Mackinnon in the IHT, January 24, 2005.

Glossary

Alliance of Concerned Teachers or ACT – a militant nationwide NGO of teachers and non-teaching employees in schools; founded sometime 1982

Above Ground activities or **AG** refers to legal mass actions by progressive forces – the opposite of the underground (UG) activities that were conducted without government permits. AGs are parts of the open mass movement

Armed Struggle also known as **AS** – considered the last strategic option by the left against the repressive state

Alternative Social Formation or ASF – is a mechanism that usually goes beyond ordinary NGO formations, for example, being a participant in decision-making, policy-determining government bodies, councils, committees and other more or less stable entities because of legal provision; such social mechanism could equally start from a private initiative

BAM – Brothers for All Men (*freres de sommes*); a French partner NGO

BONIFACIO – a lawyers' organization named after a Filipino revolutionary hero Andres Bonifacio; the acronym stood for "Brotherhood of Nationalistic Involved and Free Attorneys to Combat Injustice & Oppression"

BUNSO – a nursing mothers' NGO earlier formed by CACP; "bunso" refers to the youngest child in the family. The NGO belongs to the health and children's sectors was responsible for initiating a move for government to follow UNICEF-WHO convention on regulating artificial milk marketing

CACP – Citizens' Alliance for Consumer Protection, a nation-wide NGO in the consumer sector founded sometime 1978-79

'Civil Society' groups – used here in a pejorative sense as referring to some people during the People Power mass actions ousting President Estrada who were waiting on the wings for a juicy position in the next government

Christians for National Liberation or CNL – was an underground NGO composed of church-people believed in armed struggle against the dictatorship. It later became a part of the National Democratic Front

Cordillera Peoples Liberation Army or CPLA – was armed underground NGO in the north that used to be headed by a priest Conrado Balweg

"Development NGO" – refers to the new name of many NGOs that have abandoned their libertarian perspective as principal objective and shifted to socio-economism; calling themselves "development NGOs" when foreign assistance funds started to come beginning 1983

EDSA Uno, Dos, Tres – are the other names for the First, Second, and Third People Power risings in 1986, 2001 and 2003 respectively that occurred mostly along the Super highway named Epifanio Delos Santos Avenue a.k.a. EDSA outside Manila

EIGHTEENTH BRUMAIRE – in the old French calendar is November 9, 1799. *"The Eighteenth Brumair of Louis Bonaparte"* is Marx's long essay in classic class analysis. It describes how Napoleon's nephew seized extreme powers by a coup in 1851 placing the executive beyond the pall of parliament. The period made the dominant capitalist system losing its rule according to parliamentary means but neither can the working class at that time asserts its hegemony. Comparable acts by Marcos occurred in 1972 when the dictator placed the whole bureaucracy and military machinery under him. The attempt was a farce since Marcos could not completely control the emerging mass movement

Filipino-Irish group or FIG – was a support NGO in Ireland during the Martial Law period in the Philippines

Friends of the Filipino People, FFP – was an anti-Marcos NGO in the U.S. mostly in the east coast

International Baby Food Action Network or IBFAN – was an alliance of people and groups committed to promote the WHO-UNICEF code on marketing of baby foods; an ally of BUNSO

IBON – (bird) a progressive research group in Manila, also, a book publisher; its reading materials have become background readings of activists in the mass movement

Iglesia Filipina Indepediente or I.F.I. – is the official name of the Philippine Aglipayan church; many of its priests follow the nationalist traditions of its founding father

KM stands for Kabataang Makabayan – one of the earliest militant student groups in the 1960s

MABINI – Movement of Attorneys for Brotherhood, Independence, Nationalism, and Integrity; it flourished during the Martial Law period assisting victims of repression by the dictatorship

MTT – Mao Tsetung Thought, the Maoist ideology

"Natsit" – is an argot for national situationer, usually given during sympos by progressive NGOs describing an overview of the country's condition; given usually for agitational purposes

NDF – National Democratic Front, an umbrella organizing under whose wings were progressive groups, including the CPP and its armed elements, the New People's Army

Nuclear-Free Philippine Coalition (NFPC) – an NGO originally formed by CACP to address the issue of the overpriced, risky nuclear plant in Bataan by Westinghouse

PCGG – Presidential Committee on Good Government, an anti-graft body

People Power – a name by media to people's rising against government ; this started in 1986 then called EDSA Uno and later been universally applied in all places where people in great mass express their grievances against the state or its surrogates

Partido Komunista ng Pilipinas or PKP – was founded in early thirties but later was dismantled after arrests in late fifties of its top leaders.

Political Officer or PO – is an ideologue who usually serves as political guide to progressive NGOs during the dictatorship; PO could also mean People's Organization

"RA/RJ" – early 1990s, the group under the influence of the CPP split onto two factions: one maintained its adherence to fundamental Maoist lines and called themselves Re-affirmists or RA; from its original sense of gaining political power through armed struggle; the opposite camp called themselves Rejectionists or RJ

Rent Seeking – is a kind of economic activity that seeks profit without producing; a non-competitive search for wealth or opportunities taking advantage of its proximity to power or source of influence; a variant of crony capitalism

SCAUP – Student Council Association of U.P; sometimes Student Cultural Association of U.P., this later was founded by Jose Maria Sison

Socio-Economism – the choice for economic activities at the expense of the political agenda of many progressive groups

"Tama Na" – "Enough is enough!", usually addressed to vociferous critics or to the reigning authority abusing its power

Trapos – (literally, rags used to wipe one's dirty feet or hands) refers to "dirty politicians"; sometimes called *"tradpols"* or "traditional politicians" with similar opprobrium as *"trapos"*

Trotskyism – a school of thinking traced to Trotsky that could mean different things in different periods; it remains to be *"the theory of permanent revolution."* It was originally formulated by Marx, then re-formulated by Trotsky in 1906 and applied to Russia; he believes that the transition to socialism "is a series of interconnected, and independent social, political and economic upheavals proceeding in various levels (feudal, underdeveloped, pre-industrial and capitalist) occurring at different historical junctures. National revolutions that usually occur first are followed in the international area. Hence, *internationalism* constitutes an indelible mark of Trotskyian. The theory clashed fiercely with Stalin's *"socialism in one country."* (See p. 491 **A Dictionary of Marxist Thought**, edited by Tom Bottomore, etc.) The question as to who should be regarded as the main agent and decisive in the TW countries' liberation movements arises: the industrial proletariat (as in Russia) or the peasantry (as in Mao's China)? This kind of political aporia has dogged liberation movements in developing countries for a quick transition to socialism

ZOTO – Zone One of Tondo Organization, an NGO in the Tondo foreshore areas fighting against urban poor displacement by the Marcos government

Bibliography

Abinales, Patricio N. *Fellow Traveler, Essays on Filipino Communism*. Quezon City: University of the Philippines Press, 2001.

Aithusser, Louis. *Essays on Ideology*. London: New Left Books, Verso 1976.

Aithusser, Louis and Etienne Balibar. *Reading Capital.*, (Ben Brewster, translator) London: New Left Book, 1970.

Aithusser, Louis and Etienne Balibar *Reading Capital* (Translated by Ben Brewster) New York: Panther Books. 1970.

Amnesty International Report. *Torture in the Eighties*. London: AI Publications. 1984.

Anderson, Benedict. *Imagined Communities, Reflections on the Origin and Spread of Nationalism*. London: Verso, 1983.

Arendt, Hannah. *The Human Condition*. Chicago: The University of Chicago Press, 1958.

Arendt, Hannah. *On Revolution* New York: Harcourt, Brace & World Inc., 1970.

Bahro, Rudolf. *The Alternative in Eastern Europe* (Translated by David Fembach) London: Verso, New Left Review Books, 1978.

Bello, Walden. *The Future in the Balance* Essays on Globalization and Resistance (edited by Amuradha Mittae) Quezon City: University of the Philippines Press, 2001.

Borras, Saturnino M. Jr. "State Society relations in land reform Implementation in the Philippines", Development and Change, Vol.32 No. 3 June 2001, Institute of Social Studies, Oxford, United Kingdom: The Hague Blackwell Publishers, pp. 545-575, 2000

Bourdieu, Pierre. *Language and Symbolic Power.* Cambridge, Massachusettes: Harvard University Press, 1999.

Bourdieu, Pierre. *Outline of A Theory of Practice*, Cambridge Studies in Social Anthropology. Massachusettes: Harvard University Press, 1977.

Bourdieu, Pierre. *Practical Reason* California: Stanford University Press, 1998.

Buendia, Rizal "Edjop's Martyrdom", Trends Trimestral Journal of Ideas. Manila: Polytechnic University of the Philippines, 1988.

Canetti, Elias. *Crowds and Power.* New Yoric Viking Press, 1962.

Clarke, Gerard. *The Politics of NGOs in Southeast Asia*, Participation and Protest in the Philippines, London: Routledge, 1988.

Constantino, Renato *The Invisible Enemy*, Globalization and Maldevelopment. (edited by Joan Orendain), Quezon City: Foundation for Nationalist Studies, 1997.

Copplestone, Frederick *A History of Philosophy* Chapter XXXII "Politics". New York: Doubleday, 1962.

Coronet-Ferrer, Miriam (editor) *Peace Matters, A Philippine Peace Compendium.* Quezon City: University of the Philippines Press, 1997.

Corpus, Victor N. *Silent War*, VNC Enterprise, 1989.

Daroy, P. Bn.; Aurora Javate-de Dios, Lorna Kalaw-Tirol (editors) *Dictatorship and Revolution, Roots of People Power.* Manila: Conspectus, 1988.

De Quiros, Conrado. *Dead Aim, How Marcos Ambushed Philippine Democracy.* Pasig City: Foundation for Worldwide Power, 1997.

Eco, Umberto, Mario Santamibrogio, Patrtia Violi. *Meaning and Mental Representation.* Indiana University Press, 1988.

Franco, Jennifer, et at. *Building Alternatives, Harvesting Change: PEACE Network and the Institutionalization of Bibinka Strategy, A PEACE Institutional Study.* Quezon City: PEACE Foundation, 2001.

Freudenberg, Gunter. "Target-Oriented Or Process-Oriented Co-operation with Projects in the South?" *Focus on Philippines*, a journal of the Stiftung for Kinder (Foundation for Children): Vol.11, No. 1, June 1994.

Garcia, Robert Francis. *To Suffer Thy Brothers.* Manila: Anvil, 2001.

Godelier, Maurice. *The Mental and the Material* New York: Verso, 1986.

Godelier, Maurice *Perspective in Marxist Anthropology.* Cambridge: Cambridge University Press, 1978.

Green, Edward C. *Practicing Development Anthropology.* London: Westview Press, 1986.

Guerrero, Amado. *Philippine Society and Revolution.* U.S.A.: International Association of Filipino Patriot (IAFP), 1979.

Habermas, Jurgen. *Theory and Practice.* Boston: Beacon Press, 1973.

Habermas, Jurgen *Knowledge and Human Interest.* Boston: Beacon Press, 1968.

Havel, Vaclav et at. *The Power of the Powerless.* Palach Press, 1985.

Kaldor, Mary (ed.). *Europe From Below,* London: Verso, 1992.

Kramer, Jane *The Politics of Memory, Looking for Germany in the New Germany.* New York: Random House, 1996.

Lehmann, Jennifer M., *Deconstructiung Dukheim A Post-post Structural Critique,* London: Rutledge, 1993.

Macapagal, Diosdado. *Democracy in the Philippines.* Manila: 1976.

Marx, Karl & F. Engels. *On the Paris Commune.* Moscow: Progress Publisher, 1971.

Marx, Karl & F. Engels. *Selected Work* New York: International Publishers, 1984.

McCoy, Alfred W. (editor). *Lives at the Margins,* Biography of Filipinos Obscure, Ordinary and Heroic. Quezon City: Ateneo de Manila University Press 2000.

Miller, James. *Democracy is in the Streets.* Mass., U.S.: Harvard University Press, 2000.

Osborne, Peter (editor). *Socialism and the Limits of Liberalism. London:* Verso, 1991.

Partido Komunista ng Pilipinas, *Communism in the Philippines: The P.KP. Book 1,* Manila: 1961.

PEACE Foundation Inc. *Program Impact Evaluation Report,* (edited by Pi Villanueva et a!), Prepared by the program Impact Evaluation Team, 30 June 1992.

PEACE Institutional Study (prepared by Jennifer Franco), *Building Alternatives, Harvesting Change: Institutionalization of Bibinka Strategy.* 2001.

Phelan, John Leddy. *The Hispanization of the Philippines.* University of Wisconsin Press, 1959.

Permanent People's Tribunal Session in the Philippines, Philippine Repression and Resistance (source for the NDF Ten-Point Program). London: KSP, 1981.

Philippine Assistance for Rural and Urban Development (PARUD). *People's Alternative, Proceedings of the Second Convention of the National Assembly, 1985.*

Polanyi, Karl. *The Great Transformation.* Boston: Beacon Press 1944. *Readings in Philippine History.* Manila: Philippine Book Guild, 1979.

Rocamora, Joel, *Breakthrough.* Manila: Anvil Publishing, Inc.

Rosca, Ninotchka. *Jose Maria Sison: At Home in the World Portrait of a Revolutionary.* Manila: IBON Books, 2004.

San Juan, E., Jr. *Allegories of Resistance, the Philippines at the Threshold of the Twenty-First Century.* Quezon City: University of the Philippines Press, 1994.

Segovia, Raul E. *A Dictionary of the Crisis in the Philippine Ecosystems.* Manila: CACP/PEAN, 1995.

Serrano, Isagani it. *Civil Society in the Asia Pac~flc Region,* Civicus, 1994.

Serrano, Isagani R. *On Civil Society*. (a monograph). Quezon City: Philippine Rural Rehabilitation Movement,1993.

Sison, Jose Maria with Rainer Werning. *The Philippine Revolution, The Leader's View*. New York Crane Russak, Taylor & Francis, 1989.

Solidarity in the Nineties. Current Affairs, Ideas and the Arts, Special Issue on NGOs No.27 (July –September). Manila, Philippines: Solidarity Publishing House, 1990.

Surowiecki, James. *The Wisdom of Crowd*. U.S.: Doubleday, 2004.

"Theory, Technology, Practice: The Task of the Science of Man", *Social Research*, Vol. 44. 1977.

Today Letters to the Editorpage, July 7,2001.

Valenzuela, Arturo. *The Breakdown of Democratic Regimes*. Baltimore & London: John Hopkins University Press, 8th printing, 1991.

Verzola, Robeito (Secretary General). *Society, Ecology and Transformation*. (The Philippine Greens monograph, a working draft of their first general assembly, November 29-30) 1997, Quezon City: 1997.

Weekley, Kathleen. *The Communist Party of the Philippines, 1968-1993, A Study of its Theory and Practice*. Quezon City: University of the Philippines Press, 2001.

Werming, Rainer. *The Philippine Revolution, The Leader's View*. New York: Crane Russak, 1989.

Wood, Ellen Meiksins. *Democracy against Capitalism, Renewing Historical Materialism*. U.K.: Cambridge University Press, 1995.

Zumel, Antonio, *Radical Prose: Zumel*. Manila: published by First Quarter Storm Movement (FQSM), 2004.

Index

Business, first social sector to support Martial Law xxx, 4, 18, 42, 44, 54, 63, 64, 66, 80, 83, 85, 88, 101, 108, 112, 113, 114, 130, 132, 135, 150, 172, 187, 201, 204, 227, 228, 233, 234, 235, 237, 238, 241, 243, 253, 259, 275, 277, 284

C

CACP (Citizens' Alliance for Consumer Protection) vii, xiii, xxix, xxx, 32, 35, 45, 46, 47, 49, 54, 56, 59, 63, 72, 73, 76, 77, 78, 79, 80, 81, 90, 128, 132, 134, 135, 145, 160, 161, 164, 165, 166, 168, 179, 190, 233, 234, 236, 240, 241, 262, 263, 267

CAFA (Committee on Anti-Filipino Activities) 11, 270

Capadocia, Guillermo (and Balgos) 10

capitalism a dominant ideology 16, 89, 268

captive press alternative vi, 58

Carlos, Sixto Jr., et al 48, 69, 182, 271

Carlos, Tina Ebro 165, 271

CARP (Comprehensive Agrarian Reform Program) xiv, 163

Cash nexus. *See* money economy

Castro, Fidel 32

Catholic Church 14, 33, 51, 60, 73, 80, 271, 282

Cause-oriented Groups (COGs) vi, vii, xxi, xxii, 60, 61, 77, 80, 81, 87, 89, 95, 96, 99, 100, 135, 215, 218

centers of mass movements: Manila, Davao City, Cebu City, Baguio xiv, xviii, xxi, 5, 9, 10, 11, 12, 26, 28, 30, 31, 34, 40, 41, 43, 44, 46, 49, 52, 53, 57, 58, 59, 63, 72, 73, 74, 75, 76, 78, 80, 91, 96, 98, 104, 112, 119, 121, 131, 133, 144, 146, 148, 150, 152, 153, 156, 157, 167, 168, 169, 172, 177, 179, 182, 184, 197, 200, 201, 204, 206, 209, 210, 212, 214, 218, 225, 228, 230, 254, 257, 258, 259, 262, 263, 266, 267, 268

Central Luzon 1, 9, 19, 36, 92

Cervantes, "Behn" xxx

Charlemagne statue in Paris 205

Che Guevarra's "Foco Theory" 36

church people supported workers' strike xxiii, 9, 54, 58, 75, 84, 96, 113, 131, 167, 170, 182, 212, 221

CIA (Counter Intelligence Agency of the U.S.) messing with local militants 11, 17, 18, 26, 36, 224

Cid, Cipriano 32, 271

Citizens' Alliance for Consumer Power (2004), a creation of CACP 1978 xiii

Citizens' Assembly created by Marcos to extend his term 54, 55

Civil Rights Movement, U.S. 29

civil service 5, 153

civil society xx, xxi, xxii, 49, 104, 105, 108, 213, 218, 227, 229, 255, 258

Civil Society Groups (CSGs) xx

Clarita Roja 66, 68

Clark Airbase and Subic Bay 8, 163, 164

177, 180, 181, 186, 187, 190, 192, 230, 242, 243, 246, 247, 248, 261, 262, 263, 264. *See also* "development NGOs"

Nona, sister-in-law 199

Notre Dame, Paris 205, 210

NPAs many were college dropout xv, 36, 64, 96, 141, 143, 146, 202

Nuclear-Free Philippines Coalition (NFPC), viii, xv, xxix, xxx, 77, 90, 144, 159, 160, 161, 163, 170, 263

NUSP (national union of students of the Philipppines) xv, 50

O

Ocampo, Rep. Satur xvii, xxx, 4, 55, 59, 69, 111, 112, 132, 144, 152, 153, 225, 243, 245

October 24 Movement. *See* Garcia, Voltair

October Revolution 100th year 216

Oil firms' unconscionable pricing. *See* Three Sisters

Olalia, Bert 32, 40, 144

Olalia, Lando 93

open or Above Ground (AG) mass movement xiii, xxix, 20, 35, 59, 62, 66, 72, 73, 75, 85, 95, 102, 103, 129, 134, 138, 145, 148, 159, 169

open revolutionary mass responses. *See* AG movement

Opposite ways of organizing the national economy 7

Oppressors are a minority of 1% in 1978. *See* class analysis of Clarita Roja

Organizing people as stage 2 67, 189

Other option for the Left: go UG vii, viii, xvi, xxiv, xxix, 28, 39, 48, 49, 54, 58, 59, 62, 64, 65, 68, 71, 72, 73, 74, 75, 93, 95, 96, 97, 98, 101, 102, 103, 113, 127, 130, 139, 141, 142, 144, 145, 147, 148, 149, 150, 159, 221, 225, 227, 246, 261

P

packaging of knowledge. *See also* Rewriting of history

Padilla, Abe xvii

PANDAYAN (Pandayan para sosyalistang Pilipinas) 223

Paris Commune 47, 255, 267

Paris Nord 200

Parity Rights for Americans extended 1974 39

Partido ng Bayan (PnB) 225

Partylist xvii, xviii

Pascual, philosopher Ricardo 14

pathological anti-communism. *See* McCarthyism

pathologies and politics 179, 280

patriarchy 29, 280

PDs (or presidential decrees) by Marcos peasant movement xv, 75, 98, 107, 163, 280, 281

peasant movement 4, 7, 19, 32, 41, 81, 141, 167, 168, 170, 280

pensionados abroad, civil service exam, etc. 5, 280

People's Army or NPA in Arayat, Pampanga 36, 269, 280. *See also* HUKS